American Indians and the Rhetoric of Removal and Allotment

RACE, RHETORIC, AND MEDIA SERIES
Davis W. Houck, *General Editor*

American Indians and the Rhetoric of Removal and Allotment

JASON EDWARD BLACK

University Press of Mississippi • *Jackson*

www.upress.state.ms.us

The University Press of Mississippi is a member of the Association of American University Presses.

Portions of this work have appeared in altered forms in the following publications.

Jason Edward Black, "Rhetorical Circulation, Native Authenticity, and Neocolonial Decay: The Case of Chief Seattle's Controversial Elegy," *Rhetoric & Public Affairs* 15:4 (2012): 635–46.

Jason Edward Black, "A Clash of Native Space and Institutional Place in a Local Choctaw-Upper Creek Memory Site—Decolonizing Critiques and Scholar-Activist Interventions," *American Indian Culture & Research Journal* 36:3 (2012): 19–44.

Jason Edward Black, "Plenary Rhetoric in Indian Country: The *Lone Wolf v. Hitchcock* Case and the Codification of a Weakened Native America," *Advances in the History of Rhetoric* 11 (2011): 59–80.

Jason Edward Black, "Native Resistive Rhetoric and the Decolonization of American Indian Removal Discourse," *Quarterly Journal of Speech* 95:1 (2009): 66–88.

Jason Edward Black, "Remembrances of Removal: Native Resistance to Allotment and the Unmasking of Paternal Benevolence," *Southern Communication Journal* 72:2 (2007): 185–203.

Jason Edward Black, "Symbolic Suicide as Mortification and Transformation: The Conciliatory (Yet) Resistant Surrender of Maka-tai-mesh-ekia-kiak," *Kenneth Burke Journal* 2:1 (2005): 1–14.

Manufactured in the United States of America

First printing 2015
∞
Library of Congress Cataloging-in-Publication Data

Black, Jason Edward.
American Indians and the rhetoric of removal and allotment / Jason Edward Black.
pages cm. — (Race, rhetoric, and media series) Includes bibliographical references and index.
ISBN 978-1-62846-196-1 (hardback : alkaline paper) — ISBN 978-1-62674-485-1 (ebook) 1. Indians of North America—Government relations—History—19th century. 2. Indians of North America—Government relations—History—20th century. 3. Rhetoric—Political aspects—United States—History—19th century. 4. Rhetoric—Political aspects—United States—History—20th century. 5. Indian Removal, 1813–1903. 6. United States. General Allotment Act (1887). 7. Indians of North America—Legal status, laws, etc. 8. Decolonization—United States—History. 9. Citizenship—United States—History. 10. Indians of North America—Politics and government. I. Title.
E93.B633 2015
323.1197—dc23 2014029788

British Library Cataloging-in-Publication Data available

FOR MY FATHER,

MARTIN BLACK,

IN RESPECT,

HONOR,

AND LOVE.

Contents

Acknowledgments

THE PROCESS OF COMPLETING THIS BOOK HAS PROVIDED ME WITH AN embarrassment of riches, and the folks recognized below are testaments to the ways that an academic project is neither singularly inspired nor privately written.

To begin, this project has been supported emotionally and psychically by my colleagues, past and present, at the University of Alabama. My department chair Beth S. Bennett has offered incredible professional and personal direction during my time at Alabama, and I am far richer in confidence and ability because of her mentorship. Many of my fellow faculty members have also contributed fulsomely to this project and to my well being as a teacher-scholar. Special thanks are due to Anita Abernathy, Robin Boylorn, Marsha Houston, Mary Meares, Carol Bishop Mills, Mark Nelson, and Matt Payne for listening to my ideas and for providing enduring encouragement every step of the way.

I have been absolutely blessed with brilliant undergraduate and graduate students at the University of Alabama, and I wish to thank them all here for helping to guide the micro-arguments of this project. Students in my classes over the years, especially seminars such as Contemporary Rhetorical Theory; Critical, Cultural, and Rhetorical Theories; Rhetoric of Native America; Rhetoric, Race, and Law; African American Rhetoric; Rhetoric and Social Change; and War and Protest Rhetoric, have genuinely sharpened almost every facet of this volume.

Some students have become close friends, collaborators, and family over the past decade. I want to recognize Justin Combs, Ray Harrison, Adam Sharples, and Jeff Walker—specifically—for providing the kind of brotherhood that helped me simultaneously stay grounded and feel comforted. I mean it when I say that our friendship has meant the world to me.

Speaking of family, this book would never have seen the light of day without my academic kin. I am so very grateful to many, but particularly to William Doty, Danielle Endres, Steve Herro, Casey Kelly, James Klumpp, Shawn Parry-Giles, Trevor Parry-Giles, Belinda Stillion-Southard, Bjorn Stillion-Southard, Mary Stuckey, Mari Boor Tonn, Dan Waterman, Marilyn Young, and my Southern States Communication Association, Carolinas Communication Association, and Alabama Communication Association communities. Most of all, I would not be the scholar and person I am today without my mentor and brother Charles E. Morris III, whose love is enduring and whose patience is saintly.

I would like to thank Davis Houck, my colleague and the Race, Rhetoric, and Media series editor at the University Press of Mississippi (UPM), for all his support. He single-handedly breathed new life into this project. Throughout our time chatting about the book, I have found both a fabulous exemplar and good friend in Davis. I also found at UPM one of the best editors with whom I have ever worked. Craig Gill is, hand's down, an "author's editor." Katie Keene at UPM, too, has been both inspiring and fun to work with on the project. Copy editor Robert Jefferson Norrell sharpened the prose incredibly and taught me much along the way. Thank you, Craig, Katie, and Robert for helping to animate this project.

As I close, I want to thank two more of my families. The first is my NASCAR community, especially Mike and Angela Loveland. For roughly 40 weeks out of the year, whether on Facebook across the miles or in the stands at tracks around the country, you help make life fun. There is no way I could hold it together without my "pit crew." Our daily chats and laughs are the "stuff" that matters and the memories that count.

Finally, I want to acknowledge my personal family—my grandmother, aunts, uncles, cousins, in-laws, and nephews who have helped me to grow as a person. I offer a special heartfelt thank you to my mother and father, Cheryl Black and Martin Black, for all their care and support over the years. I am fortunate beyond words to count in my corner two humble, hard-working, and compassionate people who never relent in their unbridled affection. And, of course, to my heart and soul; my will to meaning—Jennifer, Anabelle, and Amelia. I love you so very much. I treasure every moment spent together and cherish every moment to come. Thank you for making our home warm, bright, and loving.

American Indians and the Rhetoric of Removal and Allotment

INTRODUCTION

Colonization and Decolonization in the Native-US Relationship

IN THE FIFTEENTH CENTURY, SAUK NATION ELDER NANAMAKEE PROPHesied the impending contact between a strange race of Wasichus—or Europeans—and his people.[1] Nanamakee revealed to his community, "By the end of four years, you should see a *white man*, who would be to you a father." Sauk history tells that four years later Nanamakee traveled east to meet the Wasichus. According to his descendent Chief Black Hawk (Sauk), when Nanamakee came into sight, the Wasichus "took him by the hand and welcomed him into his tent. . . . He told him . . . that the Great Spirit had directed him to come here, where he should meet a nation of people [and] that they should be his children and he should be their father."[2] The Wasichus carried with him a message of heavenly proportions, one granting to whites a providential exceptionalism regarding Native nations, whose members would soon be called "American Indians." Thus began the Sauk Nation's relationship with European settlers.

Around the time of Nanamakee's revelation, an aging Lakota holy man named Drinks Water also predicted the coming of a European band that would affect the land and those who had carved-out a life on it for centuries. Having lived contentedly in a sovereign nation his whole life, Drinks Water forecast for the Lakota Nation a changed existence. A cultural shift seemed part of his premonition, as he said, "When this [contact] happens, you shall live in square gray houses, in a barren land, and beside those gray houses you shall starve."[3] The Lakota legend told by his descendent Black Elk (Lakota) continues that Drinks Water was so entirely shocked by his vision that he soon after died of despondency, claiming on his deathbed that he would rather return to the Earth Mother than witness the transformation of his people.

The divinations of Nanamakee and Drinks Water foreshadowed some vital themes of European impact on American Indian cultures.[4] For one, the notion of a familial dynamic related by Nanamakee dominated not only early affairs between Europeans and indigenous people, but also the legal, political, social, and cultural connections between the US government and

American Indian nations during the eighteenth and nineteenth centuries. Indeed, as Vine Deloria notes, "Paternalism is always a favorite subject of the [US] government. . . . It has therefore become an accepted tenet that paternalism dominates government-Indian relations."[5]

Drinks Water's premonition, unmistakably more foreboding, alluded to the consequences of this relationship. European influences (and later US customs), though sometimes at first appearing well-intentioned, often concealed inequality and intrusion. Indeed, the other side of benevolence was a demand for subjugation in return for the gifts of protection and patronage. Often, in rhetorical strategies for imperial conquest European forces and the US government employed the language of fatherhood to rationalize their self-images as colonizers.[6] Given the power dynamics and hierarchical structures that undergirded such a kindred bond, the US government in particular predicated its control of Native populations on its own right of dominion.

But what Nanamakee's and Drinks Water's words also demonstrate is a complex colonial relationship engendered by discursive contact between European and Native cultures. To be sure, Europeans and the US government did not affect indigenous groups unidirectionally. If, when considering Nanamakee's narrative, we understand that the Wasichus "took him by the hand and welcomed him" and later stated "that they [the Sauk] should be his children," then we also recognize that the "him" and the "they" existed, spoke, and interacted.[7] The responsiveness of the indigenous "other" reflected back to, and likewise affected, those in power. There was a mirror effect in play. In this way, Native voices held the possibility of challenging and threatening those in authority.[8] In other words, the agency of Native peoples is an example of how cultures, through their institutions and conventions, can help define both Native and governmental character. The way that Natives enacted discourses within the intercultural relationship, then, affected governmental identities just as governmental voices influenced Native identities, albeit on vastly *differing* levels of impact.[9] There exists an almost hybrid rhetoric at work in the circuitry of Native-US parley, one that I maintain demonstrates how Native voices reflected, but also contributed to, US public culture.

The colonial Native-US relationship and its attendant discourses and identities reached a level of rhetorical intensity in the nineteenth century as the government began codifying into law widespread Indian policies. The word "colonial" refers here to the characteristics of an ideological system that demands and justifies "an appropriation of land, bodies, and labor followed by the insistence of [an imperial force's] governmental structures, languages, and logics."[10] One of the US government's first colonial policies involved removing American Indian nations from their homelands during the 1820s and 1830s. The reasons for removal are sundry and contested.

Some claim that the government wanted to remove American Indians as far as possible in order to foster a white nationalism. Walter Russell Mead argues, for instance, that the US government saw the nation first as a family and that it needed to expel those who did not fit into the parameters of its "all white" dictum.[11] These commitments to the country's white citizenry were confirmed early on in one of the new republic's first racialized legislative laws, the Naturalization Act of 1790. The act codified the requirement that every American citizen be "a free white person," "a person of good character," and willing to break all allegiances to other nations of origin.[12] This, of course, meant that scores of thousands of American Indians were denied consideration as full participants by the US government.

On the other hand, proponents thought that removal was a dynamic and potentially positive policy because it sought to protect American Indians from land encroachers—who would otherwise steal Native land and exterminate whole communities—while simultaneously creating a civilized group of yeoman farmers beyond the Mississippi. President Andrew Jackson claimed in 1830 that the benefits of excess land and the elimination of hostile Natives who threatened frontier communities were important to the policy's primary aim: saving American Indians. After signing the Indian Removal Act of 1830, which codified removal, Jackson reported, "The consequences of a speedy removal will be important... to the Indians themselves." He continued, "The pecuniary advantages which it promises the Government are the least of its recommendations."[13] Removal's benefits to American Indians were, according to most proponents, the primary benevolent thrust of the policy.

To proponents, failing to enact a removal policy would lead to American Indians' cultural disappearance. In this vein, Supreme Court Justice William Story worried in 1829 that "They [will] pass mournfully by us, and they will return no more."[14] The New York Board of Emigration, Preservation and Improvement of the Aborigines of America, a pro-removal anthropological research group, similarly concluded in 1830 that "the only means of preserving the Indians from that utter extinction is to remove them from [our] sphere."[15] Proponents overall justified removal through a benevolent rhetoric of protection for American Indians.

In the 1880s, the expanding nation reached the fringes of the Native reservations to which dispossessed American Indian communities had been removed some five decades before. Such expansion caused foundational conflicts between the federal government and American Indian nations fueled mostly by the "clamor [of] settlers to open a large portion of the land for sale."[16] Reservation land bases dwindled yet again as new treaties made way for rolling waves of white settlers.

In 1887 the US Congress passed the General Allotment (Dawes) Act that called for the redistricting of American Indian land. Simultaneously, the allotment policy sought the relocation of Natives to smaller parcels of acreage in part to assimilate them through agricultural means. Yeoman assimilation was expected to convert American Indians to private landowners and to promote their agricultural subsistence and self-sufficiency. Deloria argues that "it was thought, if the Indian had his own piece of land, he would forsake his tribal ways and become just like the white homesteaders" that were flooding US frontier areas.[17]

Dawes Act proponents claimed that allotment was the only way to save American Indian communities who were failing to thrive on barren reservations. To Indian Commissioner Thomas Morgan in 1889, "[The Indians] are in a 'vanishing state of things' . . . and must adjust themselves to their environment, and conform their mode of living substantially to our civilization."[18] Meanwhile, opponents argued that the US government simply wanted for its own use the land it had bequeathed in a so-called benevolent way through the policy of removal. For instance, furious over the government moving Cherokee people to unfertile parcels of land while offering whites the most lush portions of the reservations, activist Dewitt Duncan (Cherokee) could only conclude that "the Government of the United States knows that these allotments of the Indians are not sufficient!"[19]

The removal and allotment policies certainly thrust upon Native populations a variety of diminutive constructions and subservient roles. In both cases, the government displaced American Indians to make more room for frontier whites, a telltale sign of colonization. At the same time, the US government strove to assimilate Native communities to control "savage" behavior that threatened the fringes of the frontier.[20] And, of course, the paternal structure of US-Native affairs championed as a benefit the preservation of "the Indian who is in *all* cases, broadly speaking, destitute of some of these safeguards [security] . . . and in *some* cases destitute of them all."[21] For, as the Indian Rights Association claimed in 1885, the "Indian as a savage member of a tribal organization cannot survive, ought not to survive . . . but his individual redemption from the condition of savage nomad . . . is abundantly possible" with American protection.[22] This kind of policy, though, did more than provide material advantages to the benefactor and protection to the beneficiary. In addition, the policies helped shape the very identities of the groups involved in the rhetorical exchange. As Natives were saved "from white aggression," government rhetoric reaffirmed white dominance as much as it provided land to the government or aid to Native nations.

However, American Indian populations were not helpless and voiceless. In fact, as Frederick Hoxie has argued, Native groups "talked back," which helped them reconstitute their own identities, rebuke governmental policies, and reconfigure US identities in the rhetorical process. "By talking back to those who considered themselves superior," he maintains, "Indians could show that they rejected the self-serving nationalism they heard from missionaries and bureaucrats. The Natives made it clear that they refused to accept the definitions others had of them—savage, backward, doomed."[23] And they challenged the common mythos that only white people epitomized the merits of civilization. Such rhetorical tactics are herein labeled "decolonizing" (or "decolonial"), therein reflective of decolonization. Decolonization is the process by which those who are colonized attempt to critique the narratives "offered from the colonizer's perspective and [instead] champion their own narratives" in order to demystify these "master narratives." Decolonization can also mean the contemporary scholarly and activist methods of spotlighting both colonized peoples' efforts to decolonize in their own times and contexts, and Native epistemologies.[24]

Ostensibly, the shaping of US identities and Native identities across a centuries-old colonial landscape can be found in an exchange of voices. The formation of a community or nation does not involve one voice or several voices speaking alongside each other. Instead, identities come about by forging one conception out of another to give dimension and depth to an understanding of community; a public is not so much a continuity as a disruption brought about by reciprocal discourses. To this, Karlyn Kohrs Campbell notes that voices within a community are "communal, social, cooperative, and participatory, and simultaneously, constituted and constrained by the material and symbolic elements of context and culture."[25] These interactive identities and rhetorical constructions were particularly salient for nineteenth century Native-US relations.

The "participatory" descriptor is especially resonant in the rhetoric of the US government and Native nations regarding the policies of removal and allotment. Instead of solely privileging governmental texts comprising these policies or further marginalizing Native discursive efforts by labeling the protests mere "response," this book pulls at the strangulated relationship reflected in colonizing and decolonizing rhetorical exchanges. In this way, US Indian policies are studied as a fashioning of not only US, but also Native identities. And at the same time, Native rhetoric is examined as helping envision both Native and US identities. All of these interactions appear in colonial milieus and with strands of decolonial pushback.

A nation, in the thought of Benedict Anderson, "is an imagined political community" whose center flourishes within the web of discourses that constitute that same community.[26] E. J. Hobsbawm further contends that the power of people uniting into a public through governmental rhetoric "lie[s] at the heart of the nationalism of language."[27] In a nation such as the United States, which comprises and has outwardly championed a host of ethnicities, languages, philosophies, and heritages, it sometimes appears "the only things that would seem to be left are ideas and the rhetoric used to explain them."[28] That is, rhetoric exists at the complex heart of US governmental and public cultures.

Certainly, governmental bodies define, powerfully, the bulwarks of national character. In fact, conceptions of dominant ideologies with respect to the "people's" identities have tended to consume scholarly interest in the topic. Examining top-down studies undertaken by Anderson, M. Lane Bruner, Ernest Gellner, Gary Gerstle, and Ronald Takaki offers a glimpse at the way marginalized voices have been excluded from the study of national identities in contrast to the attention afforded governmental authorities.[29] Still, one cannot deny the agency of the oppressed in helping constitute governmental identities. Public identities ought to be examined with an eye toward "dual phenomena, constructed essentially from above, but which cannot be understood unless also analyzed from below, that is in terms of the assumptions, hopes, needs, longings and interests of ordinary people, which are not necessarily national and still less nationalist."[30] Even when a government's colonizing ideologies guide a nation's character, always present are voices from the margins.

Colonization is a foundational framework for the analysis of Native and governmental discourse that follows. Reading texts with such a framework is part of a much larger project in the humanities. Accordingly, Raka Shome notes that this "postcolonial condition" attends to the tragedies of colonization by exposing "the imperialism of Western discourses."[31] Colonization, to borrow from Derek Buescher and Kent Ono, begins when "colonizers appropriate land, conquer indigenous people, and found colonialist governments to oversee the efficient operation of property and labor. . . . [They then] teach the colonized the language, logic, and history of the colonizer."[32] Postcolonial studies examines the ways in which these hierarchical relationships functioned over time and continue to function through issues beyond labor and territory.

Colonialism is studied as it manifests both in the material and symbolic realms. Postcolonial scholars such as Stuart Hall, Gayatri Spivak, Homi Bhabha, and Edward Said emphasize the ways in which exploitative labor, capitalist structures, conditioned living spaces, deprivation of benefits, subsistent needs and information, and exposure to diseases and drugs affect the oppressed human subject (and cultural identities as imbrications of the body and social spaces).[33] Rationalizations of colonialism involve the symbolic, as both a generative precursor to and extension of the material realm. As Susan Silbey writes, "control of land or political organization" is important, but so is "power over consciousness and consumption."[34] In other words, representations and memories of the "other" by colonial forces can entrap as much as material conditions do. Colonialism is therefore powerful in terms of what it did (and does) to oppressed communities physically, but also what it did (and does) for representations of those same oppressed communities. This is the core of Said's arguments about Orientalism: that the linguistic symbolism and public imaginary of the oppressed comes to mean along with all material characteristics of an imperial system. Of these representations, he writes that what critics find in them almost universally is a system of discourse "by which the 'world' is divided, administered, plundered, by which humanity is thrust into pigeonholes, by which 'we' are 'human' and 'they' are not."[35] In the end, this conception lends credence to the social construction of lived colonial experiences, especially those found in exchanges between dominant forces and disempowered subjects.

Territorial expansion, a principal colonizing ideology of the early US government, dictated that there was a need for physical places and cultural spaces for the nation to thrive.[36] And, the issue of land and the rhetoric of space was core to US governmental bodies and American Indian communities. Within the complex of nineteenth-century US governmental ideologies, such territorial "place" was necessary to "the nation's rapidly-industrializing economy."[37] Additionally, the "space" that was attached to the physical land was vital to build a nation "based on the assumptions of racial and cultural superiority as well as an insatiable desire for land, expansion and empire."[38] The American public, as well, needed land for enlargement and was not above exacting the sentiments and terminologies of *terra nullius*, or "the uninhabited or unimproved wasteland commonly described by early European explorers and settlers in North America and other regions inhabited by aboriginal peoples."[39] To the nineteenth-century US government this so-called uninhabited wasteland allowed for the growth of American economies and cultural identities based on a rhetoric of space that justified such expansion.

Alternatively, land for indigenous nations was connected ontologically to cultural existence.[40] According to William Strickland, American Indians in the main consistently argued against removal from homelands on the grounds that they "should not relinquish the land of their ancestors" or the source of their spiritual worth.[41] To critics of American expansion, the so-called "settlement" of the West is in particular terribly flawed. William Robbins argues, for example, that the idea of discovery and settlement "refuses to acknowledge the presence of others who already inhabited the regions"—something that indigenous communities picked up on quickly throughout the sixteenth to nineteenth centuries.[42] Needless to say, there exist substantial disconnects between US governmental and American Indian perspectives of land.

Territory is also closely tied to citizenship as a colonizing construct. Citizenship, or the "criteria for membership in a political community," is among the most basic of American ideological tenets.[43] From the founding of the United States, membership in the republic merged with territorial ownership. According to David M. Ricci, this was because "property assured economic self-reliance which, in turn, permitted independence of mind and will."[44] In addition to the personal benefits of territory to the US public's self-reliance, property holding bolstered the nation's infrastructure itself. Recall that James Madison acknowledged in *The Federalist Number Ten* that "the freeholders of the country" would be "the safest depositories of republican liberty."[45] With a personal stake and investment in the land and the nation under which it existed, Madison and others believed that American frontiers should be both protected and steeped in the precepts of liberty. The more landed citizens that the nation could boast, the "more stable and secure the political system" would be.[46] As Michael Schudson puts it, "There was no question in the minds" of American leaders that a "property qualification" was imperative for a productive and cohesive citizenship.[47]

Citizenship woven through overarching civic identities helped hold the colonization of American Indians in place. By linking land to citizenship, the US government through its numerous naturalization acts made property a definitional quality of Americanness. The possession and control of land, writes Robert Shalhope, "meant control of an economic future of people living in an agrarian society," but access to land also "constituted the vital prerequisite for political and social" identity for the US citizen.[48] Those white citizens who owned property were considered a part of the nation. Those who could eke out a productive and economic life on the land had an unquestionable right to the land.

However, citizenship in the nineteenth century also worked through ideologies of racialism regarding the exclusion (or limited inclusion) of African Americans and American Indians. If citizenship vested in property—and the productive agrarian use of the property—then both subjectivities failed the naturalization test. For African Americans, property ownership was a non-issue that the institution of slavery made moot, oftentimes even for free blacks.[49] Though the US government admitted American Indian nations' quasi-ownership or tenantship of the land from time to time, Natives' typical subsistent modes of hunting and gathering and their cultural communalism disqualified them from citizenship. Indigenous communities were thus rarely recognized by the US government as having any claim to land, let alone the trappings that citizenship bestowed on for whites. Native nations in the eighteenth and nineteenth centuries whom the Declaration of Independence called "merciless Indian savages whose known rule of warfare is undistinguished destruction of all ages, sexes and conditions" could not be fully permitted into spaces of US citizenry.[50] The colonial language of the government was stark even in the nation's foundational documents. American Indians were typically denied because the nation sought a homogenous population that shared laws, economies, and language. Diversity was dangerous to US republicanism, as it brought to the fold "cultures close to nature and the instinctual life."[51] The uniform rule of the US government's numerous naturalization acts excluded American Indian nations based on race, to be sure, but also on their "mere" occupancy of the land and their inability to "produce" on the land as part of a larger US citizenry.

Still, US citizenship in this colonial context, and the ways that American Indians were considered for or occluded from the nation's citizenry, was not always clear and was rarely consistent. As Rogers Smith asserts, US citizenship "has always been an intellectually puzzling, legally confusing . . . and contested status."[52] When complicated by American Indians' triangulated positions (tribal, state, and federal affiliations) the naturalization processes of the US government became even less clear.

Overall, these colonial ideologies of the US government, and the ways they developed, evolved, and functioned, serve as a critical template for analyzing the governmental and Native discourses of removal and allotment. This postcolonial perspective of revealing deleterious ideologies allows critics to grapple with the ways that subjectivities were shaped by the US nation's ideologies. Vanessa Beasley argues, "Instead of continuing to ask only *what* Americans' shared beliefs are, we might also ask *how* they are . . . how they are defined and understood, and . . . [are] assumed to accompany American national identity."[53] The study of removal and allotment discourses certainly helps get us closer to understanding the Native-US relationship.

Lest history forget, American Indians were not voiceless, and the analysis that follows works through a decolonial framework to illustrate that fact. As Shome and Radha Hegde indicate, attention paid to colonial relationships is "concerned with phenomena and [the] effects and affects of colonialism" through "not only the frameworks of dominance but also . . . that of resistance."[54] Indeed, the perspective of decolonization "is centered on the assumption that American Indian (and other indigenous) philosophies of knowledge are rational, articulate, coherent logics for ordering and knowing the world."[55] Focusing on Native-centered interpretations of Native-US history and affiliations confronts and restructures dominant representations of colonized dealings within those relationships. When examining Native rhetoric, a presentation of resistance can unmask governmental cycles of abuse concerning indigenous cultures and can challenge the ways that this relationship has functioned over time.[56] This is a decolonial move that is necessary to reconceive both the colonial structures underpinning past Native-US relations and the colonial narratives deriving from that relationship that continue to constrain Native agency.[57]

One of the prevailing public and pop-cultural interpretations of Native-US relations is that interactions forced American Indians to assimilate and seemingly "kill off" their subject-positions.[58] That is, while the US government's exceptionalism became its *sine qua non* characteristic as a dominant power, Natives oppositely were scripted as what had been lost. But I, like many other scholars, challenge this unidirectional understanding of the relationship by relying on a shift toward "radical indigenism" as a part of decolonization. Simply, it would be a mistake to downplay the agency of Natives in the definition process.[59] American Indians have not just *moved* through their relations with the US government by consenting or remaining indifferent. To the contrary, radical indigenism celebrates how they have *acted* by maneuvering to possess economic modalities, sovereignty, safety, and other subsistent needs of the human experience.[60] American Indians did so, for the most part, by turning around the US government's colonial rhetorical strategies in order to invent their own decolonial rhetorical tactics.[61]

The hypocrisies of the US government's colonial policies that sought to (ironically) sustain Native nations through removal and allotment were glaring to American Indian nations. To confront these hypocrisies, American Indians worked through détournement, or using the government's language against it, as a decolonizing rupture that enabled them to create "rhetorical [tactics] for enforcing an Indian perspective in contested cultural space, in which Indians [were] at a political and cultural disadvantage."[62] The historical record indicates that such rebukes of policy probably empowered American Indians. For as Arnold Krupat argues, "To take possession of the master's 'books' is to obtain some important parts of the master's power—which then . . . may be turned to one's own purposes."[63] American Indian resistance through this rhetorically substantive appropriation was dynamic, revealing the presence and agency of Native discourses.

Détournement, according to Guy Debord, is about repurposing the rhetoric of those in power in order to drain the original language of its oppressive assaults in the service of propping up the disempowered.[64] The motivation, here, is to be able to clarify how the powerful, or *master*, rhetoric presents problems, inaccuracies, hypocrisies, distortions, and inconsistencies. Greil Marcus adds that détournement is "a politics of subversive quotation, of cutting the vocal cords of every empowered speaker, social symbols yanked through the looking glass, misappropriated words and pictures diverted into familiar scripts and blowing them up."[65] This is not just an appropriation of, or a meager mimesis related to, the dominant power's discourses, but rather a politically inventive repackaging of them for resistive purposes. There is a definite style associated with détournement, but its substantive power is what drives this mode as a kind of resistance.

Again, an examination of this decolonization (especially détournement) is instrumental to understanding the nineteenth-century activism of American Indians, especially in the face of frequent misrepresentations of their efforts by various colonial and colonizing interests. Foremost is the public and pop-cultural misconception that Natives simply disappeared without engaging in discursive appeals to resist US governmental policies.[66] This pervasive inaccuracy assumes that American Indians were simply moved and allotted without working through political channels to defy these two policies. Another common public misconception assumes that American Indians responded to government policies solely through violence.[67] Of course we know American Indians were neither helpless and voiceless nor inherently bellicose. As Hoxie offers, their back talk "did not reject governmental discourse."[68] Instead, Natives adapted to the dominant discourse so as to establish identification with a white audience prior to revealing contradictions and making demands with regard to particular policies.

The power of governmental agency, though, should not be ignored. The government certainly set the discursive strictures of the Native-US relationship. In turn, as the analysis will show, the government enjoyed a greater leverage of power than did American Indians. To avoid naiveté, we ought to assume that power differentials failed to completely balance the political and constitutive ethos of Natives and the US government during this time period.

This book situates US governmental and American Indian discourses in the constellation of nineteenth century colonizing ideologies that underpinned interactions of the Native-US relationship. Specifically, I argue that both the government's rhetoric and American Indian voices contributed to the policies of Native-US relations throughout the nineteenth century's removal and allotment eras. Simultaneously, these discourses together constructed the silhouette of both the US government and American Indian communities and contributed textures to the relationship. Such interactions—though certainly not equal between the two—demonstrate the hybrid-like potentialities of Native-US rhetoric in the nineteenth century. That is, both governmental and indigenous discourses added arguments, identity constructions, and rhetorical moves to the colonizing relationship. Ultimately, the competing voices helped shape Indian policies and organize cultural identities in the nineteenth and early twentieth centuries.

It will be shown that American Indians achieved numerous goals in terms of impeding the realization of the removal and allotment policies. Likewise, by détourning the US government's discursive frameworks and inventing their own rhetorical tactics, American Indian communities helped restyle their own and the government's identities. All along, Natives worked through the government's homogenization of indigenous culture to occasionally organize a pan-Indianism, or united front based in Native affiliations, that allowed them to unite their resistive energies in opposition to the government's oppressive policies and injurious rhetoric. Interestingly, during the first third of the twentieth century, Native agency was shown to affect the Native-US relationship when American Indians urged the ultimately successful passage of the Indian Citizenship Act of 1924 and the Indian New Deal of 1934. These acts granted US citizenship to American

Indians and also allowed them connections with their tribal cultures. The limits of these culminating laws will also be assessed in the offing.

American Indian decolonial resistance throughout the removal and allotment eras helped motivate these more emancipatory policies of the Native-US relationship leading into the turn of the twentieth century. Indigenous communities also massaged the government-instigated identity constructions of Natives as savage, childish, weak, and uncivilized into positive self-characterizations of independence, strength, and unity. On the other end of their resistance, American Indians questioned the government's self-professed identities as benevolent, paternal, just, and civilized; in the process, they illustrated how the US government acted through deception and fraud.

In the end, Native communities were granted more discursive power, though the US government still retained a powerful influence over them. Part of this authority derived from the government's territorial management of Natives, which functioned as a crucial space for constituting American Indian and governmental identities. The Indian Citizenship Act and the Indian New Deal—where this book concludes—demonstrate the prevalence of the *identity duality* of US citizenship that amalgamated American Indians to the nation, yet segregated them on reservations outside the spaces of the US civis during the twentieth century. This duality of inclusion (*controlled citizenship*) and exclusion (*controlled sovereignty*) was built incrementally through the removal and allotment periods, and existed as remnants of nineteenth century Native-US rhetorical relations.

In terms of textual authenticity, nineteenth century Native discourse was often oral in form and was recorded by either American Indian translators or by agents of the War Department and, later, the Bureau of Indian Affairs. If recorded by an American Indian translator, speeches tended to be published in popular presses by whites associated with the rhetor's nation. If recorded by government agents, discourse was either published in popular presses or stored in institutional places like the Department of Interior, Record Group 75: Records of the Bureau of Indian Affairs in the National Archives and in the Senate Committee on Indian Affairs File, Record Group 233 in the Library of Congress. Written discourse by American Indians is typically found in petitions and memorials in these public archives, as well as in secondary press books published in the nineteenth century. I have attempted, whenever possible, to analyze texts from these archival sources, but in some instances, have also accessed texts in credible academic and popular presses to secure their veracity. Moreover, I have drawn from Native-based outlets for texts from the Choctaw, Creek, Chickasaw, Seminole, and Cherokee nations and from Native personal narratives generally.

To be sure, one of the more problematic issues of studying nineteenth century American Indian discourse is authenticity. As Wayne Moquin and

Charles Van Doren claim, "There are no masses of letters, diaries, speeches, newspaper articles, pamphlets, books or tracts hidden away in tribal archives" with which to triangulate and corroborate texts.[69] Thus, authenticating texts involves comparing the extant versions of discourse in governmental archives, popular presses, academic studies, and autobiographies, or tracing a piece of discourse as far back in the historical record as possible. Despite the difficulties in authenticating pre-twentieth century Native discourse, Devon Abbott Mihesuah argues that using whatever exists in the record remains far better for American Indian empowerment than analyzing Native-US relations from an Ameri-centric viewpoint alone. This is the case, she intimates, even given translation issues and the possible corruption of Indian translators by the US government, as long as scholars are reflexive about this possibility.[70] Therefore, I am committed to using the Native discourses that exist, but am mindful of the need to corroborate and compare versions of discourse against others. As Peter Nabokov reminds scholars researching American Indian issues, "Most eighteenth- and nineteenth-century Indian-expressed accounts are unearthed from [government] documents and scholarship," which can be "haphazard prospecting."[71]

Overall, authenticity is problematic because it punctuates a Western obsession with attributing truth to a rhetor. Susan Hegeman writes that this fixation complicates a Native oral tradition that puts stock in the "word," arguing, we "can recognize that both sources of authenticity, and their corresponding desires, derive from our own cultural context, which understands validity and value primarily in terms of texts and authors."[72] Nineteenth-century contexts necessitated such rhetorical moments as American Indians and government agents met to negotiate treaties. Herein lies part of the difficulty, inasmuch as the Native-US colonial relationship obscures what was said and recorded, thus silencing to an extent so-called authentic Native voices. In terms of such cultural interactions, what we have instead, writes Arnold Krupat, are recorded moments that are "always heteroglossic and polyvocal, formed always in relation to the speech of others."[73]

So does this mean that critics should avoid studying nineteenth-century Native texts because they cannot be verified in the same way as a twenty-first century presidential speech? Krupat answers no, and exhorts that even when we have a veracious text in front of us, it could contain others' influence, or it could be redacted during its printing, or contain outright lies that undercut its so-called intent. He suggests that critics recognize the lack of lock-tight authenticity, and in so doing remain cognizant that Native texts from the nineteenth century are the result of collaboration.[74]

One main way, then, to understand Native texts is to center them as a constellation of US and Native influences, situate them in context, and seek to display how they rely on and simultaneously resist dominant discourses. Working from Krupat's ideas, if the texts are authentically Native, they will probably contain US influences given the colonial context of interactions between Natives and US officials. Similarly, if the texts are translated or recorded differently from the so-called authentically Native, then the US influence will still be there, as will be the Native arguments. These co-influences are part of the consubstantiality of this long-standing relationship.

The key is to remain somewhat cautious and balanced in one's analyses. For instance, the argument about American Indians decolonizing US discourses by both adopting and resisting them is reflective of the hybridity of Native rhetoric, which was necessitated by a colonial context, such as treaty negotiations conducted through discursive forms forced on the rhetorical situation by a dominant power. Granted, the "transformational mimesis" through which American Indians had to address the US government served as "a potent strategy for hegemonic blocs" to control Natives.[75] Still, there was undeniable accommodationism on the part of Natives. As Robert Yagelski notes, "Antagonistic kind[s] of contact . . . required Native American leaders to adopt new rhetorical techniques in order to deal successfully with their white antagonists," but also had a strong impact on Native rhetoric in general.[76] Instead of this historical consequence being used to silence, it might be used to investigate how Natives had to articulate themselves in colonial contexts in order not to be silenced. Herein lies the power of détournement.

Given all of these complexities, this volume does not attribute intent to the Native discourses under investigation, but rather performs an analysis of the records' representations of these discourses. Different interpretations of the texts by critics—or questions about the veracity of the texts—might arise as a heuristic contribution of such a study, thus enriching the conversation about American Indian resistance in the nineteenth century.

Related to the issues of text and authenticity is the western obsession with some semblance of an exact or fulsome or fine-toothed master storyline that explains it all. As decolonial scholar Linda Tuhiwai Smith (Ngati Awa and Ngati Porou) contends, colonial history gets wrapped up in "the idea that the story of history can be told in one coherent narrative." To be honest, this volume is *not* a history book in either the disciplinary sense or in the sense that it attempts to "write a true history of the world" (which, of course, cannot be done).[77] Rather, this study is a rhetorical-critical analysis of primary documents that hang together in sometimes correlative ways and, if not that, then certainly in *relative* ways to demonstrate the interstices between Native and governmental voices surrounding removal and allotment. I aim not at a totalizing chronicle or, again, at what Tuhiwai Smith frets about as the concept of finality that "assumes the possibility and desirability of being able to include absolutely all known knowledge into a coherent whole."[78] In the pages that follow, I present a larger story arc of rhetorical interactions; the story I offer allows for room and opportunity for more in-depth studies of particular Native nations and US government officials, of the specific rhetorical tactics of colonization and decolonization, and of their deeper contexts.

For instance, I approach Native voices here often as pan-Indian or, within individual nations, as holistic despite divisions between Native nations as well as intra-nation conflicts. I do my best to slate-out differences in politics among the Native voices I access through the prose and in the notes, but on occasion there are moments of authorial complication in terms of "strategic essentializing." Shome argues that one aspect of postcolonial self-reflexivity is the "problem of essentialism that a postcolonial critic is often faced with when she or he challenges the discursive constructions [i.e., large narratives] of nonwhite cultures and racially oppressed peoples of the world in hegemonic Western discourses."[79] The bottom line is that if one writes about culture, one essentializes. The key to making this strategic essentializing function responsibly is to be reflexive and gear it toward unmasking the abuses of a colonizing relationship. Gayatri Spivak reminds us that essentializing in postcolonial work is a risk we must take "in a scrupulously visible political interest."[80] She adds that we look at essentialisms "not as descriptions of the way things are, but as something one must adopt to produce a critique of anything."[81] One should always be aware that she or he is not essentializing to make total or authentic or generic or universal. Rather, it is only a "political tool that the postcolonial critic often has to adopt to resist any kind of hegemony."[82] All of this is to say that sometimes very minute variables of Native voices wind up collapsed into each other. However, in a colonial context where the larger US governmental narrative essentialized and genericized Native interests and agency, it is difficult to analyze these hegemonic moments outside of that powerful context. The difference is that the colonizing discourse essentialized, say, Native voices in order to control Native peoples; the postcolonial strategic essentializing is aimed at revealing the difficulties of colonization in order to decolonize the storylines. As Robbie Ethridge writes of her work on the larger Creek Nation, "This book is a snapshot in time. . . . But one should not mistake this snapshot for all of Creek history."[83] The same can be said of the present volume's treatment of the Native-US relationship.

Readers will notice that at no point does this work attempt to make arguments about authenticity, universality, intent, or "essence" concerning American Indian rhetoric. Rather, the texts analyzed get us close to a story of parrying and often hybridized discourses. Some of the rhetoric is popular and some is lesser known. But, taking heed from Emma LaRocque, "I am re-citing the documents because they have not been readily available to readers, nor have they received the hearing they deserve."[84] Mine is an attempt to craft a narrative of the merger between Native and US governmental voices through a rhetorical lens (versus an anthropological or historical framework). The goal is not to batten down the hatches on the story, but to throw open the sealed trapdoor to more light. When it comes to the Native-US colonizing relationship, there must always be reassessments to help make such luminescence more electric.

CHAPTER ONE

The Ties That Colonize: Rhetoric from Nationhood to Removal

THE COLONIAL RHETORICAL RELATIONSHIP BETWEEN THE US GOVERNMENT and American Indian nations did not begin in the 1830s with the Indian Removal Act. The relationship started even before the formation of the American republic, well back into the first Western-recorded contact between Natives and early European settlers. Of course, as Jill Lepore explains, the confluence of European cultures and Native populations in the New World later "would form the basis of American nationalism as it emerged in the late eighteenth and early nineteenth centuries."[1] Ostensibly, then, early interactions between European and Native cultures marked the genesis of Native-US relations. Though European-Native cultures and discourses first mingled with the arrival of the Scandinavians, Portuguese, Spanish, Dutch, and French, the story of US removal is really entrenched in the British period of contact. Specifically, the period between British settlement of North America and the Jacksonian era of the 1830s is a rich space to access as a fertile context for the removal policy and the interactive discourses extant during removal. Before delving into removal rhetoric, early characteristics of the Native-US relationship ought to be outlined, albeit briefly, before engaging in a textual analysis of the relationship itself.

The ascendance of the British Empire in the seventeenth century marked the continuation of a relationship with Native communities based on the juxtaposition of civilized and savage identities, as well as economic modalities. Differences over views of land—for the British government, it was a site of production and commodification; for Natives, it was a space of spirituality and inheritance—led to conflict among the groups. Great Britain's colonial assailment over Natives prompted the elevation of European American identities as superior to weakened Native character. Ultimately, colonizing aggressiveness became a form of tutelage, wherein the British government involved itself in guiding Native nations through conversions to Christianity, adaptations to agriculture, and dependence on trade. This latter policy arose when the British began their "benevolent policy era" following the French and Indian War.

In the wake of the settlement of Jamestown (1607) and Plymouth (1620), British colonists and Native peoples continued engaging in an assortment of relationships regarding land exchange. Natives soon realized that the colonists were remaining on the land for good, but also expanding throughout it. Captain John Smith, for instance, reminded both his fellow Jamestown colonists and a group of the Powhatan Nation in 1620 that "by reducing [Indian land], God [would] be served, His Majesties Empire enlarged by the addition of . . . large Territories . . . and the Planters themselves enriched by the trafficke and commerce."[2] The early British colonists planned to broaden their territories to the detriment of Native holdings.

Native communities typically viewed their relationships with the British as unhealthy, especially when the colonists insisted on "treating the Indians despicably" in trade and land exchanges.[3] The more Natives extended their hands to the colonists, the more the British trespassed on their lands. As tribesperson Wahunsonacock (Powhatan) explained to Smith in 1622, "Yes, Captain Smith, some doubt I have of your coming hither, [which] makes me not so kindly seeke to relieve you as I would: for many inform me your coming is not for trade, but to invade my people and posesse my Country."[4] Moreover, as Natives opened the door to the material exchange of goods, British colonists sought to trade language, Christianity, and European culture such as dress, virtues, and economic systems at a feverish pace.[5]

As the British colonials became more involved in Native cultures and the process of land exchange, aggression between British and Native groups increased. In a sense, then, the pattern of "hostility and open war" arose as a "dominant part of English-Native relations until almost the end of the nineteenth century."[6] One of the first foundational moments of aggression between British colonists and indigenous nations stemmed from white attempts to colonize Native nations. In 1675, a group of the Wampanoag Nation under the leadership of King Philip, or Metacom, rose up against the tide of encroachment in New York, Connecticut, and Massachusetts. The ensuing attacks from the British and further response from the Wampanoags garnered the title "King Philip's War."[7] Metacom eventually lost the war and was beheaded. Colonial leader Increase Mather remarked that "the memorable day" of the chief's death was "a monument of revenging Justice" that witnessed the chief's limbs "hewn in pieces before the Lord."[8] Seemingly, this violence was committed under providential watch. The war led to European acquisition of land and the re-entrenchment of British-Native identities. The war confirmed the instability of the American frontier, and set into motion an endless repeatability in which the British government advanced its influence over Natives and their land as it tramped westward.

These actions, and the rhetoric that justified the intrusions, arose from and perpetuated the identity changes facing the British colonists. They directed most of their attention toward their errand into the wilderness—the settling of the West as made manifest by providence. Part of this wilderness involved the inferior identities of Natives. Ward Churchill describes the situation as "resulting [in] rhetoric of dehumanization directed at indigenous peoples, juxtaposed as it was to a contemporaneous rhetoric of 'civilization' by which Europeans were indoctrinated to view themselves as the world's inherently superior race."[9] This became the key rallying discourse of the colonists. It remained easier for the British settlers to view themselves as civilized when, comparatively, they considered Indians, as colonist Cotton Mather labeled them, "wild, cruel, barbarous, bruitish [sic], diabolicall creatures . . . the worst of the heathen."[10]

The bond between territory and inclusion was vital during the British colonial period. And this association was rooted in the errand. The one universal requirement for inclusion as active members of colonial life was some sort of a landed property qualification for citizenship. British jurist William Blackstone, for instance, argued that colonists without property lacked the resolve to civilize the wilderness. They had neither the motivation to protect the Crown nor the connection to the land that stimulated virtuous citizenship. He wrote in 1765 that "the true reason of requiring any qualification, with regard to property" for citizenship within the British Empire, was "to exclude such persons as [were] in so mean a situation as to be esteemed to have no will of their own."[11] Blackstone's directives additionally rejected those so-called racial inferiors who occupied but did not own land.

Ironically, disastrous events like King Philip's War allowed Native communities to construct and reconstruct their identities and to understand better those of the British. This was an early form of decolonization whereby the motives of the British colonizers were laid bare by the marginalized Native groups.[12] That resistance still exists today is telling for the presence of Native back talk, even if it did not mete out material successes. At any rate, these indigenous nations realized quickly that the British could not always be trusted. Before his beheading, Metacom reminded his community of the dangers associated with the British: "You now see the foe before you, that they have grown insolent and bold; that all our ancient customs are disregarded. . . . These people from the unknown world will cut down our groves, spoil our hunting and planting grounds, and drive us and our children from the graves of our fathers."[13] Here, Wampanoag identity was centered on ancestral connections to the land; that customs would be overlooked and grounds spoiled affronted Metacom. His warning also foreshadowed the dangerous land wrangling that would soon follow.

The next pivotal moment that helped shape the British-Native landscape involved the peace treaty accorded Britain in the wake of the French-Indian War of 1756–1763. The campaigns therein witnessed the British and their American colonists battling the French and their Native supporters on the frontiers of North America. The battle lines were drawn between the British (and the colonists hoping to secure French and Native lands) and the French (along with Natives who desired the expulsion of the British).[14] The British and French empires had been battling militarily and politically for a number of years. Native-colonist tensions in North America figured in as yet another venue through which to grapple over the New World.

When the French lost the war, the Peace of Paris established the boundaries of new British areas in North America, settled former Native lands, and demarcated the boundaries of "Indian country." In his famous Proclamation of 1763, King George III reserved the right to extinguish all Indian title. That is, the British would control the land upon which Natives lived. He announced to the American colonists, "We issue this Royal Proclamation . . . to erect within the countries and islands ceded and confirmed to us by said treaty distinct governments in the Indian territories."[15] French and Spanish officials, Christian missionaries, and others tied to Natives were to remove immediately following the establishment of new British territories.

The Proclamation of 1763 set into motion a newly tweaked phase of Native-British relations: the benevolent policy era. In exchange for possessing Native lands, Britain promised to protect Natives as wards. King George III noted, "The Indians with whom we are connected, and who live under our protection, should not be molested or disturbed in the possession of such parts or our dominions and territories."[16] Notice the construction of Natives as subordinates in need of protection. Of course, as protector, the Crown made no qualms about "declaring it to be our royal will and pleasure" to seize these indigenous territories.[17]

American colonial identities, which were predicated on territorial expansion and agricultural use of the land, did not go unnoticed by American Indians. To the charge that Natives were "brutes" who "passed away their time"[18] and squandered fertile lands, Native people like Canassateego (Onondaga) argued that American Indians *did* understand land value: "We know our lands are now become more valuable. The white people think we do not know their value; but we are sensible that the land is everlasting, and the few goods we receive for it are soon worn out and gone."[19] He intimated that ancestral land was eternal, even though what the British considered of value (i.e., timber, soil, and minerals) might have been short-lived. Here, Native conceptions of land as sacred and everlasting borrowed from and disputed the common European view of land as commodity.

American Indian rebellions also challenged the governing role bequeathed to the colonists by the Proclamation of 1763. Chief Pontiac (Ottawa), for instance, confronted British forts along the Upper Mississippi Valley. He traveled from the Upper Midwest down to Creek territory (mostly in what is now Alabama) enlisting support for his coup. In a rallying call to a council at River Ecores on April 27, 1763, Pontiac exhorted a pan-Indian gathering to contest British encroachment: "My children, you have forgotten the customs and traditions of your forefathers. Why do you not clothe yourselves in skins, as they did, and use the bows and arrows, and the stone-pointed lances, which they used?"[20] In this oration, Pontiac resituated Native identities within the frames of ancestry and tradition. He continued, "You have bought guns, knives, kettles and blankets, from the white men, until you can no longer do without them . . . Fling all these things away; live as your wise forefathers lived before you."[21] He agonized that the accoutrements of colonialism had diminished the heritage of the gathered nations' ancestors. The chief's centering of customs and land within the purview of Native ancestry occluded European influence.

Pontiac was not alone in his agitation, as American Indians often met to discuss territorial grievances against the Crown. These meetings among Native nations, and also between Natives and British colonials, continued into the Revolutionary era. In such a gathering, in 1774, Mihnehwehna (Ojibway) railed against colonists to a group of kindred Native nations and some representatives of the Crown: "Although you have conquered the French you have not conquered us! We are not your slaves. These lakes and woods and mountains were left to us by our ancestors. They are our inheritance and we will part with them to none."[22] Like Pontiac, Mihnehwehna hearkened to the gathered nations' moral inheritance of their ancestral identity. Land, so vital to American Indians, was sacred in part because it was bestowed by ancestors. That the British predicated their identity on their ownership and production of the lands fell on deaf ears.

The confluence of US and American Indian discourses continued, following the American Revolution, within the parameters of economics and territoriality. Picking up Britain's lead, the US government instituted a treaty system predicated on protectionism. The government promised security to American Indians in exchange for safe passage through Indian territory and the surrender of Native lands. This was a colonizing strong-arming on the part of the US government, which led to clashes over understandings of land. As a result, the United States and Native nations negotiated the meanings of their identities through treaty meetings and councils. The US government worked from an identity of superiority, modeled after the British, while simultaneously constituting Native identities as ward-like and dependent. American Indians, however, challenged these identity constructions by asserting their sovereignty.

The treaty era arguably peaked during a 1778 exchange between the Continental Congress and the Delaware Nation. It seems, according to Francis Paul Prucha, that the government graciously inherited Britain's control over American Indian nations through "the use of treaties, carried over from British practice."[23] The idea of inheritance thus extended beyond land, capital, and independence won through the agency of the Revolutionary War.

That is, the new American nation received at the war's end a population to control.

Treaties allowed the US government to acquire land and secure peace in exchange for the protection of American Indian nations and the payment of goods and money. Working from a protectionist identity, the United States employed western contractual law as the dominant form of agreement, thus limiting the space and agency of Native treaty parties. Some scholars have viewed this as a cultural imperialism that would consistently lead to governmental interests trumping tribal liberties.[24]

Treaties hearken to the vital theme of geography within Native-US relationships. Prior to the English arriving in Jamestown in 1607, roughly 800,000 Natives lived in vicinities east of the Mississippi River. Most Native nations led insular lives replete with some system of social organization and dependence on subsistence farming and hunting.[25] Though the focus of a nation was inward, there did exist various forms of contact among groups, including both pleasant relations such as intermarriages, joint hunts, and communal spiritual practices, and antagonistic clashes related to wars and contests over land boundaries and resources. Certainly, there were always distinct characteristics of each indigenous culture, however many it seems tended to share a sense of ancestral homeland.[26] Although fringes of land were traded with other Native nations, most cherished their territories.[27]

Ancestral land represented the core of American Indian cultures. Land's importance was so great, in fact, that many nations related their own social existence and spiritual health to their homelands. A sampling of this connection to land is found in Antiwaneto's (Cowasuck) 1764 speech to the Massachusetts governor regarding the taking of Native lands:

> Your heart [is] of gall. In truth, in the moment you begin we are on our guard. . . . We have not yet sold the lands we inhabit, we wish to keep possession of them. . . . We will not, under any pretext whatsoever, let you pass beyond them. The lands we possess have been given us by the Master of Life.[28]

These sentiments, first, indicate that Antiwaneto reconstituted the identities of the US government and the Cowasuck. He challenged Native identities as "bad hearts" (an expression used by colonists) by flipping the construction to point to colonists' "heart of gall." This détourning tactic is reminiscent of what Kent Ono and John Sloop say are vernacular communities' propensities to use whatever exists of "hegemonic discourse to construct subjectivities."[29] Second, Antiwaneto expressed a desire to keep land, not for its commodity, but because only the "Master of Life" possessed it. Antiwaneto defied colonial identities predicated on the land's utility with an American Indian identity based on land's ancestral meanings.

Despite Native connections to homelands, American settlers descended on American Indian territories based on the "doctrine of discovery." According to Sidney Lens, this doctrine of eminent domain was cited as the rationale for seizing land in the Western Hemisphere. He argues that "because they were 'Christian' and 'civilized,' said the Europeans, they enjoyed the 'right of sovereignty' over the lands they claimed. They were people of a higher order endowed by the Creator with special rights."[30] Reflecting the sentiments of early European explorers, American settlers claimed dominance over any land on which they set their feet. The doctrine of discovery, then, smoothed the path of US expansion.

American settlers translated their desire for colonial conquest into a language of care, which helped form a benevolent justification. At the same time that the government could seek to civilize Native communities and later take their land, it could also ferret out dangerous Natives who threatened the American frontier. As the nation extended outward, it claimed "a care-taking quality that might counterbalance the aggressiveness and expansion for which [it was] becoming known."[31] Treaties thus became part of a rhetoric of spatial dominance that also rationalized territorial expansion and justified control over dangerous populations, while reiterating America's mission as a God-fearing people civilizing non-whites.

Some 371 treaties were negotiated between the United States and Native nations before the 1870s, but the Treaties of McIntosh (1785) and Hopewell (1785) demonstrably helped to codify the practice of land control and acquisition through a sort of hegemonic process of consent. The Treaty of McIntosh, for example, initiated the long-standing tradition of forcing tribes to submit to American superiority at the negotiating table. The treaty's second article commanded that the Wyandot, Delaware, Chippewa, and Ottawa nations "acknowledge themselves and all their tribes to be under the protection of the United States and of no other sovereign whatsoever."[32] Here, any sense that the Native nations would be treated as foreign countries on equal footing with the US government was seemingly complicated.

The Treaty of Hopewell extended US protection to commerce and trade. Couching their desire to regulate Native economies in a protectionist rhetoric, the Hopewell authors ensured that American Indians would not have the right to trade with anyone but the US government. "For the benefit and comfort of the Indians and for the prevention of injuries or oppressions on the part of the citizens or Indians," proclaimed the treaty writers, "the United States shall have the sole and exclusive right of regulating trade with the Indians." Moreover, the US government tasked itself here with "managing all their affairs in such manner as they think proper."[33] Sovereignty tended to allow for free trade, but the government's occlusion of free trade for Natives denied American Indians equal footing.[34] Slowly, these denigrating treaty articles entrenched colonization through a hegemonic relationship of economic symbiosis.

Cultural inclusion and exclusion were remnants of identities constructed by treaties. Territorial ownership played a significant role in who belonged in the US nation as active and vigorous citizen members. Typically, citizenship was only offered to white males who possessed fifty acres of land and at least two years of residence on that land.[35] And the Continental Congress's Committee on Indian Affairs celebrated the partitioning of American Indian lands as a way to quickly integrate emigrating Europeans. The committee reported in 1783 that territory would exist as a "bounty" to those immigrants in particular who were willing to relocate to the colonies, and that Native occupied (not owned) lands would make for a "speedy provision for extending" the colonies' citizenry.[36] Those whites who received the bounty would be part of the citizenry.

Furthermore, the Constitution offered little in the way of citizenship for American Indian nations. The Constitution provided that Congress "establish a uniform rule of naturalization" but did not specifically outline the qualifications for citizenship for whites, let alone Native communities.[37] Citizenship was split between individual states and the federal government. Localized white citizenship tended to take precedence, but in 1790 the US Congress began moving citizenship requirements into central form. The responsibility of separate states to establish citizenship requirements ended, somewhat officially, with the passage of the Fourteenth Amendment, in which Congress determined "all persons born or naturalized in the United States and subject to the jurisdiction thereof shall be citizens of the United States and of the State in which they reside."[38] Prior to that, both state and federal authorities negotiated citizenship. American Indians, of course, were not considered "citizens of the United States" and therefore were not protected—both prior to and following the Fourteenth Amendment. No state, then, was able to make or enforce "any law which shall abridge the privileges or immunities of citizens of the United States."[39] Native nations were left out because their lands were often viewed as not their own. Their occupation of territory and so-called misuse of "republican" land rendered them separate from the Union and the states. American Indians were neither white nor perceived to hold territory to the extent of whites; hence, Native communities were not always assured the prospects of citizenship. But, American Indians could trade their territories as tenants through treaties that favored the US government.

Just as American Indians responded to British dominance, Native nations likewise challenged the policies codified and identities constructed by the US government. These decolonizing efforts are what Peter Hitchcock writes are "dialogics of the oppressed." Certainly, while such back talk rarely induces immediate and whole-cloth successes, it does "constitute a significant logic of resistance and an array of contestatory practices."[40] Joseph Brant (Mohawk), for instance, undertook an interesting tactic of linking Native sovereign identity to US sovereign identity—creating a decolonial discourse in the process. Arguing against the typically one-sided dynamic of treaties, Brant appealed to President George Washington in 1794: "We are of the same opinion with the people of the United States; you consider yourselves as independent people; we, as the original inhabitants of this country, and sovereigns of the soil, look upon ourselves as equally independent, and free as any other nation of nations."[41] In this case, Brant confirmed American Indian sovereignty apart from the government, while also connecting the United States' recent battle for independence with the Mohawk Nation's own distinct sovereignty. Brant also added the gloss that Natives were "original inhabitants," perhaps increasing American Indian ethos as ancestral inhabitants of North America. Such an analogy worked through a common and powerful American storyline, liberty via the American Revolution, to turn the US government's colonial efforts on their head.

Similarly, Ohnawiio (Mohawk), Oteatohatongwan (Mohawk) and Teholagwanegen (Mohawk) articulated their sovereign identity apart from the US nation by appealing to key pillars of the US government. The trio contended, "Formerly, we enjoyed the privilege [that] we expect is now called freedom and liberty; but since the acquaintance with our brother white people, that which we call freedom and liberty becomes an entire stranger to us; and in the place of that comes flattery and deceit."[42] This group created an impasse for its American counterparts: dealings with Americans had severely limited Natives' freedom, thus violating an ideological building block of the United States. The use of familial language that reified a so-called kinship furthered the Mohawk grievances as the US government arguably violated the rights of fellow family members. The master's language, though Emma LaRocque writes of its "painful" use because it portends that Native "words have been infantilized, stolen, silenced, and erased," helped American Indians like Ohnawiio, Oteatohatongwan, and Teholagwanegen to fight back against spurious treaty-making.[43]

American Indian and US governmental identities transformed, once again, with the dawning of the nineteenth century. In addition to clashing over trade and land, they began negotiating the idea of American Indian assimilation. Presidents Washington and Thomas Jefferson supported the assimilation of Native communities to American agriculture, trading, education, and domestication. When assimilation seemed to falter, the US government shifted its gaze to a policy of removal. This would be the ultimate colonizing strategy. Suddenly, American Indian identities, which US assimilationist rhetoric had previously constituted as adaptable and promising, became obstinate and removable. Throughout the evolution of US Indian policy, from assimilation to removal starting in 1830, the US government further solidified its role as a paternalistic and protectionist force over American Indian nations, while Natives attempted to reconfigure and détourn these identities.

Washington and Jefferson at first publicly viewed American Indian nations with greater trust and promise than their British forebears. Natives were, to these presidents, worth helping because they could contribute to the nation by assimilating. For instance, in an 1802 Presidential Letter to Congress, Jefferson reminded leaders that they needed "to encourage [Indians] to abandon hunting, to apply to the raising of stock, to agriculture and domestic manufacture, and to prove to them that less land and labor will maintain them on this better than in their former mode of living."[44] These assimilation policies still remained controlling; both Washington and Jefferson wished to augment Native character with American cultural mores and practices.

Washington's policy involved a softening of Native-US relations, despite his personal prejudices. Washington, as Anthony F. C. Wallace reminds us, was privately reticent about trusting American Indians and placing faith in their communities as intelligent, independent, and productive. The president was "an old Indian fighter" from way back, and made no qualms about denigrating as inferior those whom he considered his Native wards.[45] In 1787, following passage of the Northwest Ordinance,[46] Washington wrote to Secretary of War Henry Knox that the Indian and the wolf, "both being beasts of prey," might be ill-affected by the United States' encroachment onto Native lands. He continued, "The gradual extension of our settlements will as certainly cause the savage, as the wolf, to retire."[47] At the same time, though, Washington was encouraged by Knox and others in his administration to take a softer line on land acquisition. The Northwest Ordinance came to represent Washington's overt policy that "the Indian tribes should be considered foreign nations" and that the United States had "a preemptive right—an exclusive option—to purchase Indian land."[48]

The Washingtonian period indicates that the Native-US relationship was built around dollar diplomacy. One of Washington's most extensive ideas for negotiating with American Indian communities was the establishment of trading houses. Such a system of trade, he said, "would be as honorable to the national character as comfortable to the dictates of sound policy."[49] This "sound policy" involved forcing American Indians to rely on goods produced by the United States, a practice that smacked of colonizing control of Native well-being. The policy was supposed to work in two ways. First, it would help assimilate Natives to American customs and cultures. Second, as Natives entered into debt with trading houses, they might be more willing to sell their land to offset the debts. As Washington put it, "The establishment of commerce with the Indian nations on behalf of the United States is most likely to conciliate their attachment" to the land.[50]

The presence of Washington's dollar diplomacy was certainly noticed by American Indian nations. Natives tended to view the US government's economic policies as contributing to diminutive indigenous identities. Speaking against the power dynamics of US-led treaties and economic plans, Corn Tassel (Cherokee) challenged US economic plans in 1795:

> How [can the president] tell me that it [land] is yours by right of conquest? . . . I should retort on him that *we* had last marched over his territory; even up to this place which he has fortified so far within his former limits. . . . If, therefore, a bare march, or reconnoitering a country is sufficient reason to ground a claim to it, we shall insist upon transposing the demand, and your relinquishing your settlements on the western waters and removing one hundred miles back towards the east.[51]

Corn Tassel called into question the control of the United States by hybridizing the government's language about occupancy. If, he contended, power over the land came from mere occupancy, then surely American Indians would have the more legitimate claim. If this were the case, the government should remove. Such a decolonial reconstitution of identities was vital to Native empowerment at this pre–removal-era stage of Native-US interactions.

Jefferson continued the program of trading houses as a way to assimilate American Indians and to siphon away more land with the Trade and Intercourse Act of 1802, which like the Treaty of Hopewell, limited all American Indian trade to the US government alone.[52] In a special message to Congress in 1803 he argued that trade would promote both Native assimilation and US expansion: "To multiply trading houses among them" and to lead "them thus to agriculture, to manufactures, and civilization; in bringing together their and our sentiments, and in preparing them ultimately to participate in the benefits of our Government, I trust and believe we are acting for their greatest good."[53] Thus, trading houses became another way to instigate Native reliance on the paternalistic US government.

The overall watchword of Jefferson's Indian policy was assimilation. Jefferson's assimilation turned on converting American Indians into yeoman farmers, a not-unexpected ambition given Jefferson's agrarian roots. Francis Paul Prucha contends that Jefferson thought, "If the Indians came to rely on agriculture and domestic manufacture for their food and clothing, they would no longer need extensive hunting grounds and would willingly give up their unneeded lands for white settlement."[54] More to the point, assimilation would lead to Natives' decreased need for land. This reduced necessity would, in turn, benefit the white land squatters who were anxious to occupy fertile American Indian lands.

Because Jefferson was far more sympathetic to American Indians, assimilation grew in importance throughout his presidency. He felt a benevolent policy of assimilation was the primary solution to U.S-Native difficulties. For instance, he assured groups of the Miami, Potawatomi, and Wea nations in 1802,

> We shall with great pleasure see your people become disposed to cultivate the earth. . . . These resources are certain, they will never disappoint you, while those of hunting may fail, and expose your women and children to the miseries of hunger and cold. We will furnish you with implements for the most necessary arts, and with persons who may instruct you how to make use of them.[55]

Jefferson also exhorted Congress that institutional intervention into Native education was crucial to Native survival. He noted in his Annual Message in 1803, "Preparing [Indians] ultimately to participate in the benefits of our Government, I trust and believe we are acting for their greatest good."[56] Overall, Jefferson exhibited the symbiotic tenor of US and Native colonial ties; the US would entrench itself in Native cultural uplift through assimilation, while Natives would benefit the US economy and expansionist goals through their assimilation.

Still, Jefferson never intimated that American Indian nations would attain the status of full inclusion in the US citizenry. He actually layered his goal of increasing white citizenship over Native communities' mere occupancy of their lands. He did this by lowering territorial requirements in order to accommodate the enlarging white population. In his first inaugural address he argued that a "rising nation, spread over a wide and fruitful land" demanded territory and yeoman farming—the latter of which could only be practiced by tying citizenship to the land.[57] Therefore, he suggested and signed into law the extended Naturalization Act of 1802, which lowered residency requirements to five years, but still maintained that land ownership was vital to US citizenship.[58] Part of Jefferson's aspirations of linking territory to citizenship can also be seen in his 1803 confidential letter to Congress asking for funds to explore the Louisiana Territory. He said then, "An extension of territory which the rapid increase of our numbers will call for" was imperative for US citizenship. This citizenship-through-land, Jefferson continued, could be had by displacing American Indians from their territories. Indigenous communities and their territories were the currency that allowed white settlers to grow, and American Indians were "excluded from the privileges and immunities of citizenship."[59]

The Lewis and Clark expedition of 1803 commenced following Jefferson's Louisiana Purchase and summarily took as its thrust a surveying of the newly acquired land west of the Mississippi River. The Purchase demonstrated US expansionist identities by allowing the government to claim a vast range west of the Mississippi River. The Louisiana Territory also came to affect Native communities by suggesting new areas onto which indigenous nations could be removed in the event that assimilation did not work.

Jefferson sponsored the Lewis and Clark expedition in part to ascertain the quality, scope, topography, and fruitfulness of the western purchase, but also to discover possible locations for removal of the five southeastern nations—Choctaw, Creek, Chickasaw, Cherokee, and Seminole nations—west of the Mississippi River. In a private memorandum to Congress in January 1803, Jefferson opined that "Indian tribes residing within the limits of the US have for a considerable time been growing more and more uneasy at the constant diminution of the territory they occupy."[60] He then crafted an economic argument showing that the joint strategy of teaching the Natives agricultural technologies and surveying the Louisiana Purchase for their possible placement would add even more area to the Purchase as indigenous groups began vacating their eastern territory. Of this, he wrote: "The portion of their [Indian] country most important to us is exactly that which they do not inhabit . . . in the interior country."[61] But Jefferson needed an agency through which to remove Natives altogether by replacing and replicating their entire holdings, both hunting acreage and settlement areas. The Lewis and Clark expedition funding was therefore partly predicated upon Jefferson's argument that Native removal would justify the cost of exploration and pay back into the American economy by seizing Native lands. The idea was "particularly interesting," wrote Jefferson. "In order peaceably to counteract this policy of theirs," the government should "provide an extension of territory which the rapid increase of our numbers [in the eastern Indian country] will call for."[62]

Hence, Jefferson actually engineered the colonizing groundwork of what would later come to be known as Indian Removal. Evidence suggests that at the conclusion of the Lewis and Clark expedition Jefferson supported a constitutional amendment to "provide among other things for the transporting of the Eastern Indians to the newly acquired territory."[63] In a letter to Louisiana Territory Governor William Henry Harrison, Jefferson averred that Indian removal might best complement US expansion by eliminating the possibility of wrangling with Natives. American Indians, he argued, would "in time either incorporate with us as citizens of the United States or remove beyond the Mississippi."[64] In other words, the president's assimilation policy involved a built-in alternative. If Natives could not succeed as yeoman farmers, thus entreating with the United States to transfer their excess land, they had better plan to remove. Jefferson's amendment never made it to Congress, but the absence of a removal bill did not quash the possibility of removal.

Jefferson's policies represented the calm before the storm. Following Jefferson's administration, the US nation found itself in the throes of the War of 1812. By this time Native-US relations began transforming into an aggressive structure that threatened not only the lives of those Natives caught up in the war's wrangling, but also the overall intercultural relationship. Whereas Washington and Jefferson viewed indigenous populations graciously, albeit with an eye toward domination, the administrations of James Madison, James Monroe, and John Quincy Adams ushered in war and increased expansion. As with the Washington and Jefferson administrations, the era between 1810 and 1828 would set the stage for eventual removal.

During the tenures of Madison and Monroe the idea of removing American Indians and colonizing them on reservations promised an efficient, entropic mechanism for purifying the US nation. As Wallace argues, "By the 1820s, the term 'colonization' had become a popular label for the concept of solving social problems" by effectively removing those races deemed "problematic."[65] Madison and Monroe both believed if Jeffersonian assimilation failed, that American Indian colonization west of the Mississippi represented the next logical solution to the "Indian problem." In this vein, Monroe claimed in 1818, "It is indispensable that their independence as communities should cease, and that control of the United States over them should be complete and undisputed."[66] Later in 1825, he argued that by colonizing Natives, "And by the establishment of such a government over these tribes ... we become in reality their benefactors."[67] Ostensibly, the ideal of removal began to take shape as the American nation, comprehending its tentative relationship with Natives, entered the war. Adding to this realization, American Indians in disproportionate numbers supported the British over what Chief Tecumseh (Shawnee) called the common enemy of America.

The war between the United States and Britain unfurled, at least in the southeastern campaigns, on lands owned by American Indians. The venues for the white dispute involved, mostly, the edges of the ever-expanding US empire. Hence, border skirmishes erupted along the US-Canadian border and, most important with regard to Native lands, on the outer fringes of the American frontier: the Midwest along the Missouri and Ohio River valleys and in the Mississippi Territory of the southeast.

Tecumseh, a chief from the Detroit encampment area, viewed the presence of settlers on Native land as a sign of aggression.[68] In October of 1812, Tecumseh gathered groups of dissenters and went on a tour to rally support against the US government. Along the way, he drew into his fold hundreds of American Indians from the Creek, Chickasaw, Choctaw, and Cherokee nations, among others. Upon arriving at an inter-tribal council in Alabama, Tecumseh delivered an oration meant to unite the spirits of his community against the United States. He exhorted, "Listen! ... Oh Muskogees [Creeks]! Brethren of my mother! Brush from your eyelids the sleep of slavery, and strike for vengeance and your country! . . . Let the white race perish! . . . Back whence they came, upon a trail of blood, they must be driven! . . . Burn their dwellings—destroy their stock—slay their wives and children, that the very breed may perish!"[69] Equating US treatment of American Indians to "slavery," Tecumseh responded to American demands for early removal by suggesting that Americans remove themselves, détourning the US government's demands. As an alternative to accepting an identity as Native outsider, the chief constructed the US government's identity as the unwelcome pariah. In the process, the chief worked through the government's own characterization of Natives as savage to inspire his audience to take up arms. By turning around this identity construction, Tecumseh conflated and appropriated the government's seemingly demeaning label with Native empowerment.

Tecumseh's decolonial oration helped ignite a battle that led to the so-called Fort Mims Massacre north of Mobile, Alabama, wherein a Red Stick band of the Upper Creek Nation defeated a settler population. Fort Mims helped maintain an ongoing hatred between the Red Sticks, in particular, and the federal government.[70] Supported by the British, Tecumseh and his supporters argued that the war offered the opportune moment to challenge the government for its past indiscretions, including the numerous broken treaties that resulted in Native losses of land. Instead of victoriously ousting settlers from Native land, Tecumseh's pan-Indian union faltered

Native-US land conflicts during the War of 1812 ended when Indian fighter General Andrew Jackson defeated the Red Sticks in 1813 at the Battle of Horseshoe Bend near Dadeville, Alabama as revenge for the Fort Mims Massacre. I have argued elsewhere that this particular battle sounded a death knell for the Creek Nation in Alabama. What Jackson did in effect "was expand the United States and expedite its successes west of the Appalachians"; his victory at Horseshoe Bend opened up all of Alabama and Mississippi territories to settlement and "bolstered the US government's colonization of Native nations."[71] As the war ended, with Jackson ascending as the quintessential military hero, the Tennessean inherited a new position: Chief Indian Agent. Beginning in 1815, Jackson took it upon himself to meet several times with the five southeastern nations in order to initiate a removal policy. Throughout these talks, Jackson strengthened the familial bond between the United States and American Indians, begun earlier with the relationships spawning from the Proclamation of 1763 and the ensuing Native-US treaties. Perhaps borrowing from the protectionist ideology of these treaties, Jackson employed parent-child metaphors in constituting Native and US identities in his 1821 address to the Creek Nation: "Your white brethren must be settled there [Indian land] to keep from you bad men and bad talks. I wish to be informed where the Red people in the Floridas are settled, that I may make it known to your Father the President, that he may be enabled to judge your situation, [so that] you may be treated as the rest of his beloved children."[72] Here, he reaffirmed an authoritarian role for the US government, noting that it would be best enabled to judge American Indians' situations. Jackson also indicated that part of US identity involved protecting Native nations; in the process, he additionally concretized American Indians as dependents of a central power.[73]

In another example of early removal rhetoric, Jackson found an opening to offer his guidance by diminishing Native identity and capacity to reason. In an 1820 talk with the Choctaw Nation, Jackson commanded: "Hear and listen well. Decide for the happiness of all your people. . . . We have labored hard to convince you of your real interests. We hope you will see them as we do, and adopt the treaty proposed. . . . Should you reject it, it will be a source of great regret."[74] It appears that American Indians had minimal choice in determining their interests. Instead, the US government would decide the real destinies of American Indians. Jackson constructed US identity as superior, and therefore the US government retained power to guide because it ruled with reason. Native identities were seen by him as closer to nature and therefore were susceptible to wild desires.[75]

The colonization of American Indians grew, not only through the office of the President and through Congressional treaties, but also through Supreme Court decisions. Chief Justice John Marshall's infamous "Indian Trilogy" set the stage for weakened Native status. Simultaneously, Marshall inscribed upon Native communities the pallor of non-citizenship; the high court held that Natives could not enjoy sovereign domain over their lands.

The first case, *Johnson v. McIntosh* (1823), denied land rights to the Piankeshaw Nation with the justification that Natives could not be involved in the US citizenry. Marshall codified the rule that "the extent of their right of alienation must depend upon the laws of dominion under which they live. . . . They are subject to the sovereignty of the United States."[76] His holding strengthened the US government's tendency to view American Indians as dependents. Moreover, racial stereotypes of the "red child" were constituted with Marshall's insistence that the government treat Natives "as an inferior race of people, without the privileges of citizens, and under the perpetual protection and pupilage of the government."[77] Seemingly, Marshall contributed to the notion that Natives could not acquire citizenship based on race. After Jeffersonian assimilation failed to convert American Indians, and as removal garnered popularity, the Supreme Court methodized the stripping away of indigenous citizenship as a rationale for dispossessing Native communities and taking more territory.

The primary legal consequence of *Johnson v. McIntosh* for Native communities was the transfer of land ownership from indigenous authority to the US government. The Court admitted Natives were occupants of land, but with the caveat that "their rights to complete sovereignty, as independent nations, were necessarily diminished, and their power to dispose of the soil at their own will, to whomsoever they pleased, was denied" by the fundamental principle of discovery.[78] The Court's rhetoric pointed to an imperialism that blocked American Indian empowerment. Moreover, Marshall's nineteenth century vision of discovery created a landlord-tenant relationship. As landlord, the US government "possessed the power to terminate the 'tenancy' of its occupants but also could materially affect the lives of Indians through its control and regulation of land use."[79] That American Indians could not hold property—in the western sense—indicated to Marshall and the broader US government the inability of Native communities to obtain full US citizenship.

Natives faced another challenge when, in 1825, President James Monroe announced a proposed policy of removal. Concerned that assimilation had not worked as planned, Monroe suggested, "Removal of the tribes from the territory which they now inhabit . . . would not only shield them from impending ruin, but promote their welfare and happiness."[80] Thus, as Indian agent Jackson strove for removal through his "talks" with Natives, and as the Supreme Court diminished Native connections to the land, Monroe set into motion Jefferson's ideas for removal.

Even prior to an official involuntary US removal policy American Indians responded with disdain to the government's early attempts at dispossessing Native nations. To one of the US government's removal talks, Black Thunder (Fox) retorted in 1815, "I have nothing new to say here in your councils. . . . You heard it, and no doubt remember it. It [is] simply this. My lands can never be surrendered; I was cheated . . . basely cheated in [US sponsored] contracts; I will not surrender my country but with my life."[81] It seems, here, that Black Thunder typified American Indian sentiments related to the land, and was willing to die for the cause of remaining on his ancestral homeland. Similarly arguing against Monroe's removal policy, Petalsharo (Pawnee) lamented in 1822: "When we did not know the whites—our wants were then fewer than they are now. . . . We had then seen nothing which we could not get. Before our intercourse with the whites . . . we would find the buffalo feeding around our camp—but now they are killing them for their skins."[82] In one fell decolonial salvo, he spoke of US character as caustic; prior to contact, Natives enjoyed their land without barrier. On the other hand, Petalsharo suggested that land, under Native care and influence, was honored for its natural abundance.

Monroe's 1825 address proposed that the acculturation of American Indians had been a somewhat flawed policy. He said then: "In [the Indians'] present state it is impossible to incorporate them . . . into our system . . . without a timely anticipation of land provision against the dangers to which they are exposed, under causes which it will be difficult, if not impossible, to control, their degradation and extermination will be inevitable."[83] Speaking benevolently, Monroe argued that American expansion and the salvation of Native nations depended on a renewed removal policy. Monroe was "impressed with the opinion that removal" would form the crux of such a new colonizing policy.[84]

Though important to both Monroe and President John Quincy Adams, removal was not officially implemented in the 1820s to the extent that it would be in the following decade. Wholesale removal would have to wait until 1828 when Jackson was elected president. Once in office, he relied less on assimilation, preferring removal as a more direct policy. Colonization was about to escalate more than most Native communities likely could anticipate.

CHAPTER TWO

Governmental Colonizing Rhetoric During Indian Removal

THE ASCENDANCE OF ANDREW JACKSON TO THE PRESIDENCY IN 1828 marked a pivotal shift in policy toward involuntary removal. The frontier character of an expanding United States was both scripted by, and layered over, his leadership. For Jackson, the key spirit of the nation was not a "revolutionary disposition as it had been understood by members of the founding generation," but rather land.[1] As his domestic policies commenced, Jackson transformed Thomas Jefferson's yeoman farmer into a pioneer, exploring the nation and widening its territory. But, before this pioneer spirit could fully flourish, Native nations on the frontier were to be moved around to allow for less-fettered white settlement. Early on as an Indian agent, Jackson did more than merely hint at the importance of overrunning Native lands. He wrote to President James Monroe in 1817: "I contend that the Legislature of the Union have the right to prescribe [Indians'] bounds at pleasure" and that the government has "the right to take it and dispose of it."[2] The dual focus of removing American Indians while usurping their land for a broadened US citizenry became the hallmark of Jackson's later presidential policies regarding Native nations. Overall, Jackson's ideas greatly influenced the government as Congress simultaneously grappled with the issue of removal.

To be sure, there was a lack of consensus among the branches of the federal government regarding American Indian identities and how Native communities should fit into the nation. On the one hand, they were considered children and part of the US nation as protected wards. As a result, American Indians could not be completely expelled due to the familial relationship fostered by the US government. Early in his career Jackson demonstrated this familial role when he told a group of the Chickasaw Nation in 1816 that "the President of the U States loves his red children, & will do justice to them" by considering their interests.[3] The protective relationship was also revealed as Monroe refused to engage in a removal policy that would "cause harm" to the nation's "wards." He addressed Congress in 1824, noting that to "remove [the Indians] by force, even with a view to their own security and happiness, would be revolting to humanity and utterly unjustifiable."[4] Native identity seemed in this rhetoric diminutive yet familial and safe.

A competing perspective, though, situated American Indians as uncivilized and in need of severance from US territories. They were, according to Governor John Forsyth (Georgia), "a race not to be admitted to be equal to the rest of the community . . . treated somewhat like human beings, but not admitted" to be men with "civil and political rights." Forsyth concluded that American Indians should be pushed aside because they possessed not "sovereignty" but "petty" and "animal" attributes.[5] This characterization had little connection to territory—except through tenancy—and was used to justify an involuntary removal plan. In a similar vein, Secretary of War John Eaton wrote to the Cherokee Nation in 1829, "No right . . . save a mere possessory one . . . is conceded to your nation."[6]

The responsibility of determining American Indians inclusion was similarly ambiguous. At times it appeared that individual states would hold sway over managing Native affairs. Thomas McKenney, Jackson's advisor on removal, echoed Eaton's sentiments when he remarked that "the General Government *will not* interfere nor should it to prevent states from extending their laws over the Indians within them."[7] And, arguments of the southern states for removal were predicated on the supremacy of states' rights over federal control. The responsibility of governing Indian affairs had always legally fallen to the US government. Even prior to the Constitution, the US government claimed pre-eminence over individual states. A notable proclamation of the Continental Congress helped forge one of the guiding tenets of Native-US relations: "The United States . . . have the sole and exclusive right and power of regulating the trade and managing the affairs of the Indians, not individual member states."[8]

These disagreements over matters of Native citizenship or sovereignty, oversight of federal versus state governments, and American Indian identities were considered by the executive, legislative and judicial branches during the removal milieu. Throughout the era, and especially with passage of the Indian Removal Act in 1830, however, such contestations were significantly lessened for the federal government. The Act reduced the government's uncertainties and codified the notion that American Indians would be treated as perpetual wards of a colonizing US government. The policy was couched in a kind of familial benevolence that appeared helpful to American Indians instead of beneficial solely to US expansion. American Indians were also constructed monolithically as dependent and, to this end, the government essentialized Native differences and overlooked geographical nuances. At the end of the day, Native communities would be viewed as reliant on the US government.

In typical fashion for a colonized relationship, land functioned as a crucial element in the contestation of Native identities. Because territory was a key criterion for citizenship and American Indians were considered too uncivilized, the government tended to dismiss Native ownership based on a lack of productivity. Instead, they were granted tenancy (or occupancy) rights. Their lack of (Western-based) territorial toil and citizenship partly resulted in removal, which was wholly justified through the doctrine of discovery.

During the removal era, the government's discourse codified the paternal Native-US relationship at the federal level to the detriment of states' rights. In the process, removal cemented the interactive identities of the US government as a dominant, supervising force and of American Indians as a homogenized mass, which further eroded Native sovereignty. In this way, the rhetoric of removal demonstrably followed the avenues of colonization. For, as Emma LaRocque argues, colonization considers civilization "illuminated, progressive, and decent. . . . [It] is repeatedly outlined against 'Indian savagery' in which savagism is seen as a psychosocial fixed condition, the antithesis of the highest human condition."[9] This sentiment represents the US government's rote colonizing map during removal.

As LaRocque's ideas above indicate, governmental identities in the Jacksonian era can be partly linked to a self-professed mission of expansion into new lands and civilizing so-called savages in the "wilderness" both with the support of divine providence. This mission was used to justify how the United States "conquered" others and "establish[ed] and perpetuate[ed] histories" that naturalized a hierarchy where the federal government possessed considerably "greater importance" than "others" like American Indians.[10] The mission of progress as a nationalistic concept has been deemed "manifest destiny."

Manifest destiny as a term derives from journalist John O'Sullivan's classic interpretation of US colonial projects sponsored under the Jackson, Tyler, and Polk administrations during the mid-century. To O'Sullivan, the nation's westward movement demanded that Americans fulfill a divine plan as central to its future.[11] In discussing expansion he worried that opponents by "thwarting our policy and hampering our power, limiting our greatness and checking the fulfillment of our *manifest destiny* to overspread the continent allotted by Providence for the free development of our yearly multiplying millions," would counteract the momentum of US nationalism.[12] O'Sullivan's term stuck.

Vestiges of this mythos can be traced back to the Puritan "errand into the wilderness," or the notion that expansion fulfilled a covenant with God to satisfy his plan.[13] The early US nation later secularized the errand as it sought divine justification for its separation from Great Britain. Sidney

Lens describes this as a grand motivation needed to remind early Americans that God was on their side both in their revolt from the Crown and in their conquest of American Indians and control of African slaves. He argues, "The Americans believed that . . . nature had given them a special right to expand. They were like the ancient Israelites, a chosen race . . . carrying progress forward wherever they went. They were not trampling on other people, they were opening up new vistas for them."[14] With God on its side, the nineteenth century US government could not only rationalize its existence, but could also commence expansion to grow the nation's economy and to secure more land for white settlers.

The broadening of the US land base inevitably led to a connection among citizenship, territory, and republicanism. That is, as the US nation expanded, and as American settlers occupied these new spaces, property holding became a vital component of a republican citizenry that would nurture the nation. Ronald Takaki claims that expansion "offered whites the promise of property ownership and [the government] a stable republican future."[15] And, though US citizenship was puzzling and unclear at times, one thing was certain: land typically affected citizenship status. As Rogan Kersh explains, federal and state grants of land "encouraged grantees to view their holding as part of a unified American territory."[16] The more citizen-freeholders there were in the newly expanded republic, the safer the US nation would prove against the external challenges of early nationhood.

Interestingly, property ties to citizenship seemed to loosen in the Jacksonian era as the populism of Republicans promoted lower classes to US citizenship in contrast to the elitist and limited citizenship suggested by the Federalists. Land was certainly considered beneficial to citizenship, but it did not have to be inherited or owned in multitudes. With Jacksonian democracy—one known for privileging meritocracy over aristocracy—came the "enunciation of the cult of the self-made man."[17] As long as people worked the land with an eye toward improving the nation, they could justly be considered republican citizens. After all, work attached people to the land, even if people lacked ownership. Pride in one's assiduousness equated with the solemn individualism upon which republican nations depended.

Such a populist vision sprang from the role of expansion in the United States and the limitations of property requirements to settling new lands. Perhaps property-holding requirements waned because yeoman farmers emigrating west could not afford land or because a large population was artisanal, mechanics-based, and shop-keeping, therefore owning little or no land. That new lands could not keep up with the surges of western movement during the Era of Good Feelings meant that relaxed and expedient citizenship rules needed to guide naturalization even more.[18] If such property requirements remained intact during the heady days of the Jacksonian era, new territories would have been virtually citizen-less.

Next to property ownership, the issue of race and ethnicity figured most prominently into Jacksonian citizenship. This seemed to exacerbate the uncertainty of who could be considered part of the nation. As Jacksonians moved toward a state-centered, populist and "*white* republic," they defended their claims to citizenship "in terms of racial superiority rather than strained doctrines" of territory.[19] Any such guilt about this was alleviated through the doctrine of discovery that placed whites on a higher cultural plane than other ethnicities. Jacksonians, in particular, used ethnic categories to define citizenship as white-only. Jackson noted in 1829 that "Indians . . . lacked the honest industry" of white citizens, and therefore "the children of the forest" could not be part of the US nation merely because "they had seen [it] from the mountain or passed it in the chase." White people, he wrote, were the "true" Americans; Natives had only "artificial distinctions" as weaker neighbors.[20]

The ambiguity of American Indians' citizenship often teetered between their rights to territory based on birthright and occupancy and the competing idea that their race precluded citizenship. Even though indigenously born to North America, American Indians would not be considered either citizens or property owners during the Jacksonian era. Rogers Smith makes the ironic point that in terms of the "*jus soli* understanding of birthright membership, no one had better claim as native-born Americans than Native Americans."[21] But, their non-white cultural markers limited their property roles as occupants, not owners. Thus, writes David Wilkins, the US government "reduced tribal claims to aboriginal lands as mere *tenancy*"—the political concept that American Indians merely existed on the territory.[22]

Paternalism likewise guided Native-US relations as a colonial mechanism. Paternalism involved a rhetoric infused with "policies and practices of treating or governing people in a [parental] manner, especially by providing for their needs without giving them responsibility."[23] Nineteenth century paternal identity in the United States was concerned with the familial relationship of "acting as a father acts with respect to his child or children" regarding American Indians.[24] Such paternalism functioned by naturalizing familial imagery within political contexts and likening "what is done by colonial powers to what goes on in the family, giving it a moral justification that it otherwise would have lacked."[25]

The paternal persona of the US government during the nineteenth century complicated the certainty of American Indians' roles in the US nation. On one hand, the United States enabled itself to assert an unnatural control over Native communities using the ironical relationship of a father to his child. In this vein, Natives were constructed as veritable wards who "as children were ignorant; they could be deceived or treated in a way that served the interests of the adults—a kind of exploitative paternalism."[26] This oppression involved the cultural status of indigenous populations. As the United States constructed its own paternal relationship with the continent's numerous Native nations, it additionally constituted these nations as inferior and less-than-civilized, or less-than-white. On the other hand, American Indians were, as familial dependents, incorporated as protected by the nation and vital to the US government's acquisition of territory. The government seemed at a loss for how to define Native character based on the competing dynamics of Native diminution and Native consideration involved in the paternal relationship.

Related to paternalism, Natives were also consistently caught between two sectional "father figures" during the Jacksonian period, which further complicated American Indian identities and how the US government would interact with them. Native sovereignty was mired in the wrangling between the federal government and individual states, which raged beyond the Federalist and Anti-Federalist debates. Under the Articles of Confederation, sovereign states possessed the "grounds for independent action" to resolve conflicts and relationships with American Indian nations.[27] However, part of the Federalists' revised plan for a more supreme central government involved limiting states' rights to encroach on Native territories. The Continental Congress's report on the Southern Department in August 1787 declared that "the laws of the States can have no effect upon a tribe of Indians or their lands within the limits of the state. . . . No particular state can have an exclusive interest in the management of affairs of any tribe."[28] Soon, the federalization of US-Indian affairs was codified in the Constitution, which asserted that only Congress possessed the power to entreat "with the Indian tribes."[29]

Individual states, typically more adverse to Native sovereignty since it impeded local expansion, attempted to regulate Indian affairs against constitutional doctrine. Such state power was overlooked as the federal government became more occupied with naturalization. As more European immigrants arrived in the United States, the federal government could not keep up with a central system of naturalization. States, especially in the South, viewed the federal government's efforts to entreat with Native nations, and also regulating immigration to the states, as too slow. Therefore the federal government "did not forbid the states to continue" to accept immigrants and "grant them citizenship rights with regard to local laws and politics."[30] And, states were not equally prevented from regulating relationships with American Indians.

But once the War of 1812 threatened national security, the federal government stepped in to regulate Native relations and naturalization. The former was necessary as a number of Native nations sided with the British. States' rights concerning American Indians were drastically reduced in the wake of the War of 1812, and this decline additionally obscured Native-US relations.

The states suffered numerous challenges to their sovereignty that complicated the sectional conflict and US governmental and American Indian identities. In 1819, John Marshall held that "it would be difficult to sustain" the proposition that "the powers of the general government . . . are delegated by the States" and, hence, "the people of a single State cannot confer a sovereignty" that would extend above and over the Union.[31] This opinion (*McCulloch v. Maryland*) put a temporary check on states' rights; according to H.W. Brands, the court "swept aside" states' rights en route to charting "the course of the republic by the Federalist stars."[32] The high court's ruling and Congress's continued privileging of federal authority over states' rights through the Missouri Compromise (1820), Tariff of Abominations (1828), and the Foote Resolution (1830) brought the Union to the brink of collapse. Jackson's vice president, John Calhoun, threatened in his South Carolina Exposition, that states would be "equally clear in the existence of a necessity to justify its exercise" of nullification should the General Government "persist in its improper assumptions of power."[33] Sectional rifts were thus widening between the South and the federal government.

Jackson became the executive mouthpiece of the federal government in dealing with the issue of removal. John Buchanan memorializes Jackson as the prime catalyst for the policy: "Monroe and others knew the answer [to the Indian question] and it was simple: Turn Jackson loose!" and then "the southern warrior Jackson" would provide the nation with its "hammer" for removal.[34] Even though Jackson's plans matured with his presidency, he long viewed removal as a viable policy. The quintessential "Indian fighter," Jackson sought to negotiate small land cessions with Native nations so that the US population could enact "the honorable toil of carrying the republican standard" of America "to the heights of Abraham."[35]

Jackson constructed American Indian identities and constituted the Native-US relationship while advocating for removal by relying on competing formations of American Indian character.[36] In his presidential rhetoric, Jackson interchanged Native identities as civilized and independent and, in contrast, as uncivilized and dependent, eventually settling on the latter pairing in order to further cement American Indians as dependent and in need of protection. Part of these identity constructions limited Native ownership rights to their territories based on their lack of production. Though Jackson hinted at Native agency in exchanging territories, he eventually entrenched the colonizing Native "tenant" identity that motivated Congress to pass the Indian Removal Act.

The pairing of American Indians as uncivilized and the government as civilized was certainly a part of Jackson's colonial administrative discourse. For instance, in discussing his removal aims in a letter to one of his subagents, he argued that Creek territory should be populated by "the civilized" of the United States. It is "essential," he reasoned, that the land "be settled by a hardy race that would defend it. . . . Our settlement [must] extend to the Mississippi."[37] Likewise, Natives were to be removed because they threatened the physical sanctuary of the nation and the purity of the US citizenry. The government then, he averred, ought to "adopt every means to populate speedily this section of the Union . . . our national security . . . and reputation . . . require it." Jackson viewed the "less advanced" American Indians as dangerous to, and undeserving of, the land.[38] In a sense, such a diminution of Native identities set the stage for their near-exclusion from citizenship and land ownership.

Jackson's characterizations of Native identity as uncivilized also connected with his insistence that American Indians were dependent. For instance, he thought that indigenous communities were equally at peril from contact with whites. Waxing paternalistic, Jackson said "*their* security require it" as well and that "the happiness and security of the whole require its salutary agreement."[39] Certainly American Indians were to be protected, but this protection was vital only inasmuch as they had lands to exchange; after the exchange, they were to be removed to the margins of US territory. Native nations were said to be land tenants due to their lack of civilization; they could not, in Jackson's estimation, "own the territory."[40] Thus, the US government was to step in to offer paternal "supervision." Jackson's continued use of the "Great Father" moniker also intimated that the government's power over American Indians would vest in the presidency.[41]

Ironically, Jackson's claims about Native territoriality still hinted at American Indian independence, thus pointing to his own internal uncertainty regarding Native communities. The expansion of US territory and removal of Native nations had to be accomplished through diplomacy to uphold republican ideals.[42] And, Jackson was still sensitive to "act humanely" and "justly" in exchanging—versus grabbing—Native territory.[43] This diplomacy speaks to the importance of American Indians being able to exchange their territory versus the federal government taking it without removal treaties. Jackson's insistence on negotiations indicated some sense that American Indians possessed agency to exchange their territories. As we will see in the following chapter, this kind of allowance opened up the doors to decolonial ruptures on the part of Native communities.

Alternatively, Jackson assumed the US government had full responsibility in rescuing Natives from eminent ruin by removing them to the far reaches of the American landscape. Not only did he view "treaties with the Indians [to be] an absurdity not to be reconciled to the principles of our Government," but he also configured a dichotomous relationship between the US government and American Indians. To him, American Indians "were subjects of the United States, inhabiting its territory and acknowledging its sovereignty."[44] Crafting a paternal governmental identity alongside dependent Native identities, Jackson reiterated that any plan in which American

Indians were granted agency to be risible. He concluded that there was nothing wrong with a relationship in which the "sovereign" decided for the "subject" their "wants and safety."[45] No matter how much American Indians had accomplished through efforts to acculturate, the expediency of US expansion required their removal.

By working through his own internal contestations over Native characterizations as both civilized and independent and uncivilized and dependent, Jackson moved toward clarifying Native and governmental identities for US leaders. As his removal plans took shape in 1829 and 1830, Jackson settled on a dependent role for American Indians in conjunction with a strong *federal* paternal character. US expansion began to take shape as a selfless effort for the benefit of dependent American Indians. While preparing his first annual address in December of 1829, Jackson elucidated this paternal benevolence. In responding to an inquiry from head US Indian Agent James Gadsen about how to "entreat" with Natives, Jackson reminded his agents, "I shall adhere to the just and humane policy toward the Indians . . . and have recommended them to quit their possessions on this side of the Mississippi." Part of his response indicated a concern for Native posterity: in the West, they would "always be free from the mercenary influence of White men and undisturbed by the local authority of the States. . . . The General government can exercise a parental control over their interests."[46]

Importantly, Jackson protected the "dependent native" by demonizing white encroachers in his paternal argument for protecting American Indian communities.[47] States wishing to take upon themselves the duty of regulating Native affairs were shown to be a detriment to Native life. In the weeks preceding his 1829 annual message, and only a few months before the passage of the Indian Removal Act in May 1830, Jackson also elevated the "General government" as the primary influence over Native nations. Historians have long assumed this break from his states-centered ideology was due to cordial relations with the Federalists to secure passage of the removal act.[48] In any case, the Native-US relationship was not to be merely paternal but exclusive to the federal government and unhindered by states' interests.

This same paternal shaping of removal continued into his first annual message in which Jackson firmly committed his administration to pursuing a bill for removal. Before crafting his solution to the "Indian problem," Jackson noted the impetus for the problem's expediency. Southern states were mobilizing against American Indians while, in tandem, supplanting federal authority over Natives. Of late, the State of Georgia had enacted several laws calling for the removal of the Cherokee Nation within the state's confines. Georgia passed a resolution in 1828 that granted it "the right to extend her authority and laws over her whole territory, and to coerce obedience to them from all descriptions of people, be them white, red or black who may reside within her limits."[49] The US government had promised the state in an 1802 agreement that the Cherokee Nation would be removed within twenty years. The Georgia legislature remarked, "All this will not do. . . . The United States will not redeem her honor," and therefore took it upon itself to entreat for removal or to "attempt violence" if other "means of redress fail."[50] Notably, Georgia had a pecuniary reason to begin its enforcement of the 1802 compact: gold had been discovered in the northeast portion of the state, especially around Dahlonega. Jackson forged his plan before Georgia threatened violence or forced American Indians to "submit to the laws of those States."[51] And, Jackson worried about appearing too sectionalist in his support of states' rights; as a politician with an eye toward passing removal legislation, he had to straddle the fence.

Ultimately, though, Jackson made unequivocal the paternal relationship between the government and American Indians by positioning the US government within the purview of the Constitution in interacting with American Indians. Again, the "Great Father" would lead the effort of the federal government. He hearkened to the provision that Congress had the power "to regulate commerce with foreign nations . . . and with the Indian tribes," and that "no State shall enter into any treaty, alliance or confederation" with outside bodies.[52] Later in his message, he underscored federal ethos by referring to the Trade and Intercourse Act of 1802 in which the US government codified the rule "that [states] could not negotiate such treaty or convention . . . to treat with any such Indian nation, or tribe of Indians."[53] Assumingly, Jackson had to appear somewhat impartial in order to get Congress behind Indian removal. As a federal official and yet an ardent supporter of state sovereignty, Jackson traipsed the line of sectional politics. Enacting a removal bill would triply: solidify the US government's controlling role in Native affairs, quell Southern antagonisms about Natives in the states, and secure more land for white settlers while pushing American Indians outside the mainstream American polity.[54]

Jackson spent the remainder of 1830 with American Indian nations entreating with them to sign removal agreements. Here, Jackson continually reified the familial relationship between the US government and American Indians. The familial relationship would soon be détourned, as Natives could claim consideration as a *very part* of the US nation. The two groups were symbiotic to Jackson; respectively, he thought that one's controlling role juxtaposed the others' lack of independence. Similarly, one's dependence strengthened the other's identity as paternalistic. Following his logic, one was to be centralized in this national imaginary while the other would be written-out. Speaking to Chief John Pitchlynn (Choctaw) in August of 1830, Jackson argued that his promotion of removal had left him feeling "conscious of having done my duty to my red children. . . . I have exonerated the national character from all imputation."[55]

As expected, the Executive was not alone in grappling with the contestation over American Indians. The twenty-first Congress also shouldered the responsibility of codifying removal. Along with Jackson's resolution of Native and governmental identities, Congress's cementing clarification of these roles did not come without capriciousness.

As Jackson rounded out his first year in office, conditions between southern states and their American Indian neighbors quickly deteriorated. Not only did Georgia and Alabama pass individual removal laws, but southern leadership also began petitioning both House and Senate Committees on Indian Affairs to get a bill onto the twenty-first Congress's docket. To this end, Georgia governor George Gilmer argued that a removal policy would be a crafty tool to induce "ignorant, intractable, and savage people" to "yield up what civilized peoples had a right to possess by virtue of that command of the Creator." He insisted that the US government allow its white population to "be fruitful, multiply, and replenish the earth, and subdue it!"[56]

Based in part on these appeals, the House Committee considered a removal bill by Representative Samuel Bell of New Hampshire that bolstered this expansionism, promoting "the claims of civilized communities over those savage tribes."[57] Actually, the Senate Committee first reported out a bill by Tennessee Senator Hugh White on February 22, 1830. Bell's bill made it out of committee two days later. The Senate debated the White bill, deliberating from April 6 to April 26. After White's bill passed, it moved into the House, where Representative Bell allowed White's bill to supplant his own removal proposal. The House took up White's bill on May 13 and passed it on May 26, whereupon the Senate received it back with a monetary-based amendment and passed it that same day. Jackson signed the bill into law on May 28, 1830.[58]

Congressional arguments surrounding removal brought to light several inconsistencies in the government's general outlook on American Indian identities. Proponents of removal in the Senate tended to characterize Native communities as uncivilized. Moreover, removal supporters in the Senate constituted American Indians as crude land tenants, thus limiting their sovereignty. Concurrently, supporters employed savage metaphors to ensure the government's control over Native territory and communities.

This view competed with anti-removal advocates in the Senate, who were inclined to discuss American Indians in childlike and dependent terms. Senate opponents therefore attempted to invalidate the reduction of Native identity to uncivilized by hearkening to paternalism. Although combating the diminutive images of savagery, such familial constructions nevertheless contributed further to American supremacy through the frame of benevolence. Native territorial rights were limited here, as well, not due to savage identities, but because of their childlike character.

The House removal debates did not deviate much in substance and style from the Senate's key speakers. Instead, the House debates replicated earlier Senate speeches since the Bell and White bills were virtually identical. Moreover, the Senate exchanges between Georgia Senator John Forsythe and New Jersey Senator Theodore Frelinghuysen have been most popularly cited as the "essential" arguments articulated by both sides of the debate and in both chambers during removal deliberations.[59] Like both counterparts in the Senate, the House debate lionized the US government to the detriment of American Indians.

The eventual passage of the Indian Removal Act helped crystallize the Native-US relationship. In so doing, however, the resolution of incoherent identity formations eroded Native sovereignty by essentializing American Indians, thereby reducing the ideological uncertainty over the Native question for the US government

Senators supporting removal tended to hail from southern states and be Jacksonian Democrats. Southerners like Forsythe were obvious champions of removal since their respective states had more at stake in the policy. His opening comments on the bill attempted to justify US rights to territory based on American Indians' so-called lack of sophisticated land ownership. Connecting Georgia's past actions to expansion, he said: "Georgia stands justified in her course . . . the condition of these remnants of the once formidable tribes of Indians is known to be deplorable; all admit that there is something due to the remaining individuals of this race."[60] Here, Forsythe diminished Native identity in order to rationalize why removal should be codified. He shrouded expansionist ends in a rhetoric of protection; American Indians, he noted, were owed their removal in order to secure their well being. In making this argument, though, he alluded to American Indians as outdated and weak. They were once powerful, but were now relicts of their ancestors. They no longer owned the land but merely "dwelled there."[61]

Forsythe employed savage metaphors, a colonizing rhetoric, to further erode Native sovereignty while pairing this diminution with constructions of a controlling governmental identity. Continuing his argument, Forsythe said that the Native-US policy of assimilation had worked in exactly the reverse of its intended effects. To allow American Indians to remain in the East, he exhorted, "You might as reasonably expect that wild animals, incapable of being tamed in a park, would be domesticated by turning them loose in a forest." Analogizing American Indians to animals, he contended that their "wild nature never was yet tamed but by coercive discipline." Such discipline was to be administered by the US government, which could "better domesticate" these "impoverished savages."[62]

Similarly, Forsythe metonymically reduced American Indians to literal territory, thus demonstrating a core feature of colonization. The United States discovered land, he said, and had *found* American Indians: "The land

and Indians are, according to the same principles, subject to the exclusive control" of state and U.S sovereignty.[63] For this reason, he declared, "The European doctrine of the right conferred by the discovery of new countries, inhabited by barbarous tribes," was a reason to take land. He basically predicated the expansion of the United States on the need to remove these "remnants" and "wild animals," but likewise based removal on territorial dominance. After all, he told the Senate, "The lands, the streams, the woods, the minerals, all living things, including the human inhabitants" were all the "property of, or subject to, the government of the fortunate navigator."[64]

Senator Robert Adams of Mississippi crafted similar territorial arguments. In fact, his avoidance of extending land rights to Native communities was the focal point. Ostensibly, he worried about those anti-removal senators who failed to trust the "the President . . . to assign a district west of the Mississippi and, by strong arm, to drive these unfortunate people from their present abode."[65] For instance, in complaining about removal opponents, he said, "It is their wish that this exchange should be left to the free and voluntary choice of the Indians themselves." He disagreed with this, as voluntary removal had progressed too slowly and as American Indians, in his estimation, were not worthy of sophisticated land use.

Adams insinuated that American Indians had no agency to decide their own fate because they were not full US citizens. Free choice, said Adams, was impossible for indigenous communities because they were "mere savage" tenants. This was so, he insisted, because over the years American Indians had "acquiesced, . . . they submitted. . . . As soon as their power was lost, and they were no longer formidable, . . . they became subject to the control and legislation" of the United States.[66] With regard to constituting identities, Adams evidenced that the US government considered American Indians "poor, ill-fated," "subdued," and "blindly compelled to yield up their territory." On the other hand, the US government had the "superiority of mental strength" to take land, and was dominant and "ably suited" to control Native nations.[67] American Indians were part of the US family so long as they could traffic land. Thus, of forced removal, Adams asked, "Is there any thing alarming in this proposition? . . . I confess . . . I see nothing in the provisions of the bill before us unbecoming the character of a great just and magnanimous nation."[68]

Opponents of removal denied the territorial arguments concerning removal and the movement of US settlers into Native territories. Speaking from paternalism, natural rights, and tenancy, removal opponents supported Native sovereignty yet strangely reified a colonizing relationship. Frelinghuysen was the first opponent to speak during the debates. He admitted that American Indians were "the original tenants of the soil," and he also elevated this right to "share in the common bounties of a benignant Providence."[69] Tenancy—though not ownership—complicated the case for removal opponents. American Indians nations, he admitted, had "some connexion" to the land, though not as strong as American citizens. He concluded therefore that American Indians had no need to remove. Instead, it would remain the US government's responsibility to motivate peace. Frelinghuysen, moreover, constituted American Indian character as equal "under natural rights" and the US government as the cause of the problem it claimed inhered in Native communities. Even if he could admit Native inferiority, Frelinghuysen argued, how could the government blame them: "The confiding Indian listened to our professions of friendship; we called him brother, and he believed us. . . . [Now we have taken] more of their land than can be cultivated in centuries. . . . We have crowded the tribes . . . and, still, like the horse-leech, our insatiated cupidity cries, give! give!"[70] Frelinghuysen's more progressive view of American Indians' natural rights conflicted with removal proponents who denied such rights under tenancy.

Despite his progressive thinking, though, Frelinghuysen's formulation of American Indian and U.S governmental identities hinted at the hierarchy of landlord/tenant and warden/ward. He argued from benevolence, but replicated the very paternalism that he claimed Jacksonians abused. For instance, speaking for why the United States should not seclude Native communities, he opined: "If the United States . . . shall withdraw their protective shield from around and above them; if the aegis, that in the days of her truth she raised, shall now be rudely and cruelly torn away, we shall refer the poor, driven, persecuted Indians over [to savagery]."[71] His insistence on demoralizing Native identity limited the fullness of an indigenous agency to resist policy.

Frelinghuysen also called into question the government's republican character as he reified American Indian identities as dependent. Through this, he urged the Senate to consider the nation's reputation should it reject its foundational precepts by removing American Indians. He employed the rhetorical tactic of moral inheritance to US forebears as authoritative support for his anti-removal goal.[72] "Sir, if we yield up this right [of letting Natives remain in the East]," he averred, "the struggles of the Revolution will have been in vain. There will be but the exchange of tyrants. . . . We should . . . resist a despotism that would despoil" the American system.[73] In this way, Frelinghuysen intimated that the colonizing US government had been replicating British imperialists from which the nation had separated. He tread on shaky ground, however, as he cemented Native limitations. He continued, "If we abandon these aboriginals, . . . these adopted children of our forefathers, how shall we justify it to our country? To all the glory of the past, and the promise of the future? Her good name is worth all else besides that contributes to her greatness."[74]

Senator Peleg Sprague of Maine also spoke from moral inheritance but, similarly, constituted Native communities as needy. To Sprague, the moral obligation involved the government retaining its honor by fulfilling past treaty obligations. With removal, a number of treaties regarding Native sovereignty to their eastern territories were going to be abrogated. Sprague contended, "We have pledged to them our protection; and instead of shielding them where they are now within their reach, under our own arm we are sending them away amongst fierce and warlike barbarians."[75] Sprague doubtlessly substantiated the familial relationship at work in Native-US affairs, but he also denigrated those American Indians west of the Mississippi. He used the presence of allegedly "uncivilized" Natives in the West—with whom eastern emigrants would mingle—as justification for failing the bill. To demonstrate American Indian dependence—and the necessity of US protection—in the East, he paired Native neediness with savagery in the West.

The trumpeting of benevolence over the material advantages of territoriality comprised another line of Sprague's argument. As with Frelinghuysen, Sprague predicated his benevolence on a diminutive Native identity. He concluded his speech on April 20 by stating, "To have secured, even to the poor and despised Indian a spot of earth upon which to rest his aching head—to give him but a cup of cold water, in charity, will be a greater treasure than to have been the conquerors of kingdoms, and lived in luxury upon their spoils."[76] Here, Sprague eschewed the prize of territory associated with removal for the benevolence of uplifting the "downtrodden" American Indian. Demonstrating charity toward Natives, he rejected the ideology of territoriality, offering a critique of US dominance. At the same time, however, he promoted a paternal relationship fused between the government and American Indians.

For all the partisan and sectional wrangling, the eventual passage of the Indian Removal Act clarified for the government a once-ambiguous relationship between itself and American Indians by scripting Natives as dependent and by granting the federal government the ultimate power in deciding removal. Rather than being considered "savage," American Indians would be demarcated monolithically as childlike. The constant reference to "all Indians" sought to homogenize Native nations, thus demonstrating an elision of individuality, geographic specificity and past relationships with the federal government. Also, though Native territoriality failed to appear as ownership, their natural rights led to removal through negotiation, thus alluding to vestiges of Native agency. Tenancy, however, no longer sheltered American Indians from removal, especially as land ownership began equating more to US citizenship. Thus, the Act noted, lands ownership "shall revert to the United States."[77] Finally, the benevolent terms of the Indian Removal Act—and the notion that Natives would agree to removal through treaties—erased the sense of hypocrisy riddling US governmental identities as imperialist. This would become a "space of dissension" through which

American Indians could enact détournement as a resistive counter to removal rhetoric.[78] Section Five stated that the government would "cause such aid and assistance as may be necessary for their support and subsistence" across the Mississippi.[79] Such protection squelched governmental identities as zealous and forceful, while reifying Native dependence. The alleged hypocrisy of the government, which connected its treatment of American Indians with Britain's treatment of the American colonies, was quelled by the paternal relationship cemented by the passage of the Act. Native resisters would most definitely pick up on this hypocrisy.

Overall, the US government would come to support American Indians as a part of the nation, albeit a part that existed separated spatially and culturally from the dominant population. The realization of American Indians' *identity duality* started to come to bear here; the limbo of their public statuses spoke of a controlling and colonizing mechanism on the part of the US government. Demonstrating the conflation of territory and citizenship, the governmental removal discourse clarified that Native land entitlement was negated, which resulted in a justification for their dislocation from these territories. Another compromise between the factions was that, if removal were to commence, the federal government and not the states would administrate the policy.

The act summarily endowed the US government with the colonial control to guide American Indian communities. It allowed the federal government "to cause such aid and assistance" toward American Indians as it deemed fit. The government also retained the duty of protecting American Indians "against all interruption and disturbance." Perhaps the most telling of the law's paternalistic rhetoric was its elasticity clause, which codified a "supervisory" role for the US government over Native nations. Section Seven clarified this role by allowing the executive "the same superintendence and care over any tribe or nation in the country to which they may remove . . . that he is now authorized to have over them at their present places of residence."[80] Overall, the act reduced the confusion and ideological contestations over the Native question for the federal government. The Native question was further solidified by the Supreme Court.

The Supreme Court under Chief Justice John Marshall is remembered as the tenure that, perhaps more than others, codified American Indian identities and the US government's relation to Native nations. The Marshall Court's decisions patently made "the Indians the only group of people in the United States who are governed by a distinct body of law."[81] Specifically, the *Cherokee Nation v. Georgia* (1831) and *Worcester v. Georgia* (1832) cases defined in large measure what it meant to be "Indian." The Marshall years are also remembered for enacting "the largest number of cases supporting American federalism."[82] This period between 1801 and 1833 witnessed the championing of federal powers over state rights that contributed to rifts between southern states and the US government. Moreover, the period propagated a rise in cases extending the power of the Supreme Court to intervene into states' rights issues (e.g., *McCulloch v. Maryland*).

The Supreme Court's decisions in *Cherokee Nation* and *Worcester* helped construct both monolithic and feeble American Indian identities while bolstering US governmental identities as exceptional and paternal. The court's discourse reaffirmed the paternal ties between the government and Native communities and ensured the dominance of the federal government—both of which were confirmed by Jackson's removal plan and the Indian Removal Act debate in Congress. To the issue of the federal government's dominance, the high court appeared to use American Indians as a cipher to fortify the federal government's influence over both states and Native nations.[83] The court's discourse illustrated an attempt to wrest control over the "parenting" of America's "red children" from individual states in order to constitute a central US identity and a monolithic Native identity. Marshall also, though, confirmed Natives as ward-like occupants of the land, which precluded them from land ownership and citizenship. This aided the US government in rationalizing removal through the doctrine of discovery.

Fascinatingly, once the removal policy gained momentum, Jackson revised his previous rhetoric that endowed the US government with removal responsibilities. The shift worked instead to endorse a territorial program of states' rights. To be sure, American Indians were to be removed by federal mandate, but Jackson hinted that individual states should encroach into Indian Country and pressure Native communities to remove. He said in his sixth annual message that all efforts had been "given by law to destroy all ardent spirits found in their [Natives'] country, without waiting the doubtful result and slow process of a legal seizure."[84] Jackson called for expediency and extra-legal means of removal. Because removal took longer than Jackson anticipated, he encouraged southerners to speed up the process.[85] He even exhorted a group of Cherokees in 1835: "You are now subject to the same laws which govern the citizens of Georgia and Alabama."[86]

Jackson's amended stance toward state sovereignty in removal clashed with the strong federalism embodied by the Marshall Court. Undoubtedly, Jackson's political influence in support of states' rights affected the ways in which the high court dealt with the colonial relationship.[87] At least from Jackson's perspective, there existed divisive animosity between his administration and the Supreme Court. Jackson worried in an 1832 letter: "If anything the Court can paralize the course of my executive. . . . [The justices] have never ceased to endeavor to put me down and the supreme court in a late decision declaring the Cherokee an independent nation, have united to embarrass me."[88] When Jackson was running for president in 1828, Marshall made an equally wry remark that "perhaps I should consider the election of Jackson as a virtual dissolution of the government."[89] There was no love lost between the men.

Marshall certainly looked askance at heightened state sovereignty. Instead, Marshall underscored the need to protect the federal government from incursions by local authorities. Specifically, Marshall disagreed with southern states over issues of internal commerce, slavery, state judicial power to abrogate Congressional and high court decisions, and state powers to forge treaties with American Indians.[90] Marshall couched his rhetoric in a reliance on constitutional intent as an argument-by-authority; in doing so, he further refined the constitutional bind between the states and US government. The Supreme Court existed in the midst of a contentious maelstrom between Jacksonians' move toward an insistence on state cooperation and the preservation of the federal government's sovereignty involving Indian removal.

Cherokee Nation v. State of Georgia (1831) strengthened US dominance and facilitated territorial expansion by confirming the Court's early construction of Native identities in *Johnson v. McIntosh* (1823) as moveable and dependent.[91] *Cherokee Nation* retains importance to Native identities in that American Indians were actual parties to the case and American Indian sovereign character was at issue. The case also generated deeper consideration as the Supreme Court valorized federalism through paternal control over American Indians. The case came in the wake of the Indian Removal Act when Georgia began designing its own laws to expedite removal. The state's removal law replicated an 1828 one that claimed "Indian lands" belonged to Georgia "absolutely" and "that the title is in her; that the Indians are tenants at her will, and that she may at any time she pleases, determine that tenancy, by taking possession of the premises."[92]

The grievance forwarded by the Cherokee Nation demanded that the Court enjoin Georgia from forcibly removing American Indians by allowing whites to overrun Cherokee land. Cherokee attorney William Wirt noted "that the Cherokees were the occupants of and owners of territory in which they now reside, before the first approach of white men of Europe to the western continent."[93] Considering this, the Cherokee Nation demanded to be recognized as "a foreign state, not owing allegiance to the United States, nor to any state of this union."[94]

Georgia responded by asking the Court to recognize the Indian Removal Act as proof that the state removal laws were constitutional. To do this, Georgia hearkened to Article IV of the US Constitution which states that "no new States shall be formed or erected within the jurisdiction of any other State" as evidence that Native groups could not claim sovereignty within Georgia's limits.[95] Marshall ruled in favor of the Cherokee: that is, the Court protected American Indians from any incursions into their land by states and their residents. However, the Cherokee victory was pyrrhic; Native nations would still be removed. Moreover, the holding positioned Natives as "dependent wards," securing territorial rights to the federal government, and not to individual states. Basically, American Indians become further essentialized. The high court codified the practice of genericizing Native culture to the detriment of inimitable Native identities, reifying federal powers over the discursively homogenized group. Condensing communities has typically been a characteristic of colonization.

In order to enjoin Georgia from touching Cherokee land, Marshall conflated American Indian dependent identities with a lack of civilization. He first argued that American Indians were once independent, but in the present remained subordinate to the "fatherly house" of the United States: "A people once numerous, powerful, and truly independent, found by our ancestors in the quiet and uncontrolled possession of an ample domain, gradually sinking beneath our superior policy, our arts, and our arms, have yielded their lands by successive treaties."[96] Marshall also, though, hinted that American Indians were uncivilized by enjoying an "uncontrolled possession" of territory. While pro-removal advocates in the Senate argued that Native communities were still uncivilized, Marshall dissociated contemporary American Indian identities from a naïve character and a "discovered" state. Instead, Marshall constituted American Indians as childlike, eking out a new life in the West with the "aid of the General Government" within whose policy, arts and arms indigenous communities were harbored."[97] He subverted Native constructions as savage or uncivilized to an American Indian identity as perpetually childlike.

Clarifying the paternal relationship between American Indians and the government, Marshall argued that the Cherokee Nation was neither a foreign entity nor a sovereign state, but rather a domestic "case of people" that the United States watched over. He denied the injunction against Georgia not based on the Cherokee claim to sovereignty; rather, he saw it fit that the Court protect indigenous populations from states that could not care for "our red children." The possessive *our* referred to the federal government's identity, not that of the individual states. Marshall continued by depicting American Indians as needy:

> They may, more correctly, be denominated domestic dependent nations. . . . They are in a state of pupilage. . . . They look to our government for protection; rely upon its kindness and power; appeal to it for relief of their wants; and address the President as their great father. They [are] . . . completely under the sovereignty and domination of the United States, that any attempt to acquire their lands, or to form a political connexion with them, would be considered an invasion of our territory and an act of hostility.[98]

The last sentence presents an inconsistency between Marshall's charge that a Native group was neither sovereign nor foreign and his charge that an attack on American Indians would qualify as an attack on the United States. Seemingly, Marshall's argument flowed from the 1823 Monroe Doctrine, which was designed to protect US interests by defending "foreign nations" from outside threats in the Western hemisphere.[99] And, yet, Marshall did not deem Native groups foreign nations. Moreover, he did not label them domestic states that the United States would have a right to protect. In this way, a dependent American Indian identity was solidified in opposition to any semblance of Native sovereignty.

Marshall also codified the notion that American Indians could be neither landowners nor citizens. Instead, they were to be considered ward-like occupants. He did this, first, by bivouacking the territorial identity associated with the US government. He argued that American Indians "occupy a territory to which we assert a title independent of their will, which must take effect in point of possession when their right of possession ceases."[100] Since American Indian nations' possession was tied to occupancy, not ownership, the US government could seize Native territory on a whim. Further, American Indians could not be considered citizens as mere tenants, but rather their "relation to the United States resembles that of a ward to his guardian."[101]

The ruling in *Cherokee Nation* alluded to a colonizing hierarchy of sorts as it simultaneously constituted the identities of American Indians and the federal government as paternally subjugated and dominant, respectively. Marshall, for instance, constructed the government as a strong federal power versus a confederation of states. James Boyd White argues that this constitutive function of the Supreme Court helped embody a central system. He maintains that constituting nineteenth century identities was "not aimed . . . at using rhetoric in a self-conscious, community building way."[102] Marshall demonstrated this constitutive rhetoric by cleverly employing the Cherokee Nation as a cipher, a vessel used for larger purposes, in order to trump federalism over state sovereignty.

Infused throughout Marshall's discourse was the homogenization of childlike American Indian identities. The Cherokee, again as flat representatives of Native people, were seen as "domestic dependents," in a continuing "state of pupilage." They were the "ward" to the American "guardian." They "relied" on the US government and "appealed" to a "great father" for permission, security, and mobility. American Indians were "under" the sovereignty—"the dominion"—of the United States. And the government wanted their land for expansionist purposes. True, Native lands were protected from rambunctious states, but *Cherokee Nation v. Georgia* reconfirmed the central and paternal stance of the United States in controlling American Indian territory and sovereignty.

The second "removal" case of the Marshall court focused on the transference of American Indian legal status from "domestic dependent" to "distinct community." In *Worcester v. State of Georgia* (1832) white missionaries, who were previously arrested by state authorities for visiting the Cherokee Nation in Georgia, brought suit to demand visitation rights. Missionary Samuel Worcester and the Cherokee Nation pleaded to the Court that American Indians could be viewed as sovereign, and thus were not subject to state law. This argument spawned from the injunction against Georgia issued in *Cherokee v. Georgia*. Incidentally, Georgia had just passed a law to prevent any white persons from meeting with the Cherokee due to white reformers' instigations of resistance.[103]

The rhetorical transformation undertaken from "domestic dependent" to "distinct community" represented Marshall's strongest threat to Jacksonian states' rights. In an inconsistent ruling, at least per *Johnson* and *Cherokee Nation*, Marshall shifted Native identities to "distinct community" in order to stop Georgia from blocking Cherokee-missionary relations.[104] American Indians, once again, appeared to have won the day, as they seemingly were awarded limited rights under the high court. However, Marshall's rhetoric pointed, yet again, to emancipating the Cherokee from a "dependent" label in order to quell states' rights and strengthen the federal government.

Moreover, Marshall's rhetoric only reified American Indian dependence in order to elide individual states' "custody" of American Indians. They were colonized for what they could do for the federal government. For instance, he argued, "The Cherokee Nation, then, is a distinct community occupying its own territory . . . in which [state laws] can have no force." He continued that states had therefore "no right to enter" unless consistent with treaties "and acts of Congress." The "whole intercourse" between the United States and Native nations was orchestrated by the federal government.[105] Here, Marshall denied Georgia access to Cherokee lands. Why? Not because the Cherokee were sovereign—Marshall never deemed the Cherokee Nation autonomous, but considered them "distinct." Instead, Georgia could not interact with American Indians; only the federal government enjoyed that right. As a result of *Worcester*, "States were excluded from the Federal/Tribal relationship, and the tribes retained a very broad grant of sovereignty" inviolate save by federalist intervention.[106]

Most poignantly, the new label of "distinct community" allowed a paternal intercourse between indigenous people and the United States, not between Native nations and sovereign states. Marshall, basically, replaced the control bequeathed to the United States by the Cherokee "domestic dependents" label with another form of control—the US government as sole administrator over American Indian territory. The "distinct community" moniker served only to clarify the state- and federal-Native relationships; American Indians were thus not "domestic dependents" of the states.

Instead of having two authorities to answer to, American Indians would eternally be controlled by one "great father"—the president of the United States.[107] Marshall's prevention of states' interaction with American Indians was so vehement that he, ironically, empowered the presidency—and particularly his arch-nemesis, Jackson—with control over Native communities. Seemingly, Marshall was willing to grant this presidential role so long as the federal government trumped states' interests.

Worcester is generally considered the strongest defense of Native sovereignty against Jacksonian localized government. As such, the case's spirit became a hypocritical gap that would later be accessed by decolonizing American Indians. But *Worcester* was simply a channel for a case that can be understood as a defense of federal power over state rights and of US governmental paternal control over American Indian nations. Amusingly, Jackson was so angered by the Marshall decision to deem the Cherokee Nation a "distinct community" that he is known to have blurted, "Well, John Marshall has made his decision: *now let's see him try to enforce it*!"[108] Jackson's ire reflected the obvious reduction of state power in Indian Removal.

The clarification of US governmental and Native identities through the colonizing removal milieu ultimately led to dire consequences for American Indians. For, as Haig Bosmajian writes, "once the Indians were successfully defined as governmental nonentities" to be exploited at the whim of the US government, "no more justification was needed to drive them off their lands" and to force them to emigrate across the Mississippi.[109] And, the ideologies of expansion, paternalism, citizenship, territoriality, and sectionalism undergirded the way the government crafted colonial US and Native identities during the removal era.

Such ideological and political resolutions to the Native question solidified the terms of the Native-US relationship for the federal government until the late nineteenth century. And as the removal policy moved beyond the halls of Congress and into practice within Native territories, resistance from American Indians complicated the Indian Removal Act. The power of decolonial Native agency and identities was evidenced in the difficulty of the government's implementation of removal. The Act cemented identities for the US government in the Jacksonian era, but Native nations rebutted this seeming lucidity by repurposing the government's own discourse. The *identity duality* of inclusion/exclusion in the US nation provided the canvas across which American Indians would détourn colonizing removal rhetoric.

CHAPTER THREE

Native Decolonial Resistance to Removal

THOUGH THE INDIAN REMOVAL ACT CLARIFIED GOVERNMENTAL AND Native identities for US leaders, it did less to satisfy a great deal of American Indians. Native disagreements with the Act heightened the intensity of their reactions to US expansion and territorialism, but it was not the first time that Natives had rebutted removal. As the administrations of George Washington, John Adams, and Thomas Jefferson crafted treaties for "protection and friendship"—beginning with the Delaware Treaty in 1778—they also called for small land cessions.[1] And, while American Indians sometimes conceded this land for the preservation of peace, there exist in the historical record plentiful signs of Native protest that speaks to decolonization. In 1825 for instance, when Indian agents under the Monroe administration attempted to negotiate a removal treaty with the Konze Nation, Allegawahu (Konze) told them: "You treat my people like a flock of turkeys. You come into our dwelling places and scare us out. We fly over and alight on another stream, but no sooner . . . you come along and drive us farther and farther."[2] Allegawahu recognized how the US government constructed Natives as animalistic and removable. Most vitally, though, to the government's typical insistence that the current treaty would represent the final request for removal ("the Indians may have full confidence in the justice of the United States, respecting their interests" to land), Allegawahu exposed the hypocrisy of such promises.[3] Public and pop-cultural impressions that American Indians exemplified the colonial mythos of the "silent Indian" crumble here when considering such responses.[4]

American Indians challenged the removal policy by working through and détourning the discursive frameworks of expansion, citizenship, territoriality, paternalism, and sectionalism in order to reconstitute Native and governmental identities. Recall that détournement allows marginalized groups to mirror powerful rhetoric in order to repurpose it for emancipatory ends. The repurposing functions by exposing the duplicities of, say, a colonizing force while also trumpeting the marginalized groups' efforts to decolonize as activists versus victims.[5] Ostensibly, the government's ideological discourses provided an entrée for American Indian resistance by addressing Native identities. And part of this involved the rift between pro- and anti-removal advocates in Congress and the initial contestation over the places of American Indians in the US nation and the government's relationship to indigenous communities. Prior to the solidification of the "Indian question," American Indians worked through this factionalism and lack of clarity regarding identities to challenge *identity duality*, and thus to combat the Indian Removal Act.

The five southeastern nations (Choctaw, Creek, Chickasaw, Seminole, and Cherokee nations), along with midwestern nations, typically sought autonomy as separate entities outside the scope of US citizenship. (These nations are discussed here, as they were the first to face removal; nations in the Northwest and Southwest, for the most part, did not experience the Indian Removal Act until later in or after the Jacksonian era when settlers moved in droves across the Mississippi River in the 1840s and 1850s.) To accomplish this, they reconstituted their identities as independent, worthy of territory, just, godly, and stable. American Indians also exposed US governmental identities, at times, as untrustworthy, sinful, and in violation of the representative government upon which it was founded. Natives opposed in varying degrees the identities clarified by the Indian Removal Act among US leaders, and thus addressed the US government's identities by decolonizing the government's own inventional strategies into fodder for resistance.

These refashioned Native tactics were primarily enacted through public speeches, but some nations also accessed the *Cherokee Phoenix* newspaper and petitions to Congress as outlets. To the latter, Alisse Portnoy argues that the genre of the nineteenth century petition allowed groups to issue grievances directly to the House of Representatives, where they were entered into the record. "Petitions were," she contends, "instruments of personal (whether individual or collective) redress."[6] That Native nations used this venue speaks to their decolonial tactic of détourning US governmental language, but also its channels, as a platform for resistance.

Native resistance thus complicated the implementation of the Indian Removal Act. Jackson anticipated in 1830 that removal would reach "a happy consummation" within one year of the act passing Congress.[7] But, the policy of removal did not translate easily into practice as American Indians opposed the Native and governmental identities clarified during the removal debates and within the act itself. Native resistance—and the verity that removal took nearly ten years to complete based partly on indigenous rebuttals—demonstrated the rhetorical impact of American Indians. An example of decolonial discourse, American Indian anti-removal rhetoric delayed removal, thus showing how they were, as Siobhan Senier contends, "bulwarks against and conceivable responses to nationalizing Euro-American traditions."[8]

The Indian Removal Act commenced through a series of treaties with American Indian nations. The first targets of the removal program were the Choctaw, Creek, Chickasaw, Seminole, and Cherokee nations.[9] These nations were targeted because their lands were the most coveted for frontier settlers who already lived in these territories and hoped to increase their land base. The Indian Removal Act did not, theoretically, force removal on the five southeastern nations. Rather, the bill explained that the President could select western lands "to be divided into a suitable number of districts, for the reception of such tribes or nations of Indians as may choose to exchange lands where they now reside, and remove there."[10]

According to the language, here, American Indian nations could opt to either remove or remain on their lands in the East. Ronald Satz argues that Jacksonians wanted to "promote removal without doing anything that would alienate public support by appearing blatantly immoral."[11] The Jackson administration and pro-removal advocates in the legislature could not unilaterally compel Natives to remove, lest the policy appear too colonizing.[12] Indeed, in Jackson's Second Annual Message (1830), he intimated that Natives had a right to choose without provocations from the US government. "We have as little right to control them as we have to prescribe laws for other nations." Of course, he also introduced in his address an irony: "We will unite in attempting to open the eyes of those children of the forest to their true condition . . . by a speedy removal."[13] Thus, many American Indians questioned the integrity of the Removal Act.

The opportunity to engage in treaties, *prima facie*, gave an important sense of decolonial agency to indigenous communities, and they seized this break to solidify their autonomy from the government. After all, treaties were formal agreements "between two or more fully sovereign and recognized states operating in an international forum."[14] The government's lack of clarity on American Indian identities also fueled Native protests. If the US government was uncertain about how it should consider and treat Native communities, then American Indians had an investiture through which to rebut removal. The Choctaw, Creek, Chickasaw, and Seminole nations worked through the government's ideological constructs and internal contention to script themselves as independent, worthy, just, and godly. Concurrently, governmental identities were characterized as iniquitous and criminal. Furthermore, the enactment of moral inheritance by the five southeastern nations rationalized their connections to homelands, demonstrating their agency rooted in ancestral and historical ties to their territories.

The Choctaw Nation became the first to begin the wholesale removal process.[15] Speaking to leaders Peter Pitchlynn (Choctaw), Colonel Webb (Choctaw), George Harkins (Choctaw), and others, War Secretary John

Eaton suggested to the Choctaw, "Keep at peace and be happy by removing, otherwise you will soon become wretched and miserable indeed."[16] To ensure the benevolent result of removal, preserving the Choctaw's fate from "misery," Eaton distributed gifts to the Choctaw leaders and people, warned that Mississippi could exert its will without federal protection should the Choctaw not emigrate, and bribed leaders with inducements including promises of choosing their own allotments.

Following such pledges of rewards and grave prophecies, the Choctaw Nation signed the Treaty of Dancing Rabbit Creek in Noxubee County, Mississippi, on September 27 and 28, 1830. The treaty codified that the Choctaw would "cede to the United States, the entire country they own and possess in the east . . . [so that] the Government [could] extend to them the facilities and comforts" it was not able to offer the nation east of the Mississippi River.[17] The connection between benevolent care towards American Indians and governmental expansion was stressed in this passage and throughout Dancing Rabbit Creek more generally. Like Jacksonian arguments for removal, the Choctaw treaty predicated expansion on some veneer or extension of protection and reassurance. Though a majority of the Choctaw leadership eventually signed a removal treaty, numerous members of the Choctaw community protested the US government's efforts to displace them from their Mississippi homeland. These protests ranged from folks whose views registered on a spectrum from overtly resistant to what at the time may have been deemed "friendly Indian." The analysis here considers voices along the spectrum of Choctaw resistance. Choctaw discourse modified the identities confirmed by the government's removal policy through the enactment of memories to past Native sovereignty and by détourning the government's paternally entrenched rhetoric. In this way, the Choctaw Nation was able to demonstrate its independence and worthiness of territory.

Choctaw resistance involved asserting independence through the building of memories to a shared past between the US government and American Indians. These memories often involved the championing of "American Creeds."[18] In this vein, Choctaw rhetors reinvented the pillars of American political culture—figures such as Washington and Jefferson and foundational texts like the Declaration of Independence and the Constitution—to secure sovereignty. Similar to the ways removal proponents hearkened to these collective histories to justify removal (especially with regard to the doctrine of discovery) Choctaw activists decolonized these memories to emphasize their rights to retain tribal homelands.

An example of Choctaw independence woven through memory arose in a newspaper editorial written by Ames (Choctaw).[19] Arguing that the Choctaw Nation had a right to choose against emigration, he reasoned that before Mississippi and the United States came into existence, "the Choctaws existed here, an independent nation, governing themselves." He continued, "the United States never attempted to impose laws upon them, but implicitly acknowledged their inability to do it by treating them as an independent nation."[20] Claiming temporal primacy, Ames directly challenged the doctrine of discovery upon which removal discourse relied. Native conceptions of their rights to territories thus worked through moral inheritance of the land instead of discovery and conquest.

Concurrently, Ames employed the Constitution to demonstrate Choctaw sovereignty. While Jacksonians contended the Constitution provided for interference into Native affairs—Congress was emboldened "to regulate commerce with foreign nations . . . and with the Indian tribes"—Ames insinuated that American Indians' being paired with "foreign nations" nodded toward Native sovereignty.[21] To this effect, Ames remarked that "the right to admission [to sovereignty for Native communities] is secured by the Constitution, and Congress cannot impose conditions. . . . For the right of admission was absolute, and could not be restricted or clogged by any law of Congress."[22]

Having framed the Choctaw Nation as historically "independent" from the United States, Ames next argued that American Indians, in general, were not exactly fully included in the US nation. Even if Choctaw communities were not protected as sovereign under the Constitution, Ames wrote, the US government could not force them, because American Indians were not truly part of the American citizenry. After all, he argued, "Were the Indians ever considered, or treated as a part of citizens? . . . Had [Indians] ever had any voice in establishing any State Government, or forming the General Government? Never!"[23] Ames channeled a memory of the Constitution and early Native-US relations in part to call into question the US government's identities as dominant. That the United States proposed to remove the Choctaw Nation for protection appeared, to Ames, colonial and misleading.

During the removal debates, Pushmataha (Choctaw) and Puckshunnubbee (Choctaw) crafted a memory of the "friendly" Jefferson Administration to juxtapose the territoriality of the US government and to hearken to Native independence.[24] The rhetors, here, challenged early governmental concepts of Native sovereignty based on Jacksonian expansion:

> It is said we have no claim to the land here. . . . How different is this from the language of the illustrious Jefferson,—"go home," said this great and good man to our fathers, "build your houses, clear your fields, and cultivate the earth." Said he, "as you live in peace with me and mine . . . you shall live upon your lands undisturbed."[25]

Pushmataha and Puckshunnubbee employed the memory of Jefferson as an authoritative figure to remain on their homelands. As early as 1803, Jefferson asked American Indian nations to remain in the East in order to "improve."[26] The Choctaw Nation had taken his advice. Thus, Pushmataha and Puckshunnubbee averred, "If ever the Choctaw character is renovated, here is the place to do it—if we are ever to experience the blessings of civilization, here is the place."[27] Here they exhibited détournement by turning the government's arguments of territoriality against the United States.

George Harkins (Choctaw) similarly made an appeal against removal by transposing US governmental and Native identities—the latter being admirable. He began by reflecting that the Choctaw Nation had attempted to fulfill its "duties" to the United States and, was thus worthy of land. He said, "Taking as an example from the American government, and knowing the happiness which its citizens enjoy, under the influence of mild republican institutions, it was the intention of our countrymen to form a government assimilated to that of our white brethren."[28] Employing the familial language of the US government, Harkins had to admit that such assimilation was all for naught. "The man who said that we would plant a stake and draw a line around us, that never should be passed, was the first . . . to draw up the stake and wipe out all traces of the line."[29] Edward Pessen remarks that Jacksonians understood such incongruity, for they "were fully aware that their doctrine [discovery] . . . was all the more specious because its assumption of Indian savagery was untrue."[30] Jacksonians knew that members of the five southeastern nations, of which the Choctaw Nation was one, had moved beyond this "savagery" when they began small attempts at assimilation—the Cherokee being the most successful at the assimilative task. Removal opponents like Senator Theodore Frelinghuysen were quick to point out the assimilative efforts of the five southeastern nations: "The confiding Indian listened to our professions of friendship; we called him brother, and he believed us . . . [now we've taken] more of their land than can be cultivated in centuries. . . . We have crowded the tribes . . . and, still, like the horse-leech, our insatiated cupidity cries, give! give!"[31]

Though Harkins' and others' rhetoric came some eighteen months following the Treaty of Dancing Rabbit Creek it is vital for the way it helped to decolonize Jacksonian ideologies and contributed to the anti-removal position. Not only are such voices of the excluded important to understanding controversy, but they are also, on their face, constructive. American Indian voices in these instances demonstrate Homi Bhabha's concept that cultures "emerge within a range of discourses as a double movement."[32] For instance, American Indian anti-removal discourse succeeded in conceiving differently the ways that American culture and the US government "read" the history and politics of identities surrounding the Indian Removal Act. As a case in point, Representative William Storrs, referring to a Choctaw memorial he had received, used Native language to call into question the US government's benevolent identity in relating with American Indians. He said in 1830 that the policy had failed "in responsibility . . . to the opinion of the world" to represent the United States as fair and just.[33] Here, Storrs worried how American Indians and the world would receive the policy.

Choctaw discourse also constituted Native identities as worthy of consideration by drawing on familial language and appropriating the government's constructions of identities. Working through the paternal relationship crystallized in the removal bill, Choctaw rhetors turned the tables on the removal policy by appealing to the very language of paternalism and protection, as well as the constructions of US supremacy and American Indian inferiority, codified by the removal policy. For instance, around the time of the Dancing Rabbit Creek council in 1830, Colonel Webb (Choctaw) redirected the US government's justification for removal, based on a weakened Native identity, toward a reason for the Choctaw Nation to seek help. "Brother, when you were young, we were strong; we fought by your side . . . You have grown large and my people have become small," Webb said, confirming US might and exceptionalism. "Brother, my voice is weak; you can scarcely hear me . . . it is the wail of an infant. I have lost it in mourning over the misfortunes of my people."[34] Because of the perception that the US government was strong and Native identities were feeble, Webb intimated that the United States should take special care to uplift Choctaw communities by leaving them alone. This matter was especially resonant as Webb reminded the US government that the Choctaw Nation had helped the government in the past and "taken you in while you were small . . . and broken."[35]

The decolonizing of paternal language also found an outlet in Pushmataha's (Choctaw) discourse during this time. Asking a council for protection against both the State of Mississippi and pro-removal officials, Pushmataha asserted:

> When we had land to spare, we gave it with very little talk . . . as children ought to do to a father. We hope our father will not be displeased; he has made us happy from our infancy; we hope the same protection will be found in the arms of our father as formerly. When a child awakens in the night, he feels for the arm of his father to shield him from danger.[36]

Like Webb, Pushmataha contended that the US "father" had always received what it wanted from its "children." As a result of this paternal relationship that seemingly benefited the government's land demands and aided Choctaw protection, the chief used the very language of the US government to ask, yet again, for more protection—this time from state incursions. Pushmataha, also, intimated that the Choctaw Nation had no more land to spare, and that they gave what they had without confrontation.

The federal government relied so heavily on paternal machinations to craft its own identities that said identities were bound to be questioned. This demystifying resistance carried over into Creek and Chickasaw decolonial rhetoric, as well.

The US government moved to quickly negotiate removal treaties with the Creek Nation in Alabama and the Chickasaw Nation in northern Mississippi during the course of 1832. In the case of the Creek Nation, several attempts at entreating had proven exhaustive to US Indian agents. The federal government then allowed settlers in Alabama to encroach illegally on Creek lands.[37] When the Creek Nation, especially the Upper Creeks, petitioned the US government for help in quelling Alabama's violations, the government strategically reiterated its argument that only removal could protect American Indians from state influence.[38] In this way, Indian agent John Coffee chided a Creek council in September of 1830: "To these laws [Alabama's], where you are, you must submit; there is no preventative—no other alternative. Your great father cannot, nor can congress prevent it. . . . Your great father's earnest desire is, that you may be perpetuated and preserved as a nation . . . in your consent to remove."[39] Couched in a rhetoric of benevolence, Coffee hinged survival on allowing expansion.

Like their Creek neighbors, the Chickasaw Nation was subjected to white encroachment as the US government looked away. As Wilcomb Washburn argues, "The threat of state jurisdiction" and violence "was the club used to intimidate the Chickasaws."[40] The combination of breaches from northern Mississippians and the failure of the US government to make good on its promises of protection finally forced the Chickasaw Nation to relent. The opening clause in the Pontitock Creek Treaty (October 20, 1832) stated that "The Chickasaw Nation find themselves oppressed in their present situation; by being made subject to the laws of the States in which they reside. . . . Rather than submit to this great evil, they prefer to seek a home in the west." And, the US government would grant them this "home" and uplift them from federal "oppression" by taking "the land which they own in the east."[41]

Perhaps viewing Choctaw appeals against removal as unproductive, some portions of the Creek and Chickasaw nations crafted a rhetoric that differed from the friendliness (i.e., Pushmataha's ideology) and paternal language of Choctaw rhetors. Specifically, they employed moral inheritance and providential authority as they offered decolonial rhetoric to confront removal and its attendant identities. One way that these nations resisted the US government's removal discourse was through a moral inheritance that alluded to Native responsibility. A kind of memory, moral inheritance ensures that "the struggles of one's ancestors are sanctified through the conscientious actions of the community." It thus pledges to take up the mantle of a culture's forebears so that those ancestors' work and struggles are "not undertaken in vain."[42] Just as pro-removal advocates hearkened to their ancestors as a way to fulfill their "errand into the wilderness," so too did Creek and Chickasaw rhetors rely on their predecessors to resist removal.

In protesting the Treaty of Ponticock Creek, for instance, Levi Colbert (part Chickasaw) couched his rhetoric in the Chickasaw Nation's responsible identity and territorial link to its ancestry.[43] He said, "we never thought of exchanging our land for any other, as we think that we would not find a country that would suit us as well as this we now occupy, it being the land of our forefathers."[44] This decolonial discourse related closely to the rhetoric of legislators like Senator Peleg Sprague, who argued that Congress should act "correctly" in order to preserve the honor of the US government and to pay tribute to the championed by the "founding fathers."[45] Colbert continued, "we cannot consent to be under your Government. If we should consent [to removal] we should be likened unto young corn growing and met with draught that would kill it" should we not remain with "our father's graves."[46] Clearly, the Chickasaw ancestors, here, sustained the tenor behind the "young corn" vehicle—Chickasaw descendants themselves. Without "roots" intact—its ancestors' "graves"—Chickasaw communities were sure to be harmed. US governmental identities were constructed alongside the reliance of Chickasaw national identity on its physical and spiritual territory. Ostensibly, should the US government succeed in removing the Chickasaw Nation, it would effectively terminate them through a kind of spiritual drought, representing the deprivation of homeland.

Tuske-Ne-Hau (Creek), Hopithle-Ho-Lo (Creek) and others connected their ancestral territory to the future of the Creek Nation (both Upper and Lower) and shaped their identities as responsible for, and generative of, their own posterity. Reminiscent of the US Constitution's Preamble ("to secure the blessings of liberty to ourselves and our posterity")[47] these protestors explained to citizens of Alabama and Georgia that the US government "acknowledged, recognized, and guaranteed to the Creek nation *forever*, all the land that we now hold . . . we never can think of moving from it. Our children are near and dear to us; we must cherish and support them . . . we wish our children to live in peace" with our fathers and after we, ourselves fill graves, and "are dead and gone."[48]

The passages above perhaps reminded US leaders that territory for nineteenth century American Indians was linked ontologically to Native culture and identity. The government's connection to land tended to relate commercial or subsistent use of the land to citizenship based in productivity.[49] The disconnect between governmental and Native considerations of territory were clear in this resistive discourse.

Creek and Chickasaw communities also spotlighted their godly identities by relying on divine authority to protect their homelands. Recall that the government bolstered its "assumptions of racial and cultural superiority as well as an insatiable desire for land, expansion and empire" with providential permission and support of its manifest destiny.[50] Creek and Chickasaw groups operationalized the "Great Spirit" argument in order to demonstrate to the US government how providence could likewise stand by American Indians. This decolonial rhetoric retains vivacity especially when we consider that the conversion of American Indians to Christianity relied on proving to Indians that the Christian God could save them. This was demonstrated by the anti-removal advocate's continual assertions that the government's paternal character required that it consider American Indians part of God's people. Even removal proponent Wilson Lumpkin of Georgia assumed Native communities to be part of a "divine structure"—albeit beneath the auspices of a "supreme" governmental persona.[51]

To safeguard their property, a council of the Chickasaw Nation protested removal by creating an identification between itself and the US government regarding godliness. Mingo (Chickasaw), M'Gilvery (Chickasaw), and Stimoluet (Chickasaw) pleaded, "We hope to be let alone where we are, and that your people will be made to treat us like men and Christians, and not like dogs."[52] Here, the council discussed its identity not as savage—taking advantage of the factional split in Congress over Native identities as either savage or childlike—but rather as closer to the so-called godly precepts of the US government.[53] They implored the government to follow its own religious philosophy of the Golden Rule. Arguably, since the US government did, in fact, accomplish a large amount of its removal efforts concerning the Chickasaw Nation, it could be critiqued as having violated its own precepts. If the government failed to consider the wrongs (sins) it committed against the Chickasaw Nation, perhaps *it* was the savage partner in the Native-US relationship. To this, Shullushoma (Chickasaw) reminded US leaders, "There is some of our white brethren as much savage as the Indian."[54]

In an 1830 memorial, Yoholo (Creek), Tuckaubatchie Hajo (Creek), Tustenuggee (Creek), Smut Eye (Creek) and others united natural rights and property to a reliance on godly identity in order to justify the Creek Nation's right to its homeland. The group claimed:

> As far back as [their fathers'] tradition is disposed to tell, long before [their fathers] saw the ancestors of this Great Council fire . . . we were a free people, in the undisturbed enjoyment of those rights held sacred among men, derived from the Great Master of Breath, who created mankind equal and in possession of an unmolested enjoyment of life, and the blessings of self-government.[55]

Here, the Creek group's argument to remain on its Alabama territory divested not in European contact and doctrines of discovery but in a higher power outside the aegis of European influence. Moreover, the "Great Master of Breath" endowed them with the natural rights of equality, freedom, the "enjoyment of life," and the "blessings of self government."[56] These natural rights to property seemed homologically similar to the Declaration of Independence, punctuating another example of Native decolonial rhetoric.

The Seminole Nation, at first, resisted removal through discursive means, but in desperation later turned more toward direct confrontation following 1833. As J. Leitch Wright summarizes, the Seminole people "were the only southeastern Indians who in any significant way violently resisted removal."[57] The path to violent resistance, however, did not inhere in the Seminole community itself. Rather, the Seminole Nation fell prey to a falsified removal treaty wrought by US-inspired colonization.

Secretary of War Lewis Cass visited Seminole territories in northwest Florida in 1832 and noted the nation's condition. "These miserable people are now reduced to the utmost necessities of life," he wrote to Jackson. "Indeed they have been in penury and wretchedness for years and many have perished from starvation."[58] In typical fashion, Cass sent Indian agents to offer food and clothing as a way to motivate the Seminole Nation's consent to remove. The benevolent tactic worked—"the promise of food and clothing in the treaty eased the negotiations"—and on May 9, 1832, a group of Seminole leaders signed the Treaty of Payne's Landing.[59] The treaty was signed by some (though not all) of the leaders, but only with the provision that before taking affect a Seminole envoy would be allowed to assess the community's tract west of the Mississippi River. At the same time, the treaty promised independent reservations for the nation, but a last minute article was added that demanded the Seminole Nation "agree to emigrate to the country assigned to the Creeks."[60] Though the Seminole community, in the main, generated from Creek roots, they were not inclined to share territorial space.[61]

Returning from their prospective reservation, most of the Seminole leadership denied the Treaty of Payne's Landing. Still, a minority portion of the leadership had approved of the treaty. These individuals confirmed the treaty in a renewal document called the Treaty of Fort Gibson on March 28, 1833. This treaty demanded that the Seminole Nation remove by March 28, 1836.[62] As the time drew nigh, Seminole removal opponents argued that an outlying minority had secured the treaty of 1833, not those representing the Seminole people. The Seminole Nation, it seemed, had fallen victim to the US government's propensity to select "friendly" minority factions supposedly representing whole Native nations.

In exploring the Seminole Nation's resistance to removal, of note are the ways in which Seminole rhetors détourned the US government's language of savagery. Seminole leaders worked through the government's lack of clarity of savage/childish Native identities to refract savagery back to the federal government. They parleyed this rhetorical tactic to resist the hierarchical relationship that removal discourse instantiated.[63] At the same time, they identified themselves as just and stable.

Perhaps due to the bellicosity between the Seminole Nation and the US government, Seminole rhetors tended to craft harsh invectives against the removal policy. In the same fashion that the US government constituted American Indians as "savage," so too did Seminole respondents turn around this "savage" label to reflect US identities. No Seminole rhetor demonstrated this turnaround tactic more than Coacoochee, who spoke to a group of US Indian agents in 1841 to rebuke Jackson's policy.[64] Combating the false promises involved in the treaties of Payne's Landing and Fort Gibson, Coacoochee constructed the government as evil and wild: "Still he [US government] gave me his hand in friendship; we took it . . . he had a snake in the other; his tongue was forked; he lied and stung us."[65] In his estimation, the government represented the serpent in a veritable Garden of Eden myth. As untrustworthy characters, US leaders, said Coacoochee, extended friendship, perhaps even familialism ("he [US government] said he was my father; he said he was my friend") on the one hand and "stung" on the other.[66] The "forked tongue" with which US Indian agents negotiated the treaties confirmed for the Seminole Nation the dishonesty extant in the government's promises.

Coacoochee continued his decolonial invective by further constituting US identities as savage. "If your hearts are bad let me see them now," he demanded of the Indian agents. "Let me know they are dark with bad blood; but do not like a dog, bite me as soon as I turn my back."[67] The chief insisted that the US government make known its motives. Instead of lying—for instance about garnering a Seminole majority in the treaties—Coacoochee exhorted the government to face up to the Seminole Nation. As it remained, though, the US government appeared to wait until the Seminole Nation was not looking to renege on its promises.

In contrast to molding savagery into an embodiment of US identities, Coacoochee described the Seminole Nation as stable. He seemingly did this to challenge the ways that removal rhetoric cemented the identities of American Indians as weakened and in need of preservation. He argued, "My word . . . is true to the heart," he reported. "[We] are not boys" and we can "die like a man" knowing we have "strong hearts and heads."[68] Warrior Chief Osceola (Seminole) also exercised this kind of back talk. He said in 1834 to General Wiley Thompson, an Indian agent, "I have done nothing to be ashamed of; it is for those who passed [the removal] policy to shame."[69] The unjust government should feel, he intimated, embarrassed by its actions to break its many promises. Again, Osceola's rebuke of governmental identities as dominant and fair worked to call into question what the removal act clarified in terms of the Native-US relationship.[70]

Perhaps borrowing from, or even informing, the rhetoric of pro-removal advocates like Senators John Forsythe and Robert Adams, Jumper turned around natural metaphors for anti-removal purposes. If the US government continued to label American Indians as natural and fettered, then appropriating its language for resistance was a sanguine anti-removal tactic. In this way, the Seminole Nation pulled at the Congress' fractious knot by hearkening to natural/savage metaphors versus the eventually solidified childlike identities attributed to American Indians.

The Cherokee Nation represents a unique case study in American Indian resistance to removal.[71] Since the close of the Revolutionary War, the Cherokee Nation followed the United States in its republican political forms. To the Jacksonian charge that American Indians should "introduce among themselves the habits and arts of civilization," the Cherokee Nation replied with aplomb. They, in fact, undertook a number of republican projects in crafting their government.[72] In addition, the Cherokee Nation assumed the practices of western dress, marriage, Christianity and agriculture.[73] These actions placed them in a curious position between the Indian Removal Act's insistence that Natives had not advanced and their efforts in fulfilling the US government's requests for civilization. All in all, their past accommodationism came to underpin their newly found insistence on a separate autonomy outside the US nation.

For these reasons, the US government's justification for removal based on a failure of assimilation fell to Cherokee scrutiny as specious. In 1835, in the midst of removal negotiations with the Cherokee Nation, Jackson declared in typical style: "I am sincerely desirous to promote your welfare. Listen to me therefore while I tell you that you cannot remain where you now ... [you cannot] flourish in the midst of a civilized community."[74] Cherokee leaders were understandably confused. In an oft-repeated line of rebuttal, less US-accommodating leaders John Ross and William Hicks pointed out the inconsistency in US removal aims: "The truth is they have seen and see daily, the rapid advances of the Indians in the arts of civilization, as well as in morals and religion ... Among the Cherokees, where the most efficient efforts have been made, the improvements are truly surprising ... What is the result of all the efforts ... to remove?"[75]

As with the other four southeastern nations, federal agents asked the Cherokee Nation to remove following the ratification of the Indian Removal Act. And as with the other four, some of the Cherokee resisted as long as possible. Negotiations with both pro-US and more skeptical leaders of the Cherokee Nation began in 1832, but were not concluded until 1835. In the face of physical threats from both the federal and Georgia governments, a portion of the Cherokee Nation agreed to a removal treaty. These threats resonated with them as they witnessed increased hostilities committed by whites in Georgia.

When the US government ratified the Treaty of New Echota on December 29, 1835, the document was criticized along the lines of the Seminole Nation's treaties. A minority faction (the Treaty Party) had signed off on the proposal. A number of the Cherokee people (identified as the National Party) rebuked the Treaty Party's concessions and nullified the treaty. Ross, leader of the National Party and officially elected President of the Cherokee Nation in Georgia, castigated the Jackson Administration for entreating with an unrepresentative Cherokee group. He said in 1835, prior to the Treaty of New Echota: "As the duly authorized delegation of the Cherokee nation, here, we do most solemnly protest against any such arrangements being entered into with these [Treaty Party] individuals . . . do not throw any of these obstacles in our way."[76] Ross's decolonial resistance helped slow the implementation of the treaty, punctuating the impact of such rebuttals to removal.

Some members of the Cherokee Nation, though, worked through these breaches and crafted identities infused with republican and assimilative dispositions. If removal advocates argued that a "failure to assimilate" necessitated the removal policy, then crafting an identity based on amalgamation and American precepts would, surely, undercut the Indian Removal Act.[77] In this way, Cherokee discourse worked decolonially. The enactment of assimilative and republicanism appeals appeared to demonstrate accommodationism. But, considering the tactic of aligning their rhetoric with the government, their discourse can be judged as resistive in pursuit of autonomy and sovereignty.

Certainly, the enactment of assimilation and republicanism indicated the Cherokee Nation's predisposition toward melding their discourses with those of the federal government. To this end, the bulk of Cherokee anti-removal rhetoric centered appeals on the Cherokee nation's assimilative aims. A Cherokee Nation council in 1829 wrote, for instance, that removal was "remarkable because it had been the professed object of the government . . . to teach them [Cherokee] knowledge and the arts of civilized life" and now "it is quite immaterial what course of life [we] pursue, provided [we] vacate our lands." The council pointed out the irony in the federal government's move to punish the Cherokee Nation for assimilating. The group continued, "a million fingers will point at us and a million tongues will hiss at us, if it [the removal question] is decided in favor of oppression and injustice."[78] Having already proven themselves amenable to Americanization, the council next turned their acculturation against the US government to demonstrate the absurdity of removal.

Through their assimilative efforts, Cherokee councils framed their identities as righteous and just, while simultaneously constructing the US government as inconsistent. To the fear that the people would "point" and "hiss," Wood Pecker (Cherokee), Roman Nose (Cherokee) and others opined: "We consider it exceedingly vexatious to be perpetually teased... to part with our inheritance, just as we are beginning to occupy a respectable standing in the estimation of the Christians who know us . . . Must our prospects be always blasted? We think [the US government] will answer, no."[79] Here, Wood Pecker, et. al. appealed to a sense of moral inheritance—their rights to territories based on ancestral connections. They also called into question the US government's aim to unite Natives and whites under the aegis of civilization. The men appealed to their white neighbors with a rhetorical question that was self-answered in the hope of moving the American public to recognize the same "hypocrisy" the Cherokee Nation observed.

More National Party-oriented Cherokee members, at times, resisted removal by separating itself from the essentialized stereotypes of American Indians who the government said was in need of assimilation. Elias Boudinot (Cherokee) admitted the Native communities' so-called past primitive character in his first editorial in the 1828 inaugural issue of the *Cherokee Phoenix*.[80] He reasoned, "There was a time . . . when darkness was sadly prevalent and ignorance abounded amongst them . . . it was thought to be a disgrace for an [Indian] to appear in the costume of the white man."[81] Boudinot, though, juxtaposed the previous Native "dark" identities with contemporary civilized Cherokee identities to illustrate how far his nation had advanced.

His non-monolithic rhetoric was enhanced by the metaphor of the "costume." The vehicle ("costume") referred to the material accoutrements of assimilation (clothing), but most vitally to American habits. The Cherokee people, Boudinot averred, built their identities around practices of republicanism, Christianity and agrarianism. At the same time, though, the "costume" could be shed, revealing a Cherokee identity wedged between Native traditions and Americanism. The power of his metaphor flourished by the way he resisted outright assimilation while highlighting assimilative identities. Boudinot further glossed his editorial by reminding his Cherokee audience to hold its culture tightly ("aris[ing] Phoenix like from their ashes") while in tandem asking them to bury their past savageries "deep under ground."[82]

Assimilative rhetoric as resistance to the Indian Removal Act also bolstered the Cherokee Nation's claims to sovereignty. The community's rise to civilization had, according to John Ridge, proven that the Cherokee people should be left to govern themselves in their homeland. Even Ridge, more accommodating than the resistive National Party, said in 1831, "You asked us to throw off a hunter and warrior state—we did so. You asked us to form a republican government—we did so. You asked us to cultivate the earth . . . we did so. You asked us to learn how to read—we did so. You asked us to cast away our idols and worship your God—we did so."[83] Here, Ridge's discourse merged with anti-removal advocates who questioned a removal policy based on a lack of assimilation. Because of these assimilationist habits, Ridge and Boudinot (also) demanded "in this land of liberty" that "we claim privileges of free men, and wish to have the right of disposing our lands" as we wish."[84] Clearly, Ridge and Boudinot amalgamated American characteristics with Cherokee lifeways. Focusing on "republican government" and the "land of liberty," both rhetors predicated Native identities on US governmental notions of civic life. Regardless of these men's particular, internal Cherokee politics, they shared rhetorical tactics of détournement.

Not surprisingly, Ridge and Boudinot's rhetoric seemed to contradict the US government's interpretation of the intersection of assimilation and sovereignty. Indian Commissioner T. Hartley Crawford reported just prior to the Treaty of New Echota that "experience has shown that, however commendable the efforts to meliorate a savage surrounded by a white population, they were not compensated to any great extent by the gratification which is the best reward of doing good."[85] Boudinot responded that any failure on the part of assimilation fell to the US government's unscrupulousness and hypocrisy. The US government had deprived Natives of "their rights—the sacred obligations of treaties and laws have been disregarded . . . [this has happened] for no other reason than that the Cherokees have so far become civilized as to appreciate a regular form of Government."[86]

Republican character and sectionalism became the frontispieces of Cherokee Nation president John Ross, who was perhaps one of the most outspoken early opponents of the Indian Removal Act. As leader of the National Party and of mixed-descent, Ross straddled the literal borderlands of white American and Cherokee nationalist identities.[87] Concurrently, he toed the political line between selling the Cherokee Nation's assimilation as a rhetorical tactic to dissuade the US government from implementing removal and using the community's assimilation as a form of resistance.

Working from his political acuity as a constant representative of the Cherokee council to Washington, Ross positioned his discourse against removal in republican language. For instance, in his 1829 annual message, Ross argued not from Cherokee identities rooted in the soil or ancestry, but in the US government itself. He explained to the Cherokee Nation that "our treaties of relationship are based in the principles of the federal constitution, and so long as peace and good faith are maintained, no power, save that of the Cherokee Nation and the United States jointly can legally change them."[88] In part, Ross spoke to the tenuous issue of Cherokee "custody" between the US government and the Georgia legislature. That is, he capitalized on the factious debates in Congress over federal power versus states' rights to position the Cherokee Nation as sovereign.

Moreover, though, Ross relied on an allusion to foundational documents of the United States and sectionalism to decolonize the importance of including Native voice in federal Indian policy. In this way, Ross too trumped federalism over states' rights. Abrogation of the US government's own recognition of treaties as two-partied would therefore violate the Constitution's tenets. Of this Prucha writes, "Treaties rested upon a concept of Indian sovereignty or quasi sovereignty . . . treaties made no sense unless based on recognition of some kind of special legal status of the Indians."[89] Denying the Cherokee Nation's sovereignty gravely stained American republicanism. Appealing to the Constitution, Ross used states' rights as a wedge issue to appear favorable to the US government. This tactic worked in two crucial ways. First, it functioned to expel state efforts to remove the Cherokee Nation. Secondly, it plied the sectional conflict, thus placing the Cherokee community on the federal government's side. Combined with assimilative appeals, his republican and sectional arguments sought to détourn and change the conception, codified by removal rhetoric, of a ward/warden relationship between the government and the Cherokee Nation.

In the year following the Indian Removal Act, and of the *Cherokee Nation v. Georgia* decision, Ross increased his decolonial resistance through republicanism and sectionalism. The *Cherokee Nation v. Georgia* case involved Ross and others forwarding a proposed injunction to prevent Georgia from encroaching on their territory. Marshall held that the high court was "of the opinion that an Indian tribe or nation within the United States is not a foreign state in the sense of the constitution, and cannot maintain an action in the Courts of the United States."[90] Ross reconfigured language akin to Marshall's decision and rooted the Cherokee community's right to petition the Supreme Court in a republican memory of the Washington Administration. He wrote in his annual message of 1831 that "President Washington and his successors well understood the constitutional powers of the General Government . . . and that the judicial power would extend to all cases of litigation that may arise under treaties . . . it was determined . . . to defend the rights of the [Cherokee] Nation before the Courts of the United States."[91] That Ross anchored Cherokee sovereignty in American law and memory problematized the US government's position on removal by bringing to bear a possible lack of moral inheritance—not to American Indian ancestors who welcomed Europeans in the seventeenth and eighteenth centuries—but to the United States' own forebears. Here, Ross demonstrated the force of Native resistance and how it complicated the realization of removal. For this reason, Senator Frelinghuysen had earlier worried that the US government would "deviate" from its epochal "ideals" should removal commence.[92]

As the negotiations of the Treaty of New Echota neared, Ross shifted his decolonial resistance to a rhetoric of "moral suasion."[93] Perhaps out of desperation or due to the Cherokee Nation's (especially the National Party's) futile attempts at forestalling removal, he saddled the federal government in 1834 with a criminal identity. That is, Ross lamented "the liberty, the freedom, and the life of the Cherokee are placed in jeopardy because they are left at the mercy of the white robber and assassin to be taken with impunity."[94] Notice how Ross enlisted the aid of key republican terms ("liberty," "freedom," "life") to clarify the identities of the US government and the Cherokee Nation. The former was a perpetrator, stealing and killing while trampling its own tenets. Meanwhile, the Cherokee people were victimized as part of the republican enterprise through connection to the government, and yet deprived of the federal government's paramount ideological principles. The deprivation of familial relations also existed in this incongruence. After all, averred Ross, the US government conferred these rights and privileges on the Cherokee Nation: "'Father' was bestowed on him [US president]. Under the fostering care and patronage of this government the arts of civilization and Christianization were successfully introduced . . . [and] improvement soon spread its happy influence over the whole country."[95] Ross thus reminded the US government of the Cherokee people's progress, appropriated Jacksonian paternalism to bolster his rebuffing of the removal policy, and portrayed the US government as wholly inconsistent. For these reasons, Ross concluded, "[We] will never voluntarily consent to remove west of the Mississippi."[96]

Finally, Ross's resistant rhetoric criticized the US government for violating representative democratic doctrine by signing the Treaty of New Echota with the unrecognized Treaty Party. Rather than solely confront Treaty Party leaders, Ross focused his reprobation on the world's exceptional example of democracy: the United States. "The will of the people was not then expressed," he told the Jackson administration, because "that meeting consisted only of a small faction." What is more, Ross wishfully suggested, "We cannot suppose that [the US government] would want us to disobey the known will of our constituents" by acceding to the falsified treaty.[97] Ross's decolonial approbation alluded to how US exceptionalism depended on the government's "status as the apotheosis of the nation-form itself and as a model for the rest of the world"—a notion that typified the removal policy's hypocrisies.[98] Part of the representative democracy supported by the US government involved "the will of the people." How could the US government deny the same republican consideration to the Cherokee Nation who had assimilated to US public lifeways? For this reason, Ross closed his letter by advising that "all is lost if the agreements of a few who arrogate themselves to power to deal with the rights and liberties and future of the Cherokee Nation" win out over truly elected representatives (i.e., the National Party).[99]

Though the Indian Removal Act focused a great deal of attention on opening lands in the southeast, areas east of the Mississippi but north of the Ohio River, as well as on the fringes of the northeastern frontier, were also cleared through removal. As Indian Commissioner William Medill noted in an 1848 annual report, Midwestern removal had to be sought "to leave an ample outlet for our white population to spread and to pass towards" the West.[100] There was little question that the government's aspirations of removing the five southeastern nations would motivate comparable and concurrent action in the Midwest.

Small land cessions had been made with these Native nations since the negotiation of the Northwest Ordinance in July 1787 that established the precedent of the US government negotiating peace for land in the Midwest.[101] It was not uncommon during this period to discern in Midwestern Native discourses expatriate sentiments such as those noted in the Chippewa's "removal song": "The sound is fading away/Freedom/The sound is fading away."[102]

The removal of Midwestern nations in the 1830s, however, proved difficult. Whereas the five southeastern nations lived on clearly demarcated land familiar to the government, the Midwest included enclaves in widespread and oftentimes lesser known areas. Adding these territories to the US land base promised to "create an extensive interior and a series of administrative headaches with which the existing bureaucratic structure was unequipped to deal."[103] Thus, the US government emboldened a new bureaucratic agency, the Department of Indian Affairs, in June 1834 to "exercise a general supervision and control over the official conduct and accounts" of Natives.[104]

Another problem with these removals was that other Native communities witnessed from afar removal's depredations for the five southeastern nations. Removing these remaining pockets would take more effort; after all, they knew the government's strategies and oft-elusive treaty methods. To this effect, a group of Wyandot chiefs told US Indian agents in 1832 that "we express a distrust of the sincerity of the President in making [treaties] and a disbelief that the Country to which we are invited to remove is such as has been represented."[105] Therefore, the US government performed a face-saving task in transferring Indian Affairs to the new Department of the Interior.[106]

To resist removal, the Midwestern nations crafted messages of irony and moral certitude to challenge removal. Typically, these discourses accompanied conciliatory addresses and surrender rituals, as tactics that decolonized governmental discourses by working through seemingly deleterious practices resulting from removal to offer resistance. By détourning both the accommodationism that the government demanded and the ironic surrender moment, these nations were able to point to the inconsistencies that were part of removal, and to forge strong identities for themselves and dastardly identities for the US government. And these inconsistencies and restructured identities aided their demands for independent status far from the influences of the government and US nation.

Native surrenders challenged the hierarchies imbricated by removal rhetoric by pairing irony with moral certitude. Chief Black Hawk's rhetoric represents a key example of this veiled resistance. Though Black Hawk's surrender unfolded through mortification, he simultaneously preserved the Sauk Nation's sovereignty through a decolonially resistive ritual that allowed him to offer a defiant double-tongued discourse. [107]

Black Hawk's conciliation to the US government's ascendancy provided him an entrée into the American imagination. That is, his surrender made him a "safe" subject for the American public to approach and consume. Black Hawk's objectification did not singularly harm him through a weakening of ethos, as some have argued.[108] Rather, his widespread and passionate American audience commanded a new presence for the chief. Black Hawk funneled his newly recognizable agency into an opportunity to address the public outside the scope of Indian agents. He accomplished the task of talking directly to the US government and the American public through his published autobiography.[109]

In the spring of 1832 the Sauk Nation journeyed back east to their former Rock River, Illinois, home. Violating a removal treaty they sought a reprieve from the separation suffered following their new life on the reservation. The return was instigated as a means of spiritual and physical survival. The US government, however, viewed the homecoming as a sign of an "aggressive warpath."[110] Major General Edmund Gaines exhorted the Sauk: "I came here, nether to *beg* nor *hire* you to leave your village," Gaines exhorted. "My business is to remove you, peaceably if I can, but *forcibly* if I must![111] Still, Black Hawk's nation refused to budge. US troops, then, engaged them in a bloody battle that ended with the Sauk Nation removed from its home.

According to popular reports, Black Hawk surrendered in early September 1832 following the Battle of Bad Axe.[112] But, Black Hawk's elegiac surrender also marked a point of resistance. Elegies, I have written elsewhere, allowed an investiture for American Indians. Nineteenth century Natives in particular "issued surrender speeches or farewells to the American public" directly, so as to pull on heartstrings outside the scope of oppressive governmental contexts.[113] Black Hawk crafted a rhetoric of moral certainty here that flipped the Sauk Nation's identity as just and the government's identity as evil. Moral certainty worked, here, as a veritable Trojan horse. That is, the chief, having secured the eyes and ears of the US public, cloaked his moral defiance in sardonic benevolence. For instance, in contrasting his present and past conditions against the current state of the United States he related:

> I am now an obscure member of a nation that formerly honored and respected my opinions. May the Great Spirit shed light on your's—and that you may never experience the humility that the power of the American government has reduced me to, is the wish of him, who . . . was once as proud and bold as yourself.[114]

On its face, his discourse appeared to be a sobering resignation. However, alternate explorations of Black Hawk's rhetoric reveal how dastardly the US government functioned: it reduced character, weakened honor, dissipated respect, and diluted pride.[115] He identified with his audience by praying to the "Great Spirit" that they would never have to suffer the disgraces and oppression lobbed by the government at the Sauk Nation. The moral certainty of pairing his own kindness with the US government's tyranny allowed Black Hawk a chance to issue a decolonial resistance that evidences, what Bhabha says, "enables a form of subversion" that "displaces the space" of the dominant.[116]

Black Hawk also wove morally certain Native identities throughout his autobiography in less covert ways. These simultaneously pegged the US government as untrustworthy. In discussing the Sauk Nation's displacement from its homeland, the chief crafted an invective against US settlers. Black Hawk, here, reversed the roles of American settlers and Sauk members. He insisted, "The whites were *complaining* at the same time that *we* were *intruding* upon *their rights*! THEY made themselves out to be the *injured* party, and *we* the *intruders*! And, called loudly to the great war chief to protect *their* property."[117] Appealing to the US public's senses of justice, Black Hawk called into question the evenhandedness of the Indian Removal Act. He closed his resistance by charging the Americans with double-crossing: "How smooth must be the language of the whites, when they can make right look like wrong, and wrong like right."[118] Black Hawk's use of antithesis—the pairing and conflation of "right" and "wrong," in this case—scrutinized whether the removal policy was, indeed, fair. And Sauk identity was crafted as innocent in the process.

The elevation of the Sauk Nation as morally certain formed the cornerstone of Black Hawk's autobiography. As a tactic of resistance, moral certitude worked on both veiled and transparent levels to refashion the identities through decolonial removal rhetoric. Clearly, for instance, Black Hawk contrasted his nation's identity as moral with the US government's depravity:

> It has always been our custom to receive all strangers that come to our village or camps, in time of peace, on terms of friendship—to share with them the best provisions we have, and give them all the assistance in our power. . . . The white man will always be welcome in our village and camps, as a brother . . .We will forget what has past—and may the watchword between the Americans and [Sauk] and Foxes ever be—*Friendship!*[119]

The Sauk were positioned as humane in addition to deserving of their homelands. In addition, despite being oppressed through removal and indignity, Black Hawk and his nation were willing to forgive the past degeneracy of the US government. Black Hawk promoted the morality of his people above the impiety of the Americans, thus challenging the identities codified in the Indian Removal Act.

Perhaps the most robust fashioning of moral Native identities came with Black Hawk's decolonial censuring of the government for its unashamed and impertinent acts of violence. He reminded the US public, for instance, "Our people were treated badly by the whites on many occasions. At one time a white man beat one of our women cruelly for pulling a few suckers of corn out of his field."[120] Also not lost in Black Hawk's translation was the notion that "whites were not satisfied until they took our village and our grave-yards from us and removed us across the Mississippi."[121] Such deprivation of American Indian moral inheritance to their territories shined a searchlight on the US government as a thief.

Under the aegis of such moral certitude, Black Hawk's rhetoric tendered a détournement by revising the historical narrative of the Sauk Nation's removal milieu and the chief's surrender ritual. Black Hawk's ability to speak as a so-called ward provided him the decolonial license to "unmask" the government's language.[122]

Although the government's rhetoric of removal neither uplifted nor sustained Native sovereignty, it ironically "provided a mechanism for resistance to [governmental] authority and an opening for critique" on the part of Native leaders in the nineteenth century.[123] American Indians resisted removal by using "an identity . . . constituted in terms of the dominant system of representation" as a conduit to reflect back and refashion US governmental and Native identities.[124] Arnold Krupat argues that such enactment, whether by a Native rhetor or through a white interpreter, suggested a concealed defiance by mingling nineteenth century American Indian voice within Western traditions.[125] Or, as Joy Harjo and Gloria Bird put it, indigenous communities reinvented the "enemy's language" in order to "turn the process of colonization around."[126]

American Indian communities resisted the relationship codified by the Indian Removal Act and its attendant rhetoric by decolonizing the ideologies that the US government set as guiding frameworks: expansion, territoriality, paternalism and sectionalism. In so doing, Native nations challenged the removal policy while also reconstituting governmental and American Indian identities through the transformation of the government's inventional strategies. The Native resistance, too, emphasized a conception of sovereignty as involving independence outside the sphere of US citizenship.[127] And, American Indian discourse influenced the removal era debate and complicated the practices of removal and the *identity duality* that Native communities suffered within the US nation.

CHAPTER FOUR

Colonization and the Solidification of Identities in the General Allotment Act

LATE NINETEENTH CENTURY US EXPANSION REOPENED QUESTIONS about Native communities by bringing western settlers ever closer to the reservations staked out for removed Native nations. US settlers caught up to the reservations in the West and every removed Native group was soon encircled by a rising tide of farmers, miners and entrepreneurs.[1] President Grover Cleveland put the Native nations' position bluntly, noting in 1886, "Civilization, with the busy hum of industry . . . surrounds these people at every point."[2] While during the removal era American Indians were isolated on the far reaches of the US nation, "all of this now changed" as no indigenous community was "outside the bounds of organized government and society."[3] The clash of stolid Natives on reservations and ever-mobile white settlers also summoned the juggernaut of colonization all over again, a precipitation of the removal era that actually never lost gumption.

As a result of the opening of the western frontier the US government and American Indian nations traditionally located in the West were forced to confront one another. Suddenly, the frontier what historian Frederick Jackson Turner called the "meeting point between savagery and civilization," came to bear as roads, railways, settlers, and industries traversed areas west of the Mississippi.[4] The meeting of these Native nations and the US government involved a number of skirmishes instigated by continued settler expansion. Quickly, American Indians who had previously avoided the US government suffered military confrontation. With each US victory between the 1850s and the 1880s came more efforts to place Natives on reservations. After some thirty years, with most western American Indians removed to reservations, General William T. Sherman concluded in 1883 that "I now regard the Indians as substantially eliminated as a problem of the Army" and that the government's victories in what came to be known as the Indian Wars had "settled forever the Indian question."[5] However, Sherman was incorrect in his assumption that the end of the Indian Wars resolved the so-called Indian question.

During the 1840s through the 1880s, such contact caused a great deal of inquiry over how the government would interact with American Indians. The question of "what to do with the Indian" troubled the government, especially as the United States continued to subsume western territories.[6] The question soon became how to treat American Indians; should they be left to their own tribal sovereignty or should they be brought into the US nation as productive citizens—albeit on reservations—owing only an allegiance to the United States? One thing was sure: "The wilderness and its Indian population were confined to reservations. . . . The land was used up," and white settlers desired American Indian territories.[7]

Few US leaders advocated for American Indian independence on the reservations, therein working from colonizing ideologies. Instead, the government's overwhelming stance was that assimilation would benefit Natives by converting them into productive members of the US nation, akin to President Thomas Jefferson's earlier goals. Such aims differed from the segregationist discourse during the removal era, wherein American Indians were to remain dependent, yet separated from the US nation. Native assimilation and citizenship in the late nineteenth century was unsurprising, however, as American Indians now lived in closer proximity to US civic spaces. Enacting paternalism, the government, wrote Indian Commissioner Henry Dawes in 1883, was "to take [the Native] by the hand and set him upon his feet and teach him to stand . . . then to walk, then to dig, then to plant, then to hoe, then to gather, then to *keep*" in order to prepare Natives for citizenship.[8] This was thought to be easier to do as there were fewer threats of Native uprisings following the end of the Indian Wars.

Assimilation was to be achieved mostly through the policy of allotment. Allotment redrew reservation lines and sectored tracts to individual American Indians. The rationale therein was to divide collectively held Indian lands into individually owned parcels to discourage communalism and so-called uncivilized modes of living. Through the colonizing practice of "individualizing" American Indians, the government endeavored to "civilize them piecemeal" by eventually eliminating "tribal" structures.[9] The allotment policy, passed in 1887 as the General Allotment (Dawes) Act, also provided that if an individual Native "adopted the habits of civilized life" he could be "declared a citizen of the United States."[10]

Ultimately, the allotment policy worked to locate the space and place of American Indians in the newly expanded US nation. The government reified its colonial role as the *republican father* that sought to train American Indians for possible citizenship through proper use of the land. Land, here, functioned as a space of commodification which, when cultivated, constituted a pathway to citizenship for American Indians—a means of civilization. The possibility of Native toil on their allotted reservations and, hence, their prospects as US citizens, pointed to the ways that Natives' moral inheritance bore fruit in the Dawes era.

Though the Dawes Act promised citizenship to assimilate Natives, the policy continued to brace a colonizing relationship through which the government retained a dominant place in deciding Native affairs. In the end, allotment fell short of granting sovereignty as its pledge of citizenship faltered. Instead, American Indians were further constituted as a homogeneous group left to the whims of the federal government. The relationship solidified between American Indians and the US government represents the ideological and rhetorical remnants of the removal policy. And this rhetoric exhibits the *identity duality* of US citizenship, especially for groups of color, where such individuals were pledged to shun past national (or tribal) commitments in exchange for citizenship rights. The possibilities of inclusion were bankrupted as American Indians were removed from the civic spaces of power, thus contradicting the government's assimilationist ideals.[11]

As with removal, national ideologies (i.e., territoriality, republicanism, paternalism) of the Dawes Era hardened the government's control over American Indian communities. Expansion certainly did not wane in the post-Jacksonian nineteenth century. Instead, the US government's extension into the West exploded as populations in the East outgrew their areas, demanded more land on which their agricultural, commercial, and ranching industries could thrive and, thereupon, relocated in fulsome numbers.[12] This expansion was a continuation of what Turner deemed "the perennial fluidity of American life, this expansion westward . . . furnish[ed] the forces dominating American character."[13]

Soon after the mid-century acquisition of lands from Mexico and Great Britain the US government set its sights on the systemization of western territories. Efforts to consolidate western American Indian communities onto reservations in order "to free the region of Indian title and thus open it for settlement" comprised the quintessence of this systemization.[14] At the same time, as whites came into increased contact with American Indians already removed to reservations, they chipped away at reservation boundaries.

For western Native nations recently defeated by the US military the reservation system became a way to organize the government's newly acquired lands. Indian Commissioner William Medill told Congress in 1848 that "material changes will soon have to be made . . . so as to leave an ample outlet for our white population to spread and pass towards and beyond the Rocky Mountains."[15] Once American Indians were cordoned onto reservations, settlers could freely move about those areas previously occupied by the removed Native communities.

The 1860s and 1870s experienced an upsurge of expansion into the West, though the Civil War years slowed growth for a short time. Following the war, a number of factors converged to increase US settlers' emboldening of their providential errand. An 1867 Senate report on conditions in the West reported that "two railroad lines are rapidly crossing the Plains" and that the settlement of farmers and miners and the destruction of forests and buffalo following them would soon "put an end to the wild men's means of life."[16] At the same time as the mushrooming of railroads, gold and silver had been discovered in California. Thereafter, emigration into California, Oregon and Washington territories was "filling every valley and gorge of the mountains with the most energetic and fearless men in the world."[17] And, this brought the US military and white settlers even closer to Native communities. Following some kind of violent exchange, Native communities were typically removed to reservations. An 1868 report on the West by the Indian Peace Commission represented well the inevitably of removal in the wake of these exchanges: "As our settlements penetrate the interior . . . white and the Indian must mingle together, . . . and one of them must abandon [territory]."[18]

Western expansion in the late nineteenth century predictably led to a connection between citizenship and territory, as was the case in the Jacksonian era. White settlers were guaranteed lands for reasonable prices if they could demonstrate their productive intentions. Jefferson's old call for a yeoman spirit did not fall on deaf ears all those years later.

A number of acts were passed to open up western lands for production and citizenship purposes to the detriment of Native land—constituting an extension of the colonizing doctrine of discovery. In 1862, for example, the Homestead Act was implemented to secure land to settlers in the public domain. Settlers who were "citizens of the United States, or who shall have filed his declaration of intention to become such, as required by the naturalization laws of the United States" were granted cheap acreage.[19] Speaking of the act, Secretary of the Interior Columbus Delano argued that homesteading would dually open land for white settlers and wreak havoc on American Indian sovereignty: "An extension . . . will rapidly break up tribal organizations and Indian communities; it will bring Indians into subjugation to our laws, civil and criminal."[20] Similarly, the Oklahoma Organic Act of 1890 gave "settlers . . . the rights and privileges of American citizens" and placed them under the protection of law if they promised to use the land for the national good.[21] These acts permitted US citizens to carry out the republican mission to populate and produce for the nation.

As American Indians were removed to reservations the US government "civilized" many of them into the ways of American culture. American Indians had been a threat to the US government since its inception. If the government could "civilize" them and offer citizenship, then perhaps future dangers would be quelled through Natives' colonial subjugation. At this point, American Indians were not a hazard, but rather an opportunity for US identity building. Assimilating Natives also spoke to the power of territory as it intersected with citizenship. Whereas African Americans had typically not owned land, and therefore did not possess a connection to US soil, Native nations had historically linked their identities to territory. While there was a difference of opinion between American Indian nations and the US government regarding how to treat the land, political leaders sensed that Natives might be better suited to engage in citizenship because they cherished and honored territory. [22]

To encourage such assimilation, the government came to embody the paternal agent of civic preparedness through a construct I call *republican fatherhood*. This ideological role allowed the government to teach its Native wards citizenship through the practice of cultivating the soil.[23] Here, the republican father "guided his children in the choice of occupational calling," property holding, and standards of morality all through laboring upon the land.[24]

Republican fatherhood brings to light the ideological configuration of *republican motherhood*. According to Linda Kerber, republican motherhood is the "proposal that women . . . play[ed] a deferential political role through the raising of a patriotic child" during the eighteenth and nineteenth centuries.[25] Women, here, were ascribed the non-governmental responsibility of nurturing the next wave of white republicans. The purpose of raising the next generation of American leaders and patriots was the continuation of the US nation's virtues. And republican mothers allowed their sons, in particular, to grow independently within the value system cherished by the US nation.

Republican fatherhood, especially regarding American Indians, functioned differently in a number of ways. First, as the US government maintained an entrenched paternal role in American Indian lives, it codified this position. Whereas republican motherhood was a non-governmental activity, republican fatherhood was cemented through legislation such as the Indian Removal Act and the Dawes Act. Hence, the construct was politically reified, further normalizing the affinitive connection between American Indians and the US government.

Second, republican fatherhood did not typically take into account the concerns of the government's Native wards. Republican mothers were "outspoken advocate[s] on behalf of the nation's children" and altruistically dedicated themselves to perpetuating their children's growth and the nation's civic character.[26] In contrast, argues Mary Jackman, the role of fathers in the early republic featured "paternalistic authority over their children" without "selflessly evaluat[ing] the best interests of the child."[27] Instead, the nation's earliest fathers demanded that their children owe an allegiance to a father's paternal whims. Children were subjugated to the interests of the family. Republican fatherhood ceaselessly helped constitute American Indians as children, which justified the US government's control over Native uses of land. In turn, the government expected American Indians to sacrifice and produce for the nation's good.

Third, though republican fatherhood—like republican motherhood—elevated education as the zenith of civic preparedness, it limited the involvement of wards. For instance, no matter how educated in the agricultural arts they became, American Indians were typically considered by the government perpetually under-aged and incapable of full citizenship. Native communities might be assimilated through their toil on the land, but their reservations were still far flung from the centers of the nation, punctuating the incongruous colonizing bind of US citizenship for groups of color with simultaneous and competing commitments to assimilation *and* segregation. Such contradictions shored-up the *identity duality* inherent in US nationalism that held out the possibility of Native citizenship, yet did so through a racialist severance that barred inclusion. Instead, American Indians were offered a restricted citizenship that kept them "productive and safe" on the nation's periphery, though never fully vested in citizenship.[28]

The government's insistence on uplifting others through civilization and protection hearkened to its self-professed character as a republican father. The late nineteenth century witnessed the rise of the government's paternalism regarding both American Indians and international communities. Concerning the latter, the Spanish-American War, through which the United States intervened into Cuba, the Philippines, Puerto Rico and other Pacific territories against the staggering Spanish Empire, exemplified well the government's paternalism.[29] Reflecting on his administration's 1900 seizure of the Philippines as a protectorate, President William McKinley asserted that "there was nothing left for us to do but to take them all and to educate the Filipinos, and uplift and civilize them."[30] The government predicated its fatherly character on shielding what it viewed as weaker groups.[31]

These civilizing programs clearly guided Native-US relations. As Indian Commissioner George Manypenny wrote in 1856, the US government should act compassionately toward "the Indian tribes now left to its oversight and guardianship, so that they shall be intelligently and generously . . . cared for in all that makes life useful and happy."[32]

By the 1880s, the pieces were in place for an allotment policy. In 1876, with most Native nations cordoned onto reservations, Indian Commissioner John Q. Smith argued that "it is doubtful whether any high degree of civilization is possible without individual [use] of the land." An American Indian, he continued, "had to feel that his home is his own . . . and needs a direct personal interest in the soil." Such connections to the land promised to protect American Indians "by the power of the Government, in [Natives'] life, liberty, property and character."[33] Bearing this in mind, the US executive and legislature measured allotment as a policy and reified the colonial relationship between American Indians and the government.

The executive branch was the main engine behind allotment. Executive discourse vacillated between American Indians as dependent and autonomous, but settled on glossing them as "problems" whose solvency depended on US republican fatherhood. Such executive discourse homogenized all American Indians as problems and, in so doing, relied on a characterization of the government as a paternal administrator led by the Interior Department and the Bureau of Indian Affairs.

Commissioner of Indian Affairs Ezra Hayt's 1879 proposal for an allotment policy exemplified the positioning of American Indian identities for the US government. First, allotment was to be implemented under the guise of protection. To Hayt, "all former methods" of safeguarding American Indians were "entirely unadequate to protect the Indians against the encroachments of the whites."[34] Constituting American Indians as dependent, he instead asserted that the "government can only retain control over [Natives]" by enacting an allotment policy that would constrict Native lands while concurrently offering white settlers the reservation land they desired.[35] Here, like removal, allotment was predicated on paternalism whereby the government controlled dependent and essentialized indigenous peoples.

President Rutherford B. Hayes echoed Hayt's suggestion of a paternal Native-US relationship in his third annual message by noting how American Indians could only survive if they were "wisely and fairly guided." Part of this paternal identity allowed a situation where the government would protect Native communities while siphoning-off more land at whim. Or, as Hayes wrote, allotment gave license "to consider in what manner the balance of their lands may be disposed of by the Government for [Natives'] benefit." Certainly American Indian uplift was reflected in Hayes' sentiments. But, he also acknowledged that "the westward movement of our population looks still more eagerly for lands to occupy" and that Natives would "do well to prepare for such a contingency."[36] In other words, the paternal relationship cloaked the government's desire to obtain Native territories.

At the same time, Hayt's proposal for allotment conflictingly demarcated American Indian character as capable of self-sufficiency. This complicated the eventual allotment policy as Native identities were shown to fluctuate between dependency and autonomy, the opening a breach for later Native decolonizing rhetoric. (This is the exact kind of fissure or gap that can be exposed as hypocritical, thus extending inventional resources for détournement.) Hayt hinted at this more enlightened view of Native identities by averring that allotment would leave Natives "to their own resources to maintain themselves as citizens of the republic."[37] As Hayt's proposal wound into the hands of Interior Secretary Carl Schurz in late 1879, the construction of American Indian identities as independent was veritably noticeable. Schurz, for instance, reported to Congress that allotment would "make [Natives] self-supporting" and, as such, the government would "treat the Indians like other inhabitants of the United States, under the laws of the land."[38] Such self-support was not part of the government's removal era discourse, mostly because American Indians were cordoned onto the farthest stretches of US territories and, hence, would not come into contact with whites. There was no reason to demand assimilation if Natives were safely removed from the nation's centers.

The conflation of dependent and self-sustaining identities would come to bear even more as the Board of Indian Commissioners deliberated over Hayt's proposal. The Board characterized the executive, once again, as a mentor of sorts. Alternatively, Native identities were typified as weakened as the Board deliberated over allotment. With "mental faculties dwarfed and shriveled" American Indians, the Board argued, were seeking "to adjust" to the "glare of civilization above and beyond his comprehension." Such cultural uplift involved Natives seeing "that the knowledge possessed by the white man is necessary for self-preservation . . . he [Natives] needs it to save him . . ." And, the government as a republican father was willing to "appreciate as it never has before our duty and responsibility in this respect."[39]

At the same time, however, the Board intimated that American Indians also possessed the ability to embrace self-sufficiency. For instance, Native communities were discussed as empowered with the "promise" of overcoming "the habits of life and thought which for generations have held him in bondage." The homogenous Native was considered enabled enough to "save him from himself" and to fight back "old currents of habit" that threatened to "sweep him to certain destruction."[40] This construction of American Indian identities as independent and capable clashed with the alleged dependency simultaneously applied to them by the US government. Such hints at autonomy were not present in the removal era, especially as Jefferson's yeoman plans for Natives were shown to have faltered.

The government's quandary over American Indian communities led to a metonymic depiction of them as maladies to be eradicated. When the government was overwhelmingly mired in the competing dependent and independent constructions of Natives, it resorted to condensing them to impediments. An 1881 article penned by Schurz in the *North American Review* demonstrated this toxic move. In arguing for allotment he noted that the policy would solve the "Indian problem . . . in such a manner that they no longer stand in the way of the development of the country as an obstacle."[41] Allotment, then, became not just a way to aid "the progress and security of our Indian wards," but it was also a colonizing conduit for obtaining Native territories.[42]

Such a construction of Native identities as problematic concurrently presumed that the US government had the fortitude to solve the problem, thus heightening its self-professed exceptionalism. The government, in addition to bolstering its paternal characteristics, became an administrator of the "Indian problem." President Chester Arthur asserted in his first annual message, "prominent among the matters which challenge the attention" of the executive "is the *management* of our Indian affairs."[43] The management/administration metaphor peppered the government's allotment discourse. Prior to the allotment policy, "fatherliness" inhered in the presidency and its role as leader of Native-US relations. As the government's Native policies took more and more bureaucratic shape, however, the Bureau of Indian Affairs and the Interior Department strengthened presidential privileges to deal with American Indians as managers. Part of this, most certainly, spawned from the abolition of treaty-making, whereby the president ultimately decided Native policy by approving treaties and issuing executive orders. Moreover, with the increased profundity of "interior" issues in the late nineteenth century—especially as the US nation expanded—the president delegated responsibilities such as Native affairs, timber and resource supervision, railroad and road management, and the like to the Department of the Interior and its attendant bureaus, of which the Bureau of Indian Affairs was part.[44]

Members of the Senate Committee on Indian Affairs took Interior Secretary Schurz's suggestion of an allotment policy to heart. Known as the Coke Bill, Schurz's plan made its way through the Committee and onto the Senate floor. The bill was debated for several days in early 1881 and passed the Senate. The Coke Bill was then sent to the House where it never quite made it out of the House Committee on Indian Affairs based on costliness.[45] Though the bill never passed Congress, it instigated a six-year public debate that by 1887 produced the Dawes Act.

The Coke Bill sought to parcel out reservation land and convert Natives into farmers. Allotment was "to prove one of the most powerful agencies in the advancement of the race."[46] At the same time, allotments would provide numerous benefits to the United States. First, individual Native land occupancy—versus communalism—pledged to "extend over Indians . . . the laws" of the government.[47] Allotment, then, made it easier for the government to corral and control Native populations as republican children.

Second, the government retained the right to intrude into both individual allotted lands and the excess land freed up by breaking apart large reservations. The Coke Bill, hence, "did not overlook the undoubted fact that it is neither wise nor right to let these great solid blocks of reservations stand in the way of traffic and settlement." The bill did enact an early example of eminent domain, as the "right of way through Indian land can be granted at any time to railroads, highways and telegraph companies."[48]

Finally, allotment extended federal protection on two levels. On the one hand, it protected American Indians "against the greed of the whites" who incessantly threatened reservation territories. Also, though, the government offered white communities protection against potentially aggressive Native communities. Allotment promised the "blotting out of the reservations as fast as it can be safely done" to ensure the security of Natives and settlers.[49]

Pro-allotment senators relied on a number of diminutive Native identities and exceptional governmental characterizations to justify the Coke Bill. These advocates operationalized the problem/administrator relationship outlined by the executive into policy. Senator Richard Coke demonstrated this relationship in his opening arguments for passage of the allotment bill. American Indians, to Coke, were a "problem" and a "question" that confronted the US government. He said Native nations had made it "impossible to preserve peace between the Indians and the whites" especially because their "immense bodies of land" spread tribes out, thus making it difficult to assimilate them "piecemeal." Here, American Indian identities were reduced to obstacles. Their presence on reservation lands was "found to be inexpedient and impolitic" to their cultural uplift and to amicable relations.[50]

Notice that the US government, just as during the removal era, was shown to share no responsibility in the clashes between American Indians and the US nation. Rather, Native obstacles were to be subverted by the government, which was identified as a manager of Native affairs. The government was a problem-solver, as pro-allotment senator, George Vest (Missouri) claimed. Addressing the construction of the government as a manager of the "Indian question," he asserted that "if anything is to be done which shall solve the problem, it must be a broad and general systematic work."[51] Not only was the government characterized as a manager capable of systemizing its solution, but American Indians were once again constituted as monolithic—a broad and general policy was going to be applied to the "problem," thus eliding any individual context or characteristics of separate Native nations. This same kind of wholesale condensation was present in the rhetoric of pro-removal legislators in the 1830s. What it did was blot-out and occlude any semblance of violence associated with a colonizing policy like allotment. The government would simply appear as a savior, one with antiseptic hands and an even cleaner conscience.

At the same time, Senate allotment proponents fortified a paternal connection between American Indians and the federal government. The Native problem was personified in these instances as American Indians were revealed to be in need of the US government's republican fatherhood.

Arguing for the advantages of converting American Indians to agriculturalists and extending federal laws over Native communities, for example, Nebraska Senator Alvin Saunders asserted that allotment would "punish them all the same" and "protect them all the same."[52] In so doing, he not only collapsed American Indians under a Native sameness, but evidenced the government's paternal role as "punisher" and "protector." Moreover, Saunders alluded to the government's responsibility to protect Native communities through allotment: "This law which shall be enacted . . . will virtually prevent" the encroachment of their territories by "sharp and designing persons." He claimed that American Indians were too "young" in development to "protect themselves."[53] Whereas the dependents of republican mothers would grow and mature into their civic roles, Natives seemed here to be stuck in an uninterrupted identity formation as too pediatric to fulfill republican duties.

Similarly, Coke predicated allotment on the government's need to uplift American Indians. Allotment would, he said, persuade them that assimilation was the best way "to place them on the highway to American citizenship."[54] He reminded the Senate that the bill would "aid them with stock and agricultural implements" and the building of "housing upon their allotments of land"—both of which would "break up tribal relations and pass them under the jurisdiction of the Constitution and laws of the United States."[55]

Allotment opponents in the Senate typically disdained the Coke Bill because they felt American Indians lacked the skills necessary to assimilate. The rhetoric of these legislators represented the status quo. They wanted the reservation system to remain intact because the government could exert its will without having to expend the extra time and money required by allotment. Colorado Senator Henry Teller predicted that allotment would fail as American Indians would "eventually [get] rid of the land." Agricultural allotments, he continued, "have been of no particular benefit to them." Natives could not assimilate because they are "undeveloped . . . wanderers over the face of this continent" and are not suitable for "practical common sense." American Indians would never "know what [allotment] is . . . certainly, very few Indians [would] understand it."[56] Here, Teller cheapened American Indian identities to childishness; they seemingly were unresponsive to the forces of republican fatherhood. Underdeveloped, they were represented as too meager to occupy their own territories and lacked a comprehension of a policy that, supposedly, benefited them.

As with Senator Theodore Frelinghuysen's rebuke of the removal bill, though, Teller expressed some semblance of agency for American Indians. For instance, he argued against the Coke Bill by admitting how a "blanketed" allotment policy could never appeal to diverse Native communities. He asserted that "Indians differ as much from one another as the civilized and enlightened nations of the earth. Legislation that is proper and just for one class of Indians will fail . . .to civilize them.[57] Tellers' reproach of homogeneity created a rupture that provided Natives an inventional tactic of détournement, as we will soon see. Still, in arguing against a homogenous American Indian identity, Teller assumed that Natives were not civilized, thereby contributing to the same kind of diminution that pro-allotment rhetors buttressed in their support for the Coke Bill.

Other anti-allotment senators likewise diminished American Indian identities in their opposition to the Coke Bill. Alabama Senator John Morgan insisted that the Coke Bill's system would not work. His rationale included the need to "march very slowly and take up tribe after tribe, section by section of the country."[58] Morgan was not so much opposed to allotment as he disagreed with Coke's timeline for a speedy process. Morgan still assumed Natives were too dependent for self-sufficiency and argued that the US government was a paternal force in leading American Indian communities toward uplift. Morgan hoped "an honest and patriotic effort for the devising of some system by which we could bring the Indian in reach of civilization" would be pondered. And he shored-up the "problem" metaphor, as well when he contended that "we need to lead the Government of the United States out of the difficulties," out of "dealing" with its "problem" and "question." Here, he referred to Native communities as barricades to a "just policy."[59] Though the bill never passed the House due to a timetable issue the ideas generated in the debate led to the eventual passage of the Dawes Act in 1887.

As time drew on, the failure of the reservation system to assimilate American Indians sparked a renewed interest in the policy. President Grover Cleveland recognized the public outcries for an allotment policy in 1885 and urged Congress to finally adopt a bill. Employing the trope of dependency, he noted in his first inaugural: "[Indians] need to be protected from purloining schemes. . . . Indians shall be . . . treated as wards of the government and their education and civilization promoted with a view toward their ultimate citizenship."[60] Thus, J. D. C. Atkins, Cleveland's Commissioner of Indian Affairs, outlined an allotment bill in his 1885 annual report. In it he aimed to solve the Indian problem by managing a new system of redistributing Native territories and converting American Indians to farmers. He wrote, "Everything done with reference to the Indian should be with a view of impressing upon them that this is the policy which has been permanently decided . . . in reference to their management."[61] Herein began renewed consideration of allotment.

Massachusetts Senator Henry Dawes had long been involved in American Indian affairs as a politician and followed closely the failed Coke Bill in 1881. With some renewed encouragement from Cleveland and the Bureau of Indian Affairs, Dawes pursued a new bill. To Dawes, the individualization of the Indian through labor was the pinnacle of the government's assimilative plans. Indeed, the time was ripe for an allotment policy. There seemed very little opposition to the measure; in fact, Robert Utley contends that the American public thought allotment "afforded the ideal incubator" for the "process" of assimilating Natives and nicking more land in a humane way.[62] And, any genuine "debate" on the issue within the federal government only involved cost and timelines. In sum, Congress was in relative agreement regarding allotment by the late 1880s.

Within this context, Dawes introduced his bill that "extended the protection of the laws of the United States" over Natives through allotted lands upon which they would toil and, assumingly, reach citizenship.[63] Dawes' insistence that labor on leased lands produced citizens reduced American Indian identities to commodified laborers. Such commodity logic resonated with the nineteenth century image of a father insisting that his children prepare for agricultural productivity to provide free labor to the family unit. Congress's debate of the Dawes Act revealed how government-led identities of problem/administrator and dependent/ward weakened American Indian sovereignty by hinging Native importance on service to, and tutelage under, the republican father.

In his opening comments to the Senate, Dawes argued that only productive use of reservation land could elevate American Indians to US citizenship. The point of labor, he said, was to lead Natives "out from the darkness and into the light" to "citizenship."[64] Such colonizing justifications pointed to American Indians as dependent in accordance with pre-Dawes rhetoric. Moreover, American Indians could only be redeemed and considered important by subjugation to a kind of yeomanry: "What [an American Indian] earns on the farm will help him learn the value" of participation in the "nation." Therefore, the promises of American Indian citizenship could only be established if the government assimilated Natives and molded them from, "the best material out of which citizenship was ever made": agricultural toil. Dawes continued by asking Congress if there was "any better work than . . . to make citizens worthy of this republic."[65] Ostensibly, the Dawes bill promised to end the "Indian problem" by assimilating American Indians into a capitalistic agricultural system. This, however, would reduce them and notions of the land that they toiled on to productivity alone. Dawes' plan differed from the Indian Removal Act's discourse as the Jacksonian period repudiated the idea that American Indians could actually assimilate. Now, however, with whites and Natives in closer contact assimilation quickly became a necessity to protect new settlers.

Meanwhile, Congress was tasked with crafting a law that allowed the executive to uplift dependent Natives through allotment. The executive could "put him [Indian] on his own land, furnish him with a little habitation, with a plow, and a hoe, and a rake, and show him how to go to work to use them."[66] Though agricultural labor promised to move American Indian individuals into public participation and autonomy, Dawes' discourse linked this liberty to a dependence on the federal government.

Dawes, though, offered American Indians a rupture for decolonial resistance by noting that Native communities choosing to toil on their allotments "might" reach independence. The predications of citizenship were the outward benevolent rationales for the Dawes bill and differed tremendously from removal era constructions of Natives as separated wards. Dawes looked forward to the possibility that "they [would] stand upon the reservations no more"—a time when "they will stand upon their homesteads as citizens of the United States." Native individuals, in this instance, held the promise of sovereignty that could feasibly "open to him the doors" of the US nation. This potential, however, only came with dire consequences for American Indians. For example, Native communities would be forced to abandon their traditional identities and heritages. Upon allotment, Dawes asserted that Natives "would pass away as an Indian . . . He is to disappear as an Indian of the past."[67]

Dawes' introduction of the allotment bill set the tone of the debate. He framed the need for allotment with paternal and administrative identities for the executive and dependent identities for American Indians. And in republican fatherhood form, he linked any scintilla of Native sovereignty and citizenship to what American Indians could produce as agriculturalists. Following suit, the Senate passed the Dawes bill easily and quickly, with very little discussion of the bill's merits, excepting the cost involved. Next, the bill traveled to the House where the cost of the policy became the genuine point of contestation.[68]

The most outspoken Dawes bill supporter in the House, North Carolina Representative Thomas Skinner began by reifying the problem/administrator identities first initiated by pre-Dawes executive and senatorial discourse. In the process he also exemplified the reduction of American Indian character to commodity. To Skinner, the Dawes bill would "lead to a correct solution to the Indian problem."[69] An ancillary result of the allotment policy, he averred, was the economic value that Native labor would add to the expanding US nation. "Let [Natives] become a citizen of the United States," Skinner said, "and the Indian will soon cease to burden the Government and in good time will help to bear its burdens and add to the material wealth of the country."[70] Skinner's discourse further revealed the fashion in which American Indians were diluted as problems. Native communities "burdened" the government, and the government as an administrator likewise held the duty of "enactment of a bill" that "managed" Native groups.[71] He also illustrated how Natives, as wards, would toil for the republican father.

The assimilation and citizenship of American Indians remained a crucial component of the Dawes bill as it moved further through the House. And the constitution of American Indians as commodity undergirded the allotment policy's pledge of citizenship and participation in the US nation. Representative Bishop Perkins (Kansas), speaking homologically to Senator Dawes, argued that American Indians "should be enabled and required to qualify themselves for the duties of American citizenship, and to support themselves by industry and toil."[72] Though such aims of self-support seemingly emancipated American Indians from dependent characterization, the aims "failed to elevate" Native identities to sovereignty.[73] That is, as allotted Natives "learned the habits of thrift and industry" through their labor, they were expected to do so "by associating with the white man" especially as whites possessed the ideal character for citizenship.[74] They were also to be treated as monolithic through the Dawes bill, as the "policy under examination" would "totalize" all Native communities as allotted "workers" under the proposed legislation.[75] Nowhere included in the House deliberations were indications of individuality among Native nations.

The Dawes Act of 1887 came to represent the new shape of Native affairs and of the Native-US relationship. The colonizing act demarcated for American Indians an enforced move away from traditional indigenous roaming, hunting, and gathering subsistence. It also signified the cessation of communally owned tribal lands.[76] Instead, the Dawes Act compelled an assimilationist commitment that led to a "compulsory turning toward white social and economic values and laws to which the individual Indian was to be increasingly subjected."[77] The Dawes Act combined the reduction of American Indian identities to commodities and wards into a policy that duly left the US government in control of Native territories as an administrator and republican father, ultimately segregating American Indians in ways counterintuitive to the assimilationist logic underscoring the bill's justification.

The Dawes Act allowed the executive branch through the Bureau of Indian Affairs and the Interior Department the authority to "cause said reservations, or any part thereof, to be surveyed . . . and to allot the lands in said reservation in severalty to any Indian located thereon."[78] Severalty involved a "trust" process wherein the federal government enacted paternalism by overseeing the conversion of American Indian "wards" to assimilated agricultural laborers. The severalty dimension of the Dawes Act should have cemented the notion that Native communities were never fully granted citizenship and autonomy through the allotment policy. Instead, the severalty process provided that "the United States does and will hold the land thus allotted for a period of twenty-five years, in trust for the sole use and benefit of the Indian."[79] American Indians thus remained dependent on the

US government for a period of no less than twenty-five years—about the length of time needed for an American boy to mature.[80] Only following the patenting of lands after the trust period—and with proof that an individual Native "has adopted the habits of civilized life"—could American Indians be considered US citizens.[81]

Overall, the severalty clause upon which the Dawes Act relied channeled the paternal and administrative identities constituted by Dawes rhetoric into a hierarchy. American Indians were alluded to as unfit to occupy their newly allotted lands without governmental intervention; they were treated as infants in terms of their civic preparedness and were forced to toil for at least twenty-five more years in order to demonstrate their suitability for citizenship. As the Dawes Act's header noted, allotment would "extend the protection of the laws of the United States . . . over the Indians."[82] In the meantime, the US government was characterized as an administrator of both Native cultures and territories—the government "executed," "contracted," "conveyed," and "regulated" all of "the lands in Indian Territory" and the "rights of any such Indian." The Department of the Interior and the Bureau of Indian Affairs were to "direct," "foster," "guide," and "manage" the new policy, as well as to "protect" those "Indians within jurisdiction."[83]

During deliberations over the Dawes Act, Congress punctuated the significance of allotment with the necessity of shedding "the old Indian."[84] Indian communalism on reservations, in particular, was argued to have "dwarfed [Natives'] minds and . . . clog[ged] [their] energies."[85] As Indian Commissioners gauged the implementation of the Dawes Act, they averred that American Indian assimilation could be hastened by breaking up Native communalism, therefore linking American Indian loyalty to the US government and occluding any future tribal influence. Such assimilation with white citizens would, the logic suggested, help foster enlightened individuals laboring for citizenship rights and privileges. According to Indian Commissioner Thomas Morgan's 1889 annual report, for instance, "tribal relations should be broken up and socialism destroyed."[86] The thought, here, was that tribal influence on a mass scale challenged allotment and its attendant goal of assimilation. The government figured that such influences could be diminished with the strengthening of assimilation through the allotment of lands constituting one part of the incongruous bind of US citizenship. As Theodore Roosevelt commented: "Allotment . . . is a vast pulverizing engine to break up this tribal mass."[87] And, yet, the government still channeled its relationship with Natives into a segregated and contained citizenship as the allotted lands functioned as spaces of control.

Indian Commissioners fortified the dependent/ward relationship by tying assimilation to individualism. Speaking one year after the passage of the Dawes Act, Commissioner John H. Oberly asserted that the "guardian must act for the ward . . . The Government must then, in duty to the public, compel the Indian to come out of his isolation . . . and into assimilation with the masses."[88] Here, the executive possessed a hierarchical identity in directing the childlike Native toward "American life." This guidance worked by stymying the power of Native nations. That is, American Indians were to be "imbued with the exalting egoism of American civilization."[89] The government sought to banish tribalism, thus reducing indigenous influences that otherwise clouded assimilation. Moreover, the "breaking up of the tribal mass" allowed American Indians to "find pleasure in the consummation of that patriotic enjoyment which is always to be found in the exercise of the high privilege of contributing to the general welfare."[90] In this way, Clark contends, capitalistic production of the allotted lands would dually assimilate Native individuals and add to the US nation's wealth.

To the issue of American Indian assimilation through allotment, Indian Commissioners and Interior Secretaries also predicated the reduction of tribal structures on Natives' agricultural work as republican children. Therefore, just as in the Dawes debates, American Indians could only show the promises of assimilating and becoming citizens if they contributed to the US national economy. US leaders supported allotment by asserting that Natives be "trained to habits of industry, thrift and self-reliance."[91] According to Interior Secretary Ethan Allen Hitchcock, labor preserved Natives "from extinction, not as an Indian but as a human being."[92] They could only be viewed as worthy "human beings" and as "participants" by "abolish[ing] tribal relations . . . and in the sweat of his brow and by the toil of his hands, carry out, as his white [neighbor] has done, a home for himself and his family."[93] In this quotation, American Indian culture was eschewed in favor of western conceptions of work and homesteading. This construction also homogenized Native identities.

Despite the clear areas of agreement, there did exist some ruptures in Bureau of Indian Affairs rhetoric surrounding the Dawes Act's efficacy. And as with governmental removal rhetoric, these moments simultaneously generated from American Indian viewpoints and provided entrées for Native communities to resist allotment. In arguing for the "destroy[ing] of tribal relations" and of dealing with American Indians "not as nations or tribes or bands," Morgan also alluded to Native agency.[94] First, he made explicit that American Indian communities may have—even if in the past—held the promise of sovereignty. This was born out by his inclusion of "nations" among those structures he wanted to eliminate. Morgan's admission that Natives may have once been considered sovereign allowed Natives an opening to resist allotment. Second, Morgan also claimed that the supplanting of tribalism pledged to move American Indians into the status of "American citizen" and granted "full participation in all the riches of our civilization."[95] Such questions of citizenship were a predictable outgrowth once the Natives were living within the spaces of the expanded US nation in the West rather than on the farthest reaches of the nation's border.

The Dawes Act never fulfilled Native citizenship promises. Instead, the government capitalized on essentialized Native constructions as dependent, commodified, and assimilated to expand its territory. The Supreme Court codified these identities by allowing for the government as a republican father figure to reign supreme in directing all Indian policies. The court's encroachment into American Indian communities and its solidifying of the *plenary doctrine* divided American Indians from any vestiges of independence and US citizenship once and for all during this allotment age. While congressional and executive discourse suggested that American Indians *might* be sovereign, the high court concretized the destabilized Native identities found in the removal era. With sovereignty hindered by the allotment policy, American Indians were basically left with an empty promise of citizenship.

The US government heightened its interventions into allotted Native territories, by way of the Court, even though American Indians who acceded to allotment were said to be "independent" and "immune" from federal encroachment.[96] And, one case in particular, *Lone Wolf v. Hitchcock* (1903), substantiated how the high court channeled the government's relationship with American Indians into a codified hierarchy of colonization.

One of the first legal cases that complicated American Indian sovereignty during the allotment era was *Elk v. Wilkins* (1884). In this case, John Elk (Omaha) was denied voting privileges in Nebraska, despite his claims of assimilation through agricultural labor and assumptions of citizenship based on his tax revenue. The question for the Court remained: "Whether an Indian born a member of one of the Indian tribes within the United States" having engaged in productive use of the land was protected "by the first section of the Fourteenth Amendment."[97] Elk satisfied the republican demands of citizenship and appeared eligible for protection under the Fourteenth Amendment. However, the high court ruled that Elk could not vote because American Indians were held as "no more 'born in the United States' than children of subjects of any foreign government born within the domain" of the United States." The plaintiff, "not being a citizen of the United States" was denied such status due to his Native identity.[98] In this instance, American Indians were placed outside the spaces of political participation in the US nation even though they held claim to the physical properties of what became the nation-state. Such ruling exemplified the incongruous bind of US citizenship whereby the executive and Congress pushed for assimilation while the US Supreme Court reified segregationist precedents, an inconsistency of Natives' *identity duality.*

Furthermore, the Supreme Court ruled that the federal government could justifiably seize and try Natives for crimes per federal law, hence limiting the autonomous character of American Indians who had begun to assimilate to the US nation. In *United States v. Kagama* (1886), Kagama (Hoopa) was accused of murder and had been tried under the Major Crimes Act of 1885, which subjected American Indian criminals "either within or without an Indian reservation" to federal criminal law. With the act, American Indians committing murder, manslaughter, rape, assault with intent to kill, arson, burglary, and larceny were "tried in the same manner . . . and with the same penalties as are all other persons charged with the commission of said crimes."[99] The inconsistency of the law, however, clouded the act's veracity. That is, American Indians could not be considered citizens or enjoy the privileges of American law but could be tried and punished under this very legal system. Here again was another space of dissension through which American Indians would eventually détourn the government's colonizing language.

Kagama brought his case to the Supreme Court to challenge the act's contradictions. Ultimately, the high court ruled that the Major Crimes Act was equitable because "Indians are *wards* of the nation . . . They are communities dependent on the United States."[100] Therefore, the US government owed a duty to protect those "wards" who might be threatened by such Native criminals. The Supreme Court's language, in addition to insulting American Indians as dependent, celebrated governmental identities as fatherly. "The power of the General Government . . . over the . . . now weak and diminished [Indians]," the court averred, "is necessary to their protection." The right of criminal intercession was extended to the government, above the sovereignty of American Indians and their supposed autonomous territories, because such power "never has existed anywhere else . . . the government . . . alone can enforce its laws on all tribes."[101] Such monolithic holdings weakened the agency of American Indians to retain independence.

The Supreme Court clarified the limited reach of American Indian sovereignty and citizenship in *Lone Wolf v. Hitchcock* (1903). The decision ended all challenges to the Dawes Act as intrusive and granted Congress the ultimate "plenary power" to abrogate Indian treaties without any limits or duties. The Court also ruled that American Indian communities had to rely on the federal government in "good faith" as a republican father. The high court affirmed that "protecting [Natives] is within the competency of Congress. These Indian tribes are the wards of the nation. They are communities dependent on the United States . . . The power of the general government . . . is necessary to their protection."[102]

Many have questioned the plenary doctrine's so-called benevolence. For instance, Ann Laquer Estin charges that the case allowed Congress to impulsively enlarge the nation's territory. To this effect, "the plenary power rule . . . effectively [left] the tribes at the mercy of shifting congressional moods and majorities . . . the rule's function was to facilitate continued congressional appropriation of tribal lands and resources."[103] Moreover, I have argued that plenary power was meant near-exclusively to challenge Native unity and solidarity and to threaten reservations.[104]

The *Lone Wolf* decision indicated that the Dawes Act's promise of independence and participation in the US nation fell short of its aim. As anti-allotment Senator Matthew Quay commented in 1903 after the *Lone Wolf* ruling, "It is the *Dred Scott* decision number two, except that in this case the victim is red instead of black. It practically inculcates the doctrine that the red man has no rights, which the white man is bound to respect, and, that no treaty or contract made with him is binding."[105] In the end, the case solidified the identity constructions instantiated by institutional discourse in the removal and allotment eras.

The case derived from a direct challenge to the Dawes Act. In June 1900 Congress ratified the Jerome Agreement between the federal government and the Kiowa Nation for the allotment of their reservation. According to Lone Wolf (Kiowa), the agreement violated a provision of the earlier 1867 Treaty of Medicine Lodge that required three-fourths of all Kiowa men to agree on allotment. Lone Wolf asserted that "[this] act of Congress is unconstitutional and void because it will deprive [the Kiowa] of their lands without their consent and against their protest."[106] Lone Wolf contended that Congress had forged Indian signatures and "tricked" leaders into signing the allotment agreement. This tactic, of course, alluded to the power of Native agency in resisting the Dawes Act. That Congress had to resort to spurious strategies meant that allotment suffered only partial complicity from Natives. Lone Wolf took his protest to the high court to determine if the Jerome Agreement was "a null and void act of Congress . . . upon . . . fraud and deception" and whether Natives had "vested rights" to their land or simply "the right to occupy" it at the "will of the government."[107]

The high court responded that it could not confront Congress when it came to "wardship" issues with American Indians. Of this, Justice Edward White wrote, "plenary authority over the tribal relations of the Indians has been exercised by Congress from the beginning, and the power has always been deemed a political one, not subject to be controlled by the judicial department of the government."[108] With the Kiowa Nation's legal challenge quashed, White suggested that "all Indians" (this phrase demonstrated the Court's view of Native identities as monolithic) had to have "good faith" in Congress as "protectors" and "possessors" of "plenary power."[109] Given this colonial identity construction, Congress retained the right to abrogate treaties at will.[110] In the process of cementing the plenary doctrine, the Court supported a dominant/subjugated relationship for the federal government and Native communities. White asserted that, "the power exists to abrogate the provisions of an Indian treaty [when] . . . the interest of the country and the Indian themselves, indicates that it should do so." Due to Congress's benevolent character, it was determined by the Court to hold always "perfect, good faith towards the Indians."[111]

Moreover, congressional identity was celebrated as moral. White's holding claimed that "it is to be presumed that in this matter the United States would be governed by such considerations of justice as would control a Christian people in their treatment of a . . . dependent race . . . a moral obligation rested upon Congress to act in good faith."[112] The federal government, here, was considered benevolent and controlling; American Indians, oppositely, were characterized as susceptible to governmental privilege. Indeed, claiming a self-righteous and morally superior character assisted the Court in justifying plenary power and, more generally, the ideology of paternalism. What is more, the ratification of the Jerome Agreement and the high court's championing of plenary authority were shrouded in the rhetoric of "good faith"—a legal tenet that remained difficult to disprove.[113]

Meanwhile, the Supreme Court's plenary doctrine further reduced American Indian territoriality to tenancy, solidifying the diminished identity constructions inherent in the Dawes Act's severalty clause. White relied on this construction to justify Congress's abrogation of the Treaty of Medicine Lodge. He argued, "Such lands and reservations are held by the Indians subject to the control and dominion of the United States, and such Indian tribes . . . have no title in the lands they occupy . . . their right is simply to occupy, at the will of the Government and under its protection."[114] Ostensibly, American Indians were legitimate for the ease with which the government could remove them if more settlers came along looking for western land. Natives were used as place-holder tenants, producing goods for the American economy until rightful citizens settled.

The federal government's power to manipulate American Indian communities and their lands undercut the promise of independence and citizenship.[115] Citizenship was difficult to maintain if Natives were never elevated to self-governance. Instead, as White noted, the Jerome Agreement was really "a mere change in the form of investment of Indian commodity."[116] The allotted territories functioned then as colonial spaces to curb Native agency and political power.

In the end, the allotment policy clarified the place of American Indian identities in the newly expanded US nation. The government took on the role of republican father and sought to train American Indians for citizenship. But inclusion in the US citizenry could only manifest through the proper use of land for the benefit of the republican father's larger family. The Dawes Act promised autonomy and citizenship if Natives accomplished their republican tasks on the allotted land, but these promises fell flat. In fact, the Dawes Act seemingly bolstered a colonizing relationship through which the government retained dominance in controlling American Indian affairs, thereby reifying the weakening of Native sovereignty and identities instigated by the government's removal discourse.

Moreover, land during the allotment era existed as a space of commodification which, when produced upon, constituted a corridor to Native citizenship. The Jacksonian era doctrine of discovery was supplanted in the 1880s, changing instead to conceptions of territory that included productivity and citizenship for American Indians. The change indicated the conflation of citizenship and territory, which was crucial to discourse surrounding the Indian Removal Act. Concurrently, the prospect of Native labor on their allotments and, subsequently, the possibility that they could qualify as US citizens showed how Natives' moral inheritance influenced the policies and identity formations of the Dawes era.

The bottom line is that allotment opened up the question of whether or not American Indians could attain citizenship and exemplified the *identity duality* of US citizenship logic for American Indians wherein the government posited a rhetoric of assimilation alongside a policy of segregation. The Dawes Act answered this question by effectively blocking Native empowerment through full inclusion in the US civic sphere. However, the government's suggestions of assimilation through yeoman and republican commitments, even if anemic at best, empowered Native communities with a sense that they could attain some veneer of power. Decolonial rhetoric soon followed.

CHAPTER FIVE

Pan-Indianism and Decolonial Challenges to Allotment

THE RATIFICATION OF THE DAWES ACT AMPLIFIED AMERICAN INDIAN decolonial responses to the government's policies, but Native nations had certainly been employing their voices throughout the course of the pre-Dawes reservation system. The primary point of contention for American Indian communities at that time was the growth of governmental influence over protected reservations. In 1854, Quinney (Mohican) argued that the US government had promised autonomous reservations in exchange for Native removal: "A residence was given—territory offered—and covenants of friendship exchanged."[1] However, Quinney lamented the ways that the government had violated its pledges by remaining involved as a "Great Father" and limiting Native sovereignty. He asserted that governmental intervention into Native affairs "convey to my mind the recollection of the transfer of the miserable weakness and dependence of my race from one great power to another." Quinney surmised that the government's deceitful character and "vacillations of policy" on the reservations were "hurrying" American Indians into subjugation.[2]

Moreover, some Native communities railed against the government for allowing settlers to encroach onto reservations and for providing miners and railroads traversal rights through preserved Native territories. Red Cloud (Oglala Sioux), speaking at a lyceum in 1870, told his audience that his nation was already "driven onto a very little land" and that to allow "strange people" to violate reservation boundaries only made American Indians "even more poor and ignorant."[3] Red Cloud pleaded with the government to prevent settlers and industries from intruding further. "I don't want any more such men sent out there . . . [to] fill their own pockets." Instead, he called for preservation and autonomy, saying "We want you to help to keep us in the lands that belong to us."[4] His discourse, in this iteration, pointed to the manner in which American Indians reconstituted themselves as independent, even in the wake of their forced removal, while simultaneously portraying the US government as untrustworthy.

Still other American Indians maintained that the end of the treaty system in the 1870s limited their access to self-determination and therefore provided the US government with an unchecked privilege to decide Native affairs. In 1871, Satank (Kiowa) asserted that the government who "once came to trade" reservation land for peace had "come now to fight."[5] Because it eradicated the treaty system's tenets of Native consent, the US government was characterized, here, as unjust. Satank considered the absence of treaties debilitating to Natives and maintained that the government's respect for American Indian consent "like the wind . . . soon dies away and leaves the sullen calm of unheeded oppression."[6] According to Frederick Hoxie, such American Indian rebukes to the reservation system helped motivate the government to reform its Native policy, and to slow down the injurious consequences of the government's identity constructions.[7]

Assessing American Indian voice for its discursive power is crucial to understanding the allotment era. Reading these Native rhetorics for decolonial resistance highlights Elizabeth Rich's assertion that "although documents from the late nineteenth century provide access to the ways in which an emerging American identity depended on a particular history and a specific perception of American Indian people," they also exemplify how Native discourses boldly faced down "the colonial record and challenged it."[8] One of the ways that American Indian discourses confronted the government's policies and identity constructions was through the reconstitution of these identities—a decolonial mechanism of détournement. Overall, Native dissent obligated the US government to reconfigure the rationales for allotment and to reassess the Native-US relationship. And Native discursive challenges exposed the *identity duality* of US citizenship that promised independence and citizenship, yet segregated American Indians from the US civis. To this effect, American Indian rhetoric added to the larger discussion of the Dawes Act that occurred within the executive, legislative and judicial branches.

Governmental discourse surrounding the Dawes Act continued the colonizing tenor of the Native-US relationship stimulated by the Indian Removal Act. And just as they had done with the removal policy in the 1830s, American Indians likewise challenged the implementation of allotment during the late nineteenth and early twentieth centuries. One of the most widespread public and pop-cultural fables that distorts our understanding of American Indian ontologies is that the allotment policy caused the destruction of indigenous culture and the eradication of Native voice. This mythic conception of the "vanishing" Native is an erroneous generalization that typifies American Indian agency as diluted and invisible.[9] Contrary to this mythos, the following analysis demonstrates that American Indians neither disappeared nor lost their voices to oppose the US government's policies and identity constructions during the Dawes era.[10]

This is not to say that American Indians faced few difficulties in empowering themselves against the government's policies and identity constructs. Lucy Maddox contends that the "combination of social and legal controls" placed over Native communities encumbered their abilities to "speak and act for themselves." Indeed, the government's "manipulations of Indian people made increasingly necessary a public articulation of Indian perspectives and responses."[11] As the US government enacted the allotment policy, American Indians faced a seismic rhetorical situation. As they were designated more as wards, the US government commensurably deemed their rebuttals childlike and peripheral. Ironically, though, the government's insistence on supporting such a relationship opened up spaces for Native protest. This breach gave them a decolonial foothold and an audience by prompting a "breakdown or defiance of the monolithic system of order" supported by the government's Native policies.[12] This empowered American Indians to respond to a policy and relationship that many Natives considered oppressive.

Here, American Indian resistance to allotment worked through pan-Indianism and challenged the *identity duality* of US inclusion. Pan-Indianism functioned here as a shared identity of American Indians that transcended tribal boundaries in order to forge an empowered position within a colonial context.[13] Oftentimes, this unification was necessitated by oppressive rhetorical situations and material conditions that were instigated and forced upon them, making them marginalized. The irony of an oppressive force essentializing, in this case, some 500 Native nations under a single legal/political label of "Indian" is that it allowed a comingling of Native voices that might otherwise never have happened. This provided ground for some decolonial critique. At any rate, American Indians gave voice to the dualism at work in identity constructions, signifying both the intertwined colonial relationship between Native communities and the US government and the power of indigenous voice in exposing nationalist contradictions. Puncturing the mythos of republicanism and paternalism, American Indians revealed the colonizer's incongruities.

At the same time, American Indians came to view territory as a rationale and means to achieve either citizenship or sovereignty outside the scope of the US civis. The use of territoriality as a line of argument here was similar to the US government's suggestion that land existed as a corridor to civilization. Of course, the difference was that American Indians predicated their rationale of land as a pathway on a moral inheritance that was exhibited in arguments during the removal era. For the government, land was distinctly connected to notions of US citizenship and commitments to commodification of homelands—the latter of which was also visible during the removal era.

In due course, American Indian responses to the Dawes Act checked the expediency and influence of the allotment policy and its alleged citizenship promises—promises that were contested about and within the spaces of terrioriality. During the Dawes era, the government's discourses of allotment and (empty) citizenship offered a decolonial rupture for American Indians to forward their protests. In this vein, Hoxie asserts that "Indians began to talk back. . . . Natives made it clear that they rejected the self-serving nationalism" they heard from the federal government.[14].American Indian rhetoric also alluded to the détourned structures of discourse as their arguments drew from and affected the Dawes milieu.

Indeed, Native pan-Indianism resituated the homogenizing impact of governmental rhetoric. This unification, writes Francis Paul Prucha, aimed at enhancing the independent identities of American Indians.[15] But, the ends of such sovereignty were not always similar among Native groups. One side enacted pan-Indianism to encourage the government to extend to them citizenship akin to US residents. These Natives hoped that the Dawes Act's pledge of citizenship would empower them with equal status among other American communities—status derived, at least in part, from their moral inheritance to the land. The other side, a more nationalist gathering of American Indians, employed pan-Indianism in the service of separating from the US government. These Natives encouraged autonomy grounded in traditional identities and did not aspire to US citizenship. Their moral inheritance to the land justified independence for Native nations.

A number of contextual strands intersected during the late nineteenth century to transform the spaces through which American Indians communicated with both the US government and public. Moving beyond nation/tribe-specific discourse, as was the standard of Native rhetoric in the removal era, American Indians in the late nineteenth century addressed the government as pan-Indian groups and often through means such as petitions, memorials, biographies, literatures, and performances.[16] The advent of petitions and memorials was especially valuable for American Indians in terms of offering a decolonial response. According to Susan Zaeske, a petition is "a request for redress of grievances sent from a subordinate . . . to a superior."[17] Embedded within such a conciliatory genre of discourse is the resistive tactic of détournement, or working through the oppressor's language; after all, the petition has to "acknowledge[e] the superior status of the recipient."[18] Of course, public speeches were, indeed, still employed during the Dawes era, but these other forays into different rhetorical mediums diversified Native messages. The allotment policy and its entailments of indigenous assimilation created new opportunities for Native agency that were, during the removal era, limited or absent altogether.

Even as the assimilative goals and essentializing remnants of the Dawes Act weakened American Indian sovereignty, they also ironically empowered Native communities to communicate their dissention of the allotment policy. For instance, American Indians tactically channeled the US government's insistence on the English language, yeoman farming, American domesticity as republican children, and land as a pathway to citizenship into a rhetorical tactics of protest. Siobhan Senier notes that Natives were "forced to learn how to speak, read and write in English" during the Dawes Era, and that they "capitalized on this strategy."[19]

The government's propensity to essentialize American Indians by dealing with the "Indian problem" as monolithic and eliding individual tribal identities also, paradoxically, worked to Natives' advantages. As once-disparate American Indian nations mingled in closer proximities to each other due to allotment, some developed a bond that increased their collective power. The US government's insistence on dismantling tribal structures actually helped American Indian communities come together on reservations. The result of collapsing all Native nations under one wholesale allotment policy was a pan-Indianism that transformed the weakening of Native agency through the very construction that tore down such sovereignty.

Thus, integrationist Native communities seeking citizenship were able to challenge the Dawes Act's inconsistent *identity duality* by using the very contrivances that the allotment policy forced upon them. These American Indians complicated the government's diminutive constructions of indigenous identities and paternal characterizations of the US nation by emphasizing their new status as "possible citizens," republican participants and a people "worthy of assimilation."[20] This kind of inclusive authority could not be enacted during the removal era, as American Indians in the 1830s were pushed away to the far reaches of the US nation and were, likewise, considered "a race not admitted to be equal to the rest of the community."[21] Their continued occupancy of the land further enhanced their rights to citizenship, especially as the larger civis began to envelop the Native reservations.

Similarly, separatist Native groups challenged the Dawes Act and called into question the *identity duality* of US citizenship by alluding to the government's implied admission that American Indians could sustain themselves. These Native nations argued not from republican appeals to citizenship, but to the autonomy that the allotment policy carved out for American Indians to support their own land holding, economies and social life. This separatist argument was part of the removal era's legacy wherein Native nations sought a detached independence from the US government. Separatist American Indians therefore supported pan-Indian unification to organize their own governments outside the US nation.

While this was going on, the US public in the late nineteenth century became intrigued by American Indian cultures. This was so because Natives were looked upon as "safe" subjects for study and inquiry. Just as allotment and assimilation could only begin once the "Indian wars" (1850s–1886) had ended and Native communities were cordoned onto pronounced reservations, so too did public consumption of the "safe" American Indian flourish during the late nineteenth century.[22] As permanent wards of the US government, the public felt secure in approaching them as mythic. American Indian dangers, affirmed Theodore Roosevelt, had been eliminated with the end of the Indian wars, the advent of reservationism, and the policy of allotment. Native threats were, he wrote, "gone, gone with the lost Atlantis . . . gone to the isle of ghosts and of strange dead memories."[23] With an increase in public attention toward Native expressions, American Indians held the eyes and ears of both the US government and the citizenry. Therefore Native communities were able to exert their voices more resonantly than they could in the removal era, during which they were constituted as isolated and undeserving anomalies.

This discursive opening granted integrationist American Indians the license to command an audience that consumed their allotment protests and calls for republican citizenship. And this promise of citizenship legitimated their abilities to talk back. Overall, the public's attraction to Native issues permitted integrationist American Indians to articulate their desire for citizenship through popular means of communication. The US public's intrigue about the "safe Indian" led to positive changes in Native agency.

American Indians seeking separatism also benefited from the additional governmental and public attention. According to Senier, indigenous nationalists parleyed their desires for autonomy "into white terms" which was a "necessary rhetorical strategy for securing some kind of cross-cultural sympathy and respect for Indians."[24] This is not to say that separatist pan-Indianism was unequivocally successful in convincing the US government to abandon the Dawes Act and allow for detached Native communities. It was, however, instrumental in demonstrating Native agency. Kathryn Shanely writes that challenging the dominant public was a "prerequisite to redefining that space—actual and intellectual—as Native American."[25] Overall, nineteenth century popular channels of communication allowed American Indians—both integrationist and separatist—to do just that: reconstitute their places in the expanding nation and punctuate the *identity duality* of US nationalism.

Finally, the ascendance of progressivism as a movement changed Native rhetorical spaces. Lewis Gould demarcates the time period between 1890 and 1914 as the "Progressive Era," an epoch that ushered in an ideology of "social critique and reflexivity" on the part of the US government and public.[26] The Progressive Era was a backlash to the industrialization of the United States, and American Indian reform became a watchword of the era. Historians often trace American Indians as a "subject" of reform during this time to Helen Hunt Jackson's 1881 *A Century of Dishonor*, an exposé on the state of Native communities in the nineteenth century. Jackson argued in her book that "the history of the United States Government's repeated violations of faith with the Indians thus convicts us, as a nation . . . of having outraged the principles of justice . . . and of having laid ourselves open to the accusation of both cruelty and perfidy." Her critique of broken treaties and "robberies done by our Government" opened the door to "friends of Indians" groups around the nation.[27] These groups enriched the US government's ideology of republican fatherhood and efforts to assimilate Native communities through yeoman farming, American domestic life, Christianity, the English language, and capitalism.[28] Clearly, the progressive movement to "kill the Indian and save the man"—an oft-quoted slogan of Richard Henry Pratt, a progressive founder of the Carlisle School for Indians—reconfirmed, and fed into, the US government's construction of dependent American Indians and a colonially powerful US nation.[29]

Though the "friends of Indians" groups only fortified the government's identity constructions of Native communities, the progressives' concerns left an opening for critique. Integrationist American Indians, at least, capitalized on the additional wave of reform to combat the policies and interrelated identity formations of the Dawes Act. The advent of the Progressive Era, combined with the influx of new rhetorical venues for American Indian discourse and the public's interest in Native subjectivities, to draw attention to American Indian issues. As the US government, the public and reform organizations sought to resolve the "Indian problem," the necessity for American Indian voices "to communicate with white audiences, especially with those white elites with access to forms of political power, was pressing and acute."[30]

For American Indians seeking sovereignty outside the scope of US citizenship, the progressive movement's assimilationism did not help them, and actually seemed to work against a separatist pan-Indianism. For instance, Maureen Konkle argues that such reform efforts did not necessarily "make life easier for Native people" or solve the problem of lost sovereignty. However, Progressivism did provide "a mechanism for resistance to EuroAmerican authority."[31] The climate of social change allowed separatist Natives a breach of critique.

The Dawes Act commenced through a battery of agreements between the executive and Native nations. As the law was ratified, allotments were to be selected by Natives and decided in a land-tenant "contract" between the Interior Department and American Indians. However, this sense of self-selection was a legal mask added to the Dawes Act to make allotment appear contractual and consensual. American Indians, for instance, were forced into allotment regardless, for if "they failed to make a selection within four years . . . the Secretary of the Interior may direct . . . that purpose." Moreover executives seized Native territories if in their "opinion any reservation or any part thereof of such Indians is advantageous for agricultural and grazing purposes."[32] The executive body, as a republican father, held the power to enact this seizure without Native approval. But so-called agreements for allotment were futile and unnecessary. The government had its way in spite of Native opinions. Layering the promise of Native decision-making over the government's plenary implementation reveals how inconsistent and short-sighted the deterministic policy was in practice.

Still, the Dawes Act's clause requiring American Indians' consent to participate in the allotment policy, along with the act's pledge to bestow citizenship upon "Indians . . . who ha[ve] adopted the habits of civilized life," alluded to Native empowerment.[33] Whereas during the removal era American Indians were asked to relocate to the far stretches of the US nation or remain on their lands and suffer from dire extirpation, late nineteenth century American Indians were viewed as potentially fit for, though ultimately unworthy of, *full* citizenship. With this new opportunity American Indians found even more decolonial investitures into the government's Native policies to unmask the inconsistencies of *identity duality*.

American Indian protests of the Dawes Act arose mostly through petitions and memorials to Congress. Congress was chosen as an audience because it purportedly represented the "voice of the people" and worked outside the executive channels with which Natives tended to disagree.[34] American Indians' main choice of memorials and petitions, a bureaucratic genre of governmental discourse, demonstrated their integrationist approach to calling for change. American Indians refuted the allotment policy by maneuvering through appeals to the government's hyprocricies, demonstrating how Native communities had fulfilled the promise of civilization and, yet, were still considered dependent and segregated. In the process, pan-Indianism was employed to counteract the government's negative identity constructions of American Indians.

The Dawes Act initially excluded the five southeastern nations from the allotment policy. This was so because the nations had confirmed to the US government that they had assimilated as agricultural and republican wards since the 1830s. Arguments of the five southeastern nations showed the impact that their initial resistance had on complicating and slowing the Dawes Act's implementation. Thereafter, the government became far more concerned with assimilating other American Indians who had only recently, following the Indian wars, come under the US government's tutelage.

Conditions for the five southeastern nations changed in 1889, however, as white settlers, railroads, progressives and entrepreneurs urged the Interior Department to reduce their territories. Capitulating to pressures from expansionists, Congress passed the Curtis Act in 1898, which pledged citizenship for those of the five southeastern nations who offered proof of "civilizing." At the consummation of citizenship, however, "the laws of the various tribes or nations of Indians shall not be enforced" and "tribal structures" shall be eliminated.[35] Seemingly, the five southeastern nations would lose a great bit of their sovereignty through the Dawes Act, as would other Native communities.

In the main, though there were exceptions, the nations disagreed with the US government's assessment that they needed to assimilate further; they claimed to be assimilated already. For instance, a Choctaw memorial to Congress in 1894 appealed that, "We are doing well, we are progressing; we are pressing on to higher education; we are following in the way of progress." The memorialists concluded by asking, "Why not just let us alone?"[36] These nations already considered themselves civilized and integrated, and could prove their case with evidence of learning English, adopting Christianity, working the land, memorizing US citizenship exams, and instituting their own state-like courts and legislatures based on the American model. For this reason, they crafted their remonstrations against forced allotment with references to their own republicanism.

A primary way that the five southeastern nations protested allotment through republican appeals involved reiterating to the government that reservation treaties promised Native autonomy on the land they now occupied. Some in the larger Creek and Choctaw nations banded together and in 1889 reminded the government, "The United States gave and guaranteed us, forever, [our] country west. . . . We were told that [if we removed] no white man would molest us. . . . We was to live long as the grass grow and the sun stand and the water runs." Having discussed the government's promises, they contended that they would "not agree to allotment. If [the government] allots our lands this is breaking the treaties." In these quotations, Natives held the US government along with its republican ideals of honor and justice accountable for its pledge to allow a "country for a future residence forever," as well as citizenship.[37]

Similarly, an 1890 memorial to Congress sent by some of the Creek and Seminole nations openly called into question the US government's fulfillment of republicanism. Akin to the Creek and Choctaw nations' petition, these memorialists repeated to the government that "the right of unrestricted self-government has been guaranteed to our people" throughout the nineteenth century. "You have recognized and respected that guarantee for many years," they argued. The groups worried that allotment would "affect the autonomy of our governments."[38] Clearly, they scripted themselves as sovereign in this iteration. Moreover, the groups attempted to persuade Congress that they had already amalgamated and thus were not in need of forced assimilation and allotment through the Dawes and Curtis Acts. They contended, "our people have advanced in all arts of civilization . . . our people are making commendable and satisfactory progress, and [our] pride and ambition are stimulated to increased efforts for higher and greater achievements." The Creeks and Seminoles proclaimed that they had followed the government's mandates and should be "given citizenship" as US residents. Their republicanism, after all, had been "encouraged by the example of [US] liberal institutions."[39]

Some members of the five southeastern nations addressed republicanism through forced agriculture. A different Choctaw memorial worried that making "a few dollars [from farming] weigh[ed] more with US officials than the breach in the honor and common honesty of any Nation as a result of breaking treaties."[40] Involuntary allotment, in this instance, characterized the government as looking inward. Not only did the Choctaw memorialists think that US leaders desired allotment for monetary advantages to the economy and white settlers, but they also suspected an "impurity of their intentions." These petitioners concluded that allotment supporters had "a secret or mental reservation that Indian treaties are not part of the laws of the United States." As such, they perceived that the Dawes Act allowed the government to "put her judicial arms around us . . . with the ultimate view of securing our lands."[41] The Choctaw Nation, in this quotation, openly interrogated the government's role as republican father. Recall that allotment was justified in part with protection for American Indians against white acts of violence. According to the Choctaw Nation, the government's purpose with allotment was "to fix our lands in severalty so that we can never be robbed." Instead, the activists continued, "You had not kept . . . your solemn obligations," reiterating images from the removal era of the US government as robbers of the land.[42]

Furthermore, this Choctaw memorial exemplified the fashion in which the five southeastern nations reconstituted their republican identities. First, the Choctaw Nation conveyed a sense of pan-Indian strength. In "firmness" and "stubbornness," they asserted, "We have a combination that cannot be moved." Such fortitude inhered in "any Indian" whether "Choctaw or full blood or half breed."[43] For these reasons, it was "no idle word or boast when the Indian says that we are opposed to land in severalty or sectionizing." Maneuvering through the general figures of "Indian" and "we," this Choctaw memorial verified for the government that some in the five southeastern nations were united against any further endorsements of the Dawes Act. They continued that the government might be able to convince individuals "to divide their personal property" or "to work instead of hunt," but "no Indian" would consent to allotment. Rather, "whenever you touch our 'land in common' we will meet you with all the opposition in [our] power."[44] In this memorial, the Choctaw Nation détourned the government's homogenization of Native identities to empower American Indians in their resistance to allotment.

A Seminole Nation memorial in 1897 echoed the Choctaw memorialists' republican sentiments. Seminole leader John F. Brown argued therein, "the Indians are a patriotic, religious, industrious and self-supporting people, loyal and faithful to the United States." They claimed to "have given the United States no cause of complaint."[45] Therefore, the five southeastern nations questioned what it was about their republican identity and its fulfillment of governmental expectations that led US leaders to "deeply wound" them with "punitive legislation" when they "had done nothing to justify harsh or ungenerous treatment." This "wicked waste"—as a Cherokee memorial dubbed allotment in 1897—conflicted with the government's duty "to protect our people" from the "grave wrongs" of denying assimilated Native nations any semblance of sovereign US citizenship, as codified in the Dawes Act.[46] The Seminole Nation asked that a "fair opportunity for [citizenship] be given our people."[47]

Overall, the petitions and memorials of the five southeastern nations operated through republican appeals to question allotment's citizenship promises. Appealing to the government's republican sensibilities, these nations influenced the Dawes Act by delaying its implementation in their territories for eleven years, until the passage of the Curtis Act. Slowing down what is perceived by activists to be interrogations of colonial policies is a hallmark of decolonization.

The US government also expected assimilation of the western Native nations, who were most recently cordoned onto reservations.[48] The reservation system expanded in large part prior to the Dawes Act because the government sought a way to control these so-called hostile Natives. Reservationism was to, in the words of Indian Commissioner George Manypenny, "designate suitable tracts for reservations of land, in proper localities, for permanent homes for, and provide the means to colonize, them, thereon."[49] The reservation system magnified in importance and swelled in scope during the course of the Indian wars. Consequently, as the western nations were subdued by warfare they were removed to constricted areas under the paternal eye of the US government.

The US government considered the five southeastern nations relatively safe, but it viewed western nations as primary targets in need of allotment. With allotment, these communities would "conform to the white man's ways, peaceably if they will, forcibly if they must." Indian Commissioner Thomas Morgan certified that allotment was "the best the Indians can get. They can not scape it, and must either conform to it or be crushed by it."[50] This context, especially the Dawes Act's temporal proximity to the Indian wars and forced reservationism, might explain why western nations protested allotment by enacting a pan-Indianism that typically sought separatist sovereignty (though there were exceptions).[51] To them US citizenship would reify the government's paternal hierarchy. These Native nations' rebuttals included appeals through a trope of oppression that reconstructed the government as fraudulent and damaging. Overall, western American Indians based their separatism on the inconsistency of the allotment policy regarding Native sovereignty and their continued belief in a moral and autonomous inheritance to the land.

One component of Native decolonial tactics involved analogizing the government's disastrous reservationism to similar conditions of allotment. A Winnebago petition to Congress in 1889, for instance, linked the reservation system to the Dawes Act through a negative perception of the Native-US relationship. Instead of lauding the paternal character constituted by the federal government, the community asserted that the treatment of "the Winnebagos as it related to the dealings of the government . . . has been for the most part one of *oppression*, wrongs and fraud." Why then, the petitioners asked, should the Winnebago Nation assume the allotment policy would lead to different results? Though the reservation system sought to "promote civilization by giving [Winnebagos] a fixed habitation . . . the course of that has been a reverse of that intended, and has tended to make them more nomadic, illiterate and lazy—to degenerate instead of regenerate them."[52] Here, the Winnebago memorialists resisted allotment by saddling the government with an oppressive identity.

Partly scrutinizing the "justness of Congress" and couching resistance in reservationism's shortcomings, the Winnebago Nation authors next argued against allotment because the thought of further oppression propagated through citizenship would be disastrous. Allotment, they avowed, would "keep and maintain the Indians in a state of serfdom and hence, [the US government] would neglect" the Winnebago Nation. They continued that the "evils and wrongs snffered [sic] and endured" on the reservations would percolate through the Dawes Act, henceforth shunning the sovereignty "to which [Winnebago] conditions, needs, law and justice require."[53] This quotation demonstrates how the Winnebago Nation challenged the US government's "just" character by overlaying governmental identity with the failures of previous Native policies. In the end, the government was depicted as a degenerative leader. And the Winnebago memorialists demanded that "all Indians" have a right to retain their autonomous tribal governments on their own land outside the scope of US citizenship.[54]

Such separatism was also carried into western nations' characterizations of the US government as deceptive in securing allotment contracts. These contracts, writes David Wilkins, were supposed to place American Indians on an "equal plane" with allotment negotiators.[55] Governmental power, though, trumped any decision contrary to the Dawes Act. However, the Dawes Act's insinuation of a contract allowed the pan-Indian Kiowa, Comanche and Apache nations in 1903 to refute the government's persistence that they take up allotted lands. These moments of resistance oftentimes complicated the Dawes Act's implementation by forcing the government to resort to lying. To this governmental strategy, the Kiowa, Comanche and Apache nations exhorted the government: "[We] were induced by false interpretations and misrepresentations to sign what purported to be an agreement between [us] and the United States."[56] This agreement—what would become the "Jerome Agreement" that Lone Wolf (Kiowa) later challenged in his Supreme Court complaint—included forged American Indian signatures and redacted territorial terms that benefited both the government and white settlers.[57] Because of US leaders' fabrication of the Jerome Agreement, the Kiowa, Comanche and Apache nations deemed the government "oppressive" in "forcing against the Indians" a harmful act that diminished Native sovereignty. Then they rejected the Dawes Act and instead demanded an independent status akin to foreign nations, asserting that they desired territory "in common . . . of validity and force."[58]

The Rosebud Sioux Nation, writing along with and for the Hunkpapa Sioux and Minneconjou Sioux nations, enacted a similar pan-Indian separatism in an 1897 petition in response to allotment's oppressive residues. In 1889 the government promised these Sioux nations that they would never be displaced again following their removal to a reservation.[59] However, as the allotment policy gained steam, Dee Brown notes, the government demanded that Sioux communities "slice off . . . a fifty mile strip" of land, participate in yeoman farming, and assimilate to US customs and ways of living.[60] The Rosebud Sioux responded "our treaties provide that our lands shall not be taken from us without our consent . . . yet these *oppressive* provisions of law ignore our rights, and appropriate portions of our land to others . . . without our consent." They wanted an "independent . . . holding" of territory outside the "arm" of the United States.[61] The memorialists continued that the Bureau of Indian Affair's abrogation of these territorial rights "stood there as a disturbing cause to our people." In the process of their admonishment of the government's promotion of "disquietude and unrest," the Rosebud Sioux depicted the US government as "unconcerned" with Native "lands and rights." In fact, the government's character was argued to be "counter" to and "against" the "work of improving our condition upon the lands that have been set apart for our use."[62] Although they communicated a continued entitlement to the land, citizenship through allotment to these nations would spell out further oppressive control on the Interior Department's part.

Some pan-Indian western nations likewise demanded separate autonomy by calling into question the government's benevolence as oppressive. Congress and the executive rationalized allotment and its related aim to assimilate American Indians as commodity farmers based on the objectives of "uplifting Indians to the exalted egoism" of US citizenship.[63] To Native nations like the Leech Lake, the Dawes Act's purposes were scurrilous. And as the government supported the allotment policy so fervently, American Indians associated the federal government's republican fatherhood to the hollowness of *identity duality*. The Leech Lake Nation asserted in 1898,

"We firmly believe that the proposed [allotment] of our land is more in the interests of a certain Rail Road corporation than in the interests of our people."[64] According to Francis Paul Prucha, the Leech Lake Nation was onto something. He writes that lands throughout Minnesota, where Leech Lake communities were settled, became targeted as prime railroad real estate.[65] The Leech Lake Nation worried that consolidating their territories through the Dawes Act "would deteriorate" their tribal "value" and that the government would benefit most from "the standing pine timber" and "railway land" made available from the surplus land siphoned off through allotment. In this petition, the government was characterized as a monster in its pursuits of "devouring" the Leech Lake's territory. Citizenship, they averred, would not help "Indians' conditions" but rather would "harm us further." Only separate statuses as sovereign political bodies controlling their own land and borders would prevent such damage to Native culture, identity, and agency. They argued that "we singly and collectively offer our strongest protest" against integration.[66]

American Indian petitions and memorials to Congress summoned pan-Indian unity to refute the allotment policy by revealing the government's incongruence in extending further jurisdiction over Native lands despite contrary treaties. The five southeastern nations maneuvered through republican appeals to the federal government's foundational tenets to insist on citizenship. Meanwhile, western Native nations tended to dissent from the Dawes Act by pointing to the discrepancies inhering in the government's *identity duality*. These western nations moved directly to a separate autonomy by banding together outside the parameters of US citizenship.

The *identity duality* present in the US government's allotment policy did not escape American Indians who expressed their discontent with the Dawes Act publicly in print. Senier argues that American Indians' printed remonstrances garnered attention and popularity as white settlers came into closer contact.[67] During the late nineteenth century in particular alternatives to direct American Indian resistance through petitions and memorials attracted the masses and were influential in representing Native cultures and identities. American Indians took advantage of this new-found agency and public curiosity to express their disapproval of the Dawes Act. They also used the popularity of their viewpoints in print to reconstruct their own identities and those of the US government. This was accomplished through a reconstitution of their histories by addressing non-governmental audiences, freeing them from the constraints of formality and possible repercussions. Retelling the story, rupturing the master narrative, pulls from a decolonial tradition of resistance. Concerning this new opportunity for published protest, Louis Warren asserts that American Indians "shaped their performances to subvert, reinforce, or otherwise influence American ideas of Indianness."[68]

The primary way that American Indian publications articulated their dissent of the allotment policy, and took umbrage with the government's constitution of a dependent/paternal relationship, was through the employment of collective memories. Collective memory, according to Barbie Zelizer, refers to "recollections that are instantiated beyond the individual by and for the collective . . . it comprises recollections of the past that are determined by the group."[69] In this way, memory served a constitutive function for indigenous communities protesting the allotment policy. American Indian memories summoned past events of the Native-US relationship to shape Native "ethos and sense[s] of identity" as resistive.[70] Remembrances of past Native policies and conditions evoked a past to frame a present, thereby allowing American Indians to analogize and challenge the US government's questionable identity constructions during the allotment era with historically similar examples. American Indian memories in the Dawes era "appropriated the negative constructions of Native identity and exceptional formations of American identity" as entrees to communicate back to the US government."[71]

Memory as a site of decolonial rhetoric was familiar to nineteenth century American Indian communities. According to Randall Lake, Native discursive struggles have always been "infused with temporal concerns: thoroughly (and painfully) cognizant of the history of native/Euramerican relations on this continent."[72] American Indian rhetorics of the past, though, were not solely "consummatory" or reflective.[73] In addition to helping build community, identity and a shared vision, collective memories were simultaneously pragmatically utile. That is, Native collective memories appealed to the US government for change. I have written elsewhere that Native voices "held the power to construct Native and governmental identities"—a mode of rhetoric that functioned outside of the consummatory alone. Resistance-through-memory in American Indian anti-allotment discourses "exists as an instance in which the dominance of the US government was weakened by Native agency."[74]

American Indian biographical accounts were especially resonant during the late nineteenth century. The resurrection of Native citizenship questions, part and parcel to the Dawes Act, only heightened the public's desire to learn about these indigenous wards. Since biographies tied protests to personal narratives, they tended to work through amicable appeals, such as familialism, to secure US citizenship for American Indian communities. These familial appeals evidenced the hegemony of republican fatherhood while also alluding to Native resistance in détourning the government's domestic language.

One tactic that American Indians employed through biographical memories was the questioning of the government's republican fatherhood. The Dawes Act was related to the deleterious Indian Removal Act in these memories as a way to show how Native citizenship had yet to unfold. The promise was there, however, if Natives could be included as residents equal to other US citizens. For instance, Young Joseph (Nez Perce) emphasized in a *North American Review* article that the removal policy was falsely benevolent to "all of us Indians." The US government had certainly given protection to American Indians, but, said Young Joseph, "Our father did not say anything about white men wanting to settle on our lands [afterward]."[75] Young Joseph wrote that suddenly, regardless of removal treaty stipulations of Native autonomy, "a number of white people came into your children's country and built houses and lands" during the late nineteenth century. During removal the Nez Perce Nation found that "the white men were growing rich very fast, and were greedy to possess everything the Indian had."[76] Their consent to the promises of republicanism exhibited both the oppressive components of republican fatherhood and the emptiness that such familial promises contained.

With the coming of allotment Young Joseph and others worried that their graven memories of removal would come to life in the 1880s. "I have learned," he grieved, "that we are but few, while the white men are many. . . . We are contented to let things remain. They are not and would change the rivers and mountains if they did not suit them."[77] He suggested that US citizenship would set Natives on an "equal level" with these "white brothers." Appealing to a sense of familialism and fairness with the land, he asked "my father in Washington" to consider allowing the Dawes Act's promise to come to bear as "we all in your family" had assimilated as the executive requested. Young Joseph's father-child metaphors and familial tactic suggested that he considered American Indians part of the government's family.[78]

His resistance also showed how strong and unified Native communities were despite being threatened by another wave of land encroachers supported by the allotment policy. Recall that Section Five of the Dawes Act allowed "the United States the sole purpose of securing homes to actual settlers" by taking up the surplus land left by Native allotments.[79] This clause threatened the sanctity of American Indian lands initially protected by removal treaties. In the 1880s, the government abrogated its promises of protection with the implementation of the allotment policy. Native citizenship, and the parity it engendered, was thought to mollify this inequity among "red brothers" and "white brothers."[80]

Simon Pokagon (Pottawattamie) noticed the dubiousness of republican fatherhood and crafted similar familial metaphors in his call for an amelioration of the "Great Father's" wrongs. He noticed that US citizenship was the benefit traded by the government for Native lands and that this was the "proper" exchange between "child and father."[81] Without citizenship fulfillment, he said the government would appear as "strangers" demanding that

Natives "'Give us gold, give us gold.' 'Where find you gold? Where find you gold?'" The image of the government failing its promises as a republican father by denying its wards US citizenship showed how the Dawes Act was anything but benevolent. Also unmistakable in Pokagon's discourse were capitalist constructs that he maintained led the government to pursue allotment. In sum, the government's aim to usurp white violence and to assimilate Natives seemed a sham, especially as citizenship guarantees fell flat. But, wrote Pokagon, the inclusion of American Indians as "family members" and citizens of the US civis could alleviate this problem.[82]

However, Pokagon then shifted his discussion of Native-US relations from familialism to a rhetoric of home-wrecking on the part of the government. To accomplish this Pokagon employed natural metaphors—once popular in the government's own removal discourse—throughout his removal memories. Pokagon, though, refracted the US government's use of natural imagery in a more conspicuous way. He overtly pinned these metaphors back on the government as he détourned the memories. For instance, reflecting on the removal era he said of the government: "Locust-like they swarmed on all our coasts . . . then they robbed our homes of fathers, mothers, sons and daughters."[83] The period of the Indian Removal Act, it appeared to Pokagon, had shown American Indians just how pestilent the government had acted throughout its expansive errand and encroachment onto indigenous lands. His memory also suggested that, in spite of paternal and familial promises of benevolence, the government managed ironically to destroy the Native family unit. Here, his decolonizing of familial language revealed a resistive tactic of détourning the government's paternal rhetoric through notions of moral inheritance to the land. Pokagon was therefore suspicious of the US government's allotment policy with its purported benevolent aims. The United States was not being helpful in allotting Native land, said Pokagon, if US citizenship was not extended to "all Indians" (his totalizing of Natives pointed to a pan-Indian expression of indigenousness).[84]

Some biographical memories hearkened to how American Indians remained strong and united even in the direst conditions of the removal era. Because Native communities had survived removing from their original homelands, these memories intimated that American Indians as a pan-Indian family could also survive the late nineteenth century challenges of allotment. Such memories bolstered the strength of unified Native communities in their contemporary protests of the Dawes Act. For instance, Carlos Montezuma's (Pima) essay in the *Quarterly Journal* insisted that the removal policy and its subsequent reservationism had done nothing but "debar us as a race from acquiring that knowledge to appreciate our property."[85] Removal did "not make [Natives] free any more than you can . . . free those prisoners who are in the penitentiary." However, American Indians were able "to free themselves" by binding together as "brothers" and fighting back further white encroachments. He continued, "Our peoples' heritage is freedom. Freedom reigned in their whole make-up."[86] He insisted that Native resistance had slowed down the destructive impact of the removal and reservation policies. And working as a family across Native nations helped these efforts.

Similarly, in his autobiographical experiences with the Dawes Act, Montezuma perceived the allotment policy to continue a similar denigration of autonomy within Native territories. Though Natives had consented to the hegemonic space of republican fatherhood, they were still denied rights. He therefore configured the government as a greedy colonizing "father" by denying US "citizenship": "The Indian Department has drifted into commercialism at the expense of our poor benighted people. So, the father [goes] on and [says] 'let us not allot those Indians on that sweet flowing water because there are others who will profit by damming it up and selling it to white newcomers.'" In this quotation, Montezuma referred to the government's emblematic colonial tactic of allotting Natives to barren or undesirable lands. Though threatened by the Dawes Act, he exhorted American Indian nations as a whole (his use of "us," "we" and "all Indians" alluded to his pan-Indianism) to resist further allotment and assimilation. He wrote, "being caged up and not able to develop *our* facilities has made us a dependent race." The paternal government looked upon them "as hopeless to do anything for [themselves]," and therefore justified taking more Native lands.[87]

Montezuma, then, urged American Indians to take up their forebears' mantle to be independent "in the whirl" of allotment and to aspire to equal citizenship with "other Americans." He suggested that they unite and "get into [the land] . . . and use it . . . and live up to its requirements and take our chances" as sovereign "family" and "residents" of the United States, clearly conflating ties to the land with the rights of citizenship.[88] In the end, his rhetoric pointed to a decolonizing of the *identity duality* surrounding the allotment policy and its attendant negative depictions of Native character. That is, Montezuma called into question the uniformity of the government's support of both assimilation and segregation. However, he also "reconstructed" American Indian empowerment through unification and strength.[89] He left his Native family with a final thought to this end: "We must be independent!"[90] But, the memory also suggested that American Indians could exist as a part of the US family, as long as it could boast some semblance of "independence" outside the scope of infantilization.

These biographical memories held the potential to affect the larger debate over the condition of American Indians. In this vein, Konkle concludes that American Indian anti-allotment rhetoric influenced progressives and the US government: Natives redefined "public and institutional spaces by first establishing their ability, and their right, to inhabit these spaces alongside other Americans."[91] In so doing, they "changed the nation" and perceptions of American Indianness for themselves and the broader American public. Moreover, they demonstrated that they desired sovereignty as US citizens, but that the Dawes Act had faltered in this assurance of inclusion into the US family.

As American Indians in the West assimilated further throughout the late nineteenth century, they also embraced the value of disseminating their viewpoints through literature. Literature allowed American Indians to détourn the enemy's language by assembling resistance in a form that was accepted by the masses as art or entertainment. Literary channels provided for higher degrees of radicalism as individual authors' identities were not tied directly to such invective and separatism. Thus, working outside of familialism (which Native biographies utilized as a demonstrable tactic) literature was freer from governmental constraints to demand separation.

Given this freedom, American Indian rebuttals to allotment worked through literature to brand the government's side of the Native-US relationship ungodly and violent. The memories enacted therein reshaped the identities of Native communities and the US government within the context of the Dawes Act's dismal consequences for American Indian sovereignty. American Indians promoted a pan-Indian resistance in these literatures that demanded a separatist sovereignty.

Women penned a number of American Indian literary resistance to allotment. The proliferation of women's literary accounts was perhaps prompted by two primary factors. First, government-run boarding schools during the allotment era tended to teach Native men agricultural and mechanical skills while instructing Native women in domestic projects such as sewing, cooking, housekeeping, and child rearing. According to David H. DeJong, part of the "child rearing" project involved teaching American Indian children how to read and master the English language.[92] Therefore, women maintained closer ties to a literacy tradition. Second, Native women who published literature tended to be considered "safe" subjects.[93] Publishers often approached women, versus their male counterparts, to give their accounts of US-Indian affairs. This is so, writes Peter Nabokov, because Native men, especially those of western nations who were recently "conquered," were still linked to the "warrior" persona in American popular imaginaries.[94] Thus, Native women were looked upon as mildly palatable.

These conditions undoubtedly reflected the diminutive gendered dynamics of the late nineteenth and early twentieth centuries. However, literature demonstrated a transformed turn in Native resistance for women.

During the removal period Native women were rarely given the chance to speak against governmental policies. With literary accounts, though, Native women held a crucial role in engaging the American public. To this effect, women speaking against allotment employed literature as a way to resist the Dawes Act and the *identity duality* it inspired. They did this by crafting narrative memories surrounding spiritual and familial issues. These substantive topics certainly reflect an overlap of American Indian women's voices with what Bonnie J. Dow and Mari Boor Tonn call the *feminine style*, or "a synthesis of form and substance that works to promote an alternative political philosophy reflecting traditionally family values."[95] Part of the feminine style includes a reliance on examples and anecdotes regarding the personal sphere, which involves subjects such as spirituality and family. Whether deriving from a feminine style, memories of the familial Native-US relationship, or a conscious resistance using the government's paternal language against itself, many American Indian women emboldened indigenous voice, especially in support of separate sovereignty.

These literary memories characteristically reflected back to creation and Native-US contact myths to reconstruct the government as ungodly, while reshaping Native identities as affable. According to Frederick Hoxie, authors spotlighted optimistic Native characteristics as a way to persuade the US public that involuntary allotment was not needed.[96] Instead, they illustrated how American Indians could support themselves by sustaining economies, governments, and tribal traditions. These myths were used to evidence how allotment and assimilation violated both providential mandates and harmonious relationships between the US government and American Indian communities. As a case in point, Sarah Winnemucca (Paiute) illustrated in her 1883 denunciation of proposed allotment just how horrendously the US government had breached God's covenant of peace and Native friendship. She ironically pointed out:

> Of, for shame! . . . Yes, you, who call yourselves the great civilization; you who have knelt upon Plymouth Rock, covenanting with God to make this the land of the free and brave. Ah, then you rise from your bended knees and seizing the welcoming hands of those who are the owners of this land, which you are not, your carbines rise upon the bleak shore, and your so-called civilization sweeps inland . . . but, oh, my God! leaving its pathway marked by crimson lines of blood, and strewed by the bones of two races: the inheritor and the invader.[97]

This passage reveals how Winnemucca connected her present exigency of allotment to a memory of the US government's impingement of Native lands. She argued that allotment and US citizenship would only revitalize this oppression. In the process, she invoked removal era assumptions of Natives moral inheritance to the land that was inexcusably stolen from her ancestors. Her commentary, like most in this genre, claimed that the US government seemingly defied its precepts of republicanism as the "land of the free and brave" over time, demonstrating the means by which Natives spotlighted the *identity duality* inherent in US nationalism.[98]

Concurrently, Winnemucca turned on their heads the identities of American Indians and the US government. Native peoples were "welcoming" and "godly" and had, as "owners" of North American lands, offered the US nation the aids of subsistence and territory. Puncturing the mythos surrounding a national imaginary predicated on providence, the US government had rewarded such friendship with "violence" and "ingratitude." She said the so-called "equal status with whites" would not change this; rather, a "return" to separate nationhood as the only way to refurbish Native sovereignty. When Winnemucca wrote, "we beg of you to give us back our people" and "let us have our own homes" she spoke of such separatism.[99]

Dawes era memories of the federal government's depravity in its relations with American Indians potentially resonated with US audiences for a number of reasons. Since the US government based its expansion on providential permission and heavenly support of its errand, it assumed the presence of a god. Winnemucca détourned the "manifest" argument by authority to demonstrate how providence could likewise turn away from the United States in the face of the government's violence. This rhetoric retained vivacity, especially considering that US publics honored Judeo-Christian traditions and might have found difficulty rebutting Native claims before God. The US government rooted its republican fatherhood in these Christian principles; to violate God's guidelines was, then, to violate its own ideologies.[100]

American Indian literary memories also indicated a guardedness toward, and separation from, the violent government as a way to protest the allotment policy. This distrust rested on Native interpretations of their bellicose colonized relationship with the government. Zitkala Sa (Yankton Sioux), for instance, wrote in her 1900 "Impressions of an Indian Childhood" that prior to allotment "we were once happy." She referred, here, to her own Yankton Nation and its neighboring Sioux groups. Following the Dawes Act, though, she argued, "There is what the paleface has done! . . . [He] has stolen our lands and driven us hither . . . and has killed."[101] Sa contextualized her resistance to allotment in the forced reservation system and the historical images of the US government as a land thief. Having defrauded them of our land and hurt them and forced them to assimilate, she said, "[Now] the paleface is forcing us away [again]." Sa's caginess regarding allotment rested on this tale of a mother imparting to her daughter the importance of refusing allotments and the assimilation that resulted from the elision of Native traditions. Citizenship, she argued, would only "make strong" the government's continued "violent" control.[102]

In her classic novel *Wynema*, S. Alice Callahan (Muscogee/Creek) reverberated Sa's suspicion of the US government's benevolent intentions in the Dawes Act due to past violence and thievery of Native homeland. And she glossed her mistrust of the government's libelous identity with hints of a bold pan-Indianism. Her 1891 fictionalized account of a Creek woman's uncertainty over choosing assimilation predicated Callahan's doubts of the Dawes Act on the wisdom of other Native elders. Writing of an aged Cherokee neighbor's advice on dealing with the US government, Callahan's protagonist (Wynema) recounted, "They told me we had suffered long enough at the *hands* of the white man . . . they told me to fight the palefaces . . . but, they told me to *never*, NEVER listen to a tale of peace, even if told by a friend. Peace! Let those talk of peace who live in quiet homes. . . . peace is no watchword of the oppressed."[103] In this quotation Wynema refused to negotiate with allotment officials based on other Natives' rebukes of assimilation and its dire effects on American Indian well-being. Instead, she promoted independence in the form of a separate pan-Indian group that would exist apart from US citizenship and the violence that came with struggles to achieve it. According to Senier, Callahan hoped to persuade other American Indians through cultural identification to reject allotment.[104] Callahan said that Natives desired "a home like unto the one of [sic] your forefathers owned before the form of the white man came upon the scene and changed your quiet habitations into places of business and strife."[105] Natives were already, Callahan insinuated, self-sufficient and "solid"; increasing their reliance on a violent federal government by way of citizenship would only encourage Native "suffering" and victimization.[106]

The empowerment cherished in Callahan's narrative of diverse Native communities coming together to resist the Dawes Act demonstrated her persistence in decolonizing the government's essentializing American Indian identity constructions. Moreover, Callahan's pan-Indian sentiments reminded the US public and federal government that American Indians possessed unified identities in their fused reprobations of the allotment policy. According to Callahan, for all the benevolence the US government's allotment plans promised, there was levied upon American Indians, as a whole, only "oppression" and "violence"—precipitations of *identity duality*. Callahan also indicated the power dynamics of peace. That is, it remained far easier for those in a comfortable position (i.e., US leaders) to call for harmony. Peace was more difficult for American Indians to support because they were not, wrote Callahan, "surrounded by friends and loved-ones [and] the happiness and affection . . . of the American people."[107]

In addition, Native anti-allotment literature restructured American Indian identities through a memory of warfare. Warfare was not a safe subject in biographical accounts, as biographies sought citizenship through familialism; memories of violence would hinder such arguments. Reservationism and the need to assimilate by piecemeal through the Dawes Act was predicated on the (past) violent character supposedly inhering in Native people. To this stereotypic identity formation, Winnemucca appealed that American Indians were usually drawn into battle by the government. She wrote, "Now you must not suppose that my people are weak or uncourageous. They are not what you call 'slouches.' ... We helped the Bannacks and the Umatillas in war, because we are all kindred. They are our cousins. ... Now you say, Why did they make war? I will tell you: You white men are too greedy."[108] In this iteration, Winnemucca revised the history of Native-US warfare and did so by reconstituting American Indian identities as united while portraying the government as gluttonous. Akin to Callahan, she emphasized the empowerment of American Indians as they gathered in numbers as "Indians," revealing to her audiences how resistance to allotment was shared among previously separate nations. Simultaneously, her rhetoric alluded to the power of détourning the government's homogeneous construction of Native identity to the ends of fortifying rebuttals to the Dawes Act.

Throughout both forms of publications, the US government (especially the executive branch) was shown to be in violation of its own republican fatherhood promises by promoting allotment. Seemingly in both biographical and literary memories Natives decolonized and unmasked the government's colonizing rhetoric to help empower American Indian resistance to the Dawes Act. In the process, such discourse called-out the *identity duality* at work in the US government's citizenship constructs, evidencing the empowered co-contribution of American Indian voices to the Native-US relationship.

As with Native responses to the Indian Removal Act during the 1830s and 1840s, American Indian anti-allotment discourse also coalesced through oratory. Some of these speeches were externally directed to the executive as the principal republican father. Whereas Native communities in the removal era typically accessed the executive through Indian agents and translators, though, American Indians in the late nineteenth century seemed to take their messages directly to the Bureau of Indian Affairs and the Interior Department.[109] Another kind of oratory was issued to internal Native audiences and involved the building of core aims to raise the consciousness level of American Indians across indigenous communities.

Whether external or internal, American Indian anti-Dawes oratory organized a pan-Indianism among various, and oftentimes culturally separate, Native nations. Native orators used the government's monolithic condensation of American Indian identities as diminutive and dependent, hence reworking it to foster unity. According to Richard Morris and Phillip Wander, the degree to which the government "has displaced tribal identities in favor of the 'Indian' has at times been so severe that Native Americans become unrecognizable."[110] Their critique, ironically, limits the empowerment of Native alliances. American Indians during the allotment era actually channeled the government's homogenization into a way to build resistant blocs, thereby directing their rhetoric at "other Indians for the purpose of gathering the like-minded" and only tangentially addressing "the [governmental] establishment."[111] This consummatory function, though inward, still alluded to the power of Native voice.

Native pan-Indian oratory questioned how the Dawes Act dually limited Native identities and failed to grant American Indians sovereignty, punctuating the *identity duality* of US nationalism. Ostensibly, this oratory communicated Native worries about the Dawes Act's fortification of paternal connections between indigenous nations and the government. And it showed how American Indians conflated land and citizenship, just like the US government; but Natives did so through a moral inheritance to their territories, not by suggesting a commodification of these lands. Integrationist American Indians resisted the executive's paternalism as ruinous to American Indian autonomy through economic appeals. These integrationist speeches suggested that economic self-sufficiency through state-like citizenship statuses would remedy the despair of paternalism. Pan-Indian oratory was also part of the Ghost Dance Movement that sought unity to regain their lands by rebutting the allotment policy and, thereupon, to lead a renewed virtuous and peaceful life. Ghost Dance leaders challenged the Dawes Act by gathering Natives to craft a radical separatism that not only purported to detach Natives from US citizenship, but also to squelch American influences. Ghost Dance rhetoric did so by depicting the government as virulent within the contexts of allotment and assimilation.

During removal, American Indians typically did not address the executive directly. However, as both the Interior Department and the Bureau of Indian Affairs set up shop on the reservations in the 1880s Natives gained the access to speak directly to the executive. This modification in protest channels between the eras brings to mind two vital points, aside from the observation that Natives began mastering English. First, it spotlights the consolidation of governmental management of Native affairs within the executive branch. According to Prucha, the heightening of executive influence "formalized [the executive] as an institution—and its bureaucracy grew tremendously" regarding Native policies.[112] Second, Native abilities to address the executive directly speaks to the enlargement of discursive agency granted to American Indians in the latter stages of the nineteenth century. Part of this agency derived from governmental promises to bestow citizenship on American Indians.

As noted, the Dawes Act's citizenship guarantees provoked a breach in the executive's language, which allowed American Indians a foothold in their oratorical resistance. Hoxie argues, in this vein, that "Indian political leaders" used this rupture to define "a set of 'rights' they believed Native Americans should enjoy as citizens of their communities and residents of the United States."[113] Therefore, integrationist Native leaders typically decolonized the Dawes Act by pointing out how allotment's weakening of American Indian sovereignty through the government's dependent/paternal identity constructions clouded their prospects as US citizens.

Generally, integrationist American Indians who spoke to the executive argued that the Dawes Act's assurance of Native citizenship had, thus far, produced appalling economic results. They queried, then, how the government could expect American Indian cooperation with the allotment policy when land ownership still rested with the government through the Dawes Act. Washakie (Shoshone), for instance, asked in 1888: "Knowing all this [how allotment still diminished Native sovereignty], do you wonder, sir, that we have fits of desperation and think to be avenged?"[114] Washakie, however, did not stop with his rhetorical question about failed uplift through agricultural labor. He provided an answer that positioned his resistance to the Dawes Act at the interstices of both the allotment policy's alleged civilizing efforts for American Indians and the act's opening of homesteads for settlers. He alleged that "the white man's government promised that if we ... would be content with the little patch allotted us ... [the federal government] would see that no white man should cross our border ... *But it has not kept its word!*" Allotment's citizenship pledge still did not protect Native rights to territories or economic self-sustenance. Washakie thus made it clear why Native communities had fits of desperation: "I say again, *the government does not keep its word!*" Hence, he demanded that a US citizenship predicated on Native self-sufficiency through cultivation of the land and equal to state residents be extended to "all of us ... Indians."[115]

The inconsistencies of *identity duality* also resonated for other Native rhetors as they interrogated how labor had failed to stand as a true test of citizenship. This resistance exposed the government's allotment policy as devious in its "masking" of "economic gain" in the act's alleged efforts to "uplift" American Indians to citizenship.[116] For Thomas Sloan (Omaha), allotment was just another falsehood tendered by the federal government. Akin to reservationism, he asserted that allotment could not be trusted to support Native sovereignty, civilization, or independence. He addressed a gathering of executive officials in 1912 saying, "it became evident that the Indian could not rely upon the statements of the Indian Service officials, the laws made by Congress for their protection, nor the treaties made. . ." With the Dawes Act, he continued, "these lands are administered in a manner that is a shame and disgrace to any civilized nation . . . and we ought to ask for such reform as will guarantee to us the protections and laws promised" by the United States.[117] That Sloan felt compelled to ask for protection signified how the policy's pledge of citizenship for all Indians who could prove their civilization had not yet transpired. Sloan was willing to accept the commodification of Native citizenship: that US inclusion could only come about through "labor in the fields." But, when such labor produced little results in terms of proving Natives' assimilation, Sloan argued that allotment was a "complete" charade.[118]

In the process of his economic critique, Sloan decolonized governmental rhetoric by transposing the executive's self-deemed benevolent character and republican fatherhood with its production of negative Native identities. The executive representing a "civilized nation," he said, had become discomfiting and "wrong."[119] He asserted that the failure of the Interior Department and the Bureau of Indian Affairs to honor its guarantees of Native citizenship was rooted in a desire to make more room for white settlers, and thus to make more money. The executive, characterized by Sloan as scheming, enacted "the most extreme disregard for property rights and interests . . . and decency" in its implementation of the Dawes Act. Interestingly, Sloan's and others' speeches, which sometimes wound their way into Interior Department and Bureau of Indian Affairs reports, helped persuade the federal government to investigate the efficacy of assimilation on allotted lands.[120] Citizenship (or what he called "inclusion") was "desired," Sloan said, but allotment was not the means through which Natives were receiving the warranty of equal inclusion in the US family.

Another protestor, Dewitt Duncan (Cherokee), spoke to the government's inconsistency in taking American Indian lands—under the guise of granting citizenship—for economic gain. He asserted at a 1906 Interior Department meeting that "the Government of the United States knows that these allotments of the Indians are not sufficient" and that the system as a whole "absolutely destroys" Native progress and "labors."[121] Both Sloan's and Duncan's discourses it seems resonated with the executive. Sloan's exhortation to "investigate for the benefit of the Indian" the allotment system was accepted by the Interior Department, which promptly sent agents to the reservations.[122]

Vital in American Indians' anti-assimilation oratory were efforts to unify diverse American Indian nations into a pan-Indianism. The thought here was that with a decrease in population resulting from the Indian wars and low birth rates due to disease and malnutrition on the reservations, citizenship could only be gained by traversing tribal boundaries and challenging the allotment policy as a front. Not only was the "power in numbers" formula vital here, but also American Indian unification détourned the government's own homogenous discourse to, instead, embolden Native identities. According to Lucy Maddox, this kind of decolonial rhetorical tactic helped the government identify with American Indian protest because it was crafted through similar substantive and structural means.[123]

Native anti-allotment oratory reminded US leaders that American Indians were, indeed, working through the government's essentialist Native identity constructions in order to fight for US citizenship. Albert Yava (Hopi), for instance, told the executive that it could "individualize" and force "him to consider 'I' instead of 'we'" all it wanted, as Indian Commissioner John Oberly avowed in 1888.[124] Regardless, Yava said American Indians were banding together to fight back allotment's failure to provide sovereignty in exchange for economic and social assimilation. Prior to the reservation system, he said, "villages never had a tradition of working together. Each one considered itself to be an independent group . . . as separate village communities . . . separate political entities."[125] With the collapsing of Native lands and the genericizing of Native identities, though, "none of us [want] that our lands should be measured into separate lots, and given to individuals." Rather, Yava explained that American Indians hoped to preserve Native-centered identities and lands by "gathering" and developing "one continuous boundary ring enclosing all" Native lands.[126]

These pan-Indian groups sought a quasi-state that would exist under the purview of US citizenship. Mitchell Deroin (Otoe) echoed Yava's sentiments, claiming that he would rather be "naked and have our toes sticking out" than to lose independence by a failed citizenship promise. Without citizenship, Deroin feared remaining economically dependent and reduced, therefore "running after a home like calves running on a prairie."[127] If it took unification, even among former "enemy" nations, then he was willing to do that which was necessary to ensure that the Dawes Act "granted equal citizenship" and prevented Natives from being cordoned on "a piece of land about as big as a hog pen."[128]

These anti-allotment American Indians decolonized the Dawes Act's diminution of Native identities and spotlighted how the act failed in its pledges of Native citizenship by way of the *identity duality* construct. These Native speeches worked through economic appeals to resist the allotment policy as injurious to American Indian autonomy, while also stressing the unified and empowered Native identities associated with the pursuit of citizenship.

While integrationist American Indian anti-allotment oratory united to demand citizenship through economic appeals, the Ghost Dance Movement sought to transform that unity into stark separatism. Protestors of assimilation were not always "primarily interested in representing tribal practice for the non-Indian . . . who comprised much of their audience." Rather, some Native rhetoric was "most interested in restructuring the relations [among] Indians" as an internal rhetoric.[129] The Ghost Dance movement built a pan-Indianism that united American Indians by an investment in a joint "messiah" and through shared stakes to territory and cultural traditions. This kind of unity was important to contesting the allotment policy and urging for independent American Indian entities outside the scope of US citizenship. Unity was especially resonant as the worship of indigenous deities was viewed by nineteenth century US leaders to "retard the advancement of the Indians and what effect it has on their morals."[130] Thus, the Ghost Dance, with its emphasis on fusing Native nations through the "Great Spirit," functioned to resurrect American Indian spiritualities displaced by the Dawes Act's emphasis on assimilation.

Pan-Indianism represented a larger ideological construct for the Ghost Dance movement than for other unified Native groups. In essence, the movement united the past, present and the future—working through notions of ancestry and moral inheritance to indigenous territory in the process.[131] Other pan-Indian discourses tended to be rooted solely in the present and did not transcend the past through to the future. Temporality was the *sine qua non* tenet of the Ghost Dance.

At the same time, the Dawes Act's oppressive impact on Native identities and independence was channeled into an empowered venue for Native resistance. The Ghost Dance Movement resisted allotment based on a *radical separatism* that raised the allotment policy as a flag issue, or an "event . . . susceptible to the charges made against the establishment by the agitator's ideology."[132] Ghost Dance advocates mostly championed separate Indian nationalism over US citizenship.

The Ghost Dance instigated a return of American Indian lands and political sovereignty. Participants, literally, danced while building unification through pleas to both the "Great Spirit" and deceased Native forebears (called "fathers" by the movement). The movement also encouraged the expulsion of Dawes era influences, such as yeoman farming and the adoption of American customs—as well as white settlers—from Indian Country. The latter was a radical departure from the pro-citizenship discourse of Native oratory and even the pro-separatist rhetoric of western memorials and petitions and literary publications. Self-professed disciple Wovoka (Paiute) began the pan-Indian movement by summoning American Indian leaders to his Utah home in 1890 where participants committed themselves to spreading the communal dance among their respective nations.[133] At the council, he foretold "a promising new world, a world in which all the white people would soon disappear and the buffalo would return and all the dead Indian ancestors of long ago would rejoin the living in a new way of life."[134] His peers believed that dancing in the fashion that he taught would usher in this new world of Native empowerment. According to Wovoka, the more the participants danced, the sooner the Great Spirit and the Native "fathers" would descend to the earth, thus ousting the government's "impediments" to American Indian autonomy.[135] Such images not only linked pan-Indianism in the present but also the past and future as its memories collectivized the binds of Indian ancestry as one people.

Ghost Dance rhetoric, above all, united American Indians through providential identities, an indigenist version of the U.S government's self-entitled "manifest" ethos. Kicking Bear (Minneconjou Sioux), for instance, told a gathering of the Cheyenne and Sioux nations that we "are [God's] chosen people for all future time."[136] As the chosen people, American Indians were encouraged to perform the Ghost Dance as a way of doing away with governmental influences.[137] He identified with other American Indians by offering them a spiritual errand that decolonized the larger US story line about Puritanical errands into Native land. "[Wovoka] told us to return to our people," Kicking Bear narrated, "to tell them, and all the people of the red nations" to unite and only then "the ghosts of our fathers . . . meet us" and bring us sovereignty. Only through the communitarian undertaking of the Ghost Dance could American Indians, he said, overcome the deleterious and hierarchical effects of the Dawes Act. He exhorted them therefore to join together against the "wave" of governmental reforms "plaguing" Native reservations.[138] Instead of taking up allotments and individualizing on separated plots of land, Kicking Bear suggested re-adopting the communalism on their ancestral lands that remained such a vital component of Native identities prior to the ratification of the Dawes Act.

Ghost Dance rhetoric especially as espoused by Kicking Bear, its most notable disciple, furthermore constructed the US government as evil in having encroached onto American Indian reservations through the Dawes Act. As a result, Kicking Bear related that the "Great Spirit" would "cover the earth with new spoil to a depth of five times the height of a man, and under this new soil will be buried all the whites, and all the holes and rotten places will then be filled up."[139] Kicking Bear, here, inverted the allotment policy's denigration of Native identities with a reduction of white character to malevolent "ground dwelling." He sought both separation from the government and, in time, the eradication of US settlers in Indian Territory. So adamant was he in his arguments for Native unification and governmental remonstration that he anticipated the Ghost Dance would "fill in . . .the rot and dirt" of allotted territories, leaving in its wake "sweet-grass and running water and trees, and herds of buffalo and ponies." Engaging in the separatist pan-Indian movement also promised to refurbish American Indian autonomy over their morally inherited homelands and senses of identity.[140]

Finally, Ghost Dance discourse united American Indian nations against allotment by suggesting that Native communities owed a moral inheritance to the Great Spirit and their "fathers the ghosts."[141] This internal rhetorical tactic was successful at garnering unity for American Indian protestors during the removal era by tightening common bonds. To this end, Wovoka's message urged other American Indians that the Great Spirit had "neglected the Indians for many moons, but . . . will make them my people now if they obey me in this message. The earth is getting old and I will make it new for my chosen people, the Indians, who are to inhabit it and among them will be all those of their ancestors who have died."[142] Wovoka said, though the Great Spirit may have sided with the US government in the past, that a unified pan-Indianism would win over the Great Spirit. Wovoka then argued "we should unite now" lest "our ancestors, who died fighting" back the ebb of white encroachment "will have perished" in vain. Ostensibly, American Indians were bonded through their common ancestries. If they united, their ancestors would return to them "avenged and satisfied" and therefore "bring with them" a return of sovereignty and self-sustenance.[143]

Native resistance to allotment enacted a pan-Indianism that challenged the cementing of identities supported by the Dawes Act. The government's blending of several Native nations together under a blanketed identity construction allowed American Indians to find an invigorated common ground where they could be heard. Unification made it possible "for Indians to communicate with outsiders and each other in new ways" and to reconstitute governmental and Native identities.[144] And, in the end, American Indian remonstrations against allotment slowed the implementation of the Dawes Act, thereby spotlighting the strength of Native agency and helping to decolonize US cultural ideologies. American Indians also addressed the *identity duality* of US citizenship, demonstrating the interactive relationship between indigenous communities and the US government. The power of Native voice was exhibited by exposing the government's contradictions, thus perforating the ideologies of republicanism and paternalism. Ostensibly, American Indians unearthed the hypocrisy of assimilating Natives, yet segregating them from the core of the US civis. Natives, like their governmental counterparts, envisioned land as the pathway for either Native citizenship or autonomy. Such constructions reveal a fusion of historical commitments—the US government's conflation of land/citizenship with American Indians' assumptions of moral inheritance to land.

The government's Dawes era discourses of allotment and supposed citizenship promulgated a decolonial break through which American Indians forwarded their resistance. Nowhere was American Indian decolonial resistance made more electric in the Progressive Era than in the passage of the Indian Citizenship Act of 1924. The act was closely aligned with the integrationist pan-Indianism that demanded citizenship through the Dawes Act. Later, the Indian Reorganization Act of 1934 was passed, which stripped away the allotment policy altogether, allowing for quasi-separate tribal status. This latter change was more parallel to pan-Indian arguments for separatist autonomy. Within this ten-year period, the amalgam of pan-Indianism (integrationist and separatist) influenced the statures and identities of American Indian communities. American Indians became quasi-citizens: included in the US nation, but likewise permitted to reorganize as independent nationalist bodies. As Colin Calloway emphasizes about this change in the Native-US relationship, "in spite of past population losses and legal constraints, the [early] twentieth century was to be a time of endurance and survival, not decline and disappearance." The ways that American Indians went about "surviving the dark years" helped them to fashion decolonial possibilities for later resurgence.[145]

CONCLUSION

Identity Duality and the Legacies of Colonizing and Decolonizing Rhetoric

IN 1906, AFTER EIGHT YEARS OF WORKING HIS LAND THROUGH ALLOTMENT, activist Dewitt Clinton Duncan (Cherokee) concluded that the Dawes Act had not improved his condition as either a self-sufficient American Indian or a US citizen. Duncan took particular umbrage with how the Interior Department intruded on Native lands, thus violating any semblance of sovereignty or citizenship. Of this colonial travesty, he exhorted a congressional committee, "Suppose the federal government send a survey company into the midst of some of your central counties of Kansas or Colorado or Connecticut and run off all the surface of the earth into sections and quarter sections . . . rescinding and annulling all title."[1] Appealing to a sense of fairness and equity he then asked, "Would Colorado submit to it? Would Kansas brook such an outrage? No! . . . There is not an American citizen in any of these states [who] should submit to it, even if it cost him every drop of his heart's blood." Expressing his discontent with the government's license to encroach on Native lands as a dominant force, Duncan concluded that such oppressive actions would ultimately amount to "ruin, immeasurable ruin; devastation."[2]

Vitally, Duncan's resistance represented one of the ways that American Indian remonstrations to allotment spoke to the colonizing and decolonizing discourses extant in the Native-US relationship and to the *identity duality* that continued into the twentieth century. He worked through the policy's pledges of citizenship to construct American Indian and US citizen identities as equally included. To this end, Duncan's scenario analogized Native communities to "American citizen[s] in any of these states," drawing the two together as joint identities under the government's aegis. Emancipating opportunities like these allude to the empowerment that American Indians experienced in the twentieth century. According to Frederick Hoxie, political leaders such as Duncan demonstrated how Natives had a "say" in Native-US affairs along with their governmental counterparts. This talk "produced results" and eventually led to both American Indian citizenship and a retraction of the Dawes Act.[3]

Around the time of Duncan's decolonial rebuke of allotment, Ruth Muskrat Bronson (Cherokee) was experiencing the same lag in the so-called benefits of the Dawes Act. As with Duncan, she addressed the government's lapses in fulfilling its republican aims by parceling Native lands and assimilating American Indians. According to Peter Nabokov, Bronson's 1910 essay to the Interior Department likely sparked some thought about "revising the allotment policy," especially when combined with other decolonial protests from the era.[4] In her essay she told the story of Jim Runningwolf who "typical of much of the Indian population" lost his land to the US government.[5] The failure of American Indians to work the land did not factor into the government's rationales for the Dawes Act. Similarly, an extraction of Native territories was not part of the government's benevolent justification for allotment. But, Bronson argued that the Interior Department in particular prompted these difficulties. She wrote that, "the Indian agent [came] along" and said to Runningwolf, "You are not using your land ... why don't you let me lease it for you to that white farmer who was looking it over the other day?" Wheedling away at Runningwolf's land, the government cajoled him to "live in idleness on an annual rent" that was "barely sufficient to hold off starvation—never enough to lift the shadow of malnutrition."[6] Duncan's and Bronson's resistance contributed to the formation of US Native policy alongside the federal government's rhetoric of control as such voices were integrated into discussions of the Native-US relationship within the bounds of a colonized context.

In *Culture and Imperialism*, Edward Said sets the groundwork for this prototypal understanding of colonial language clashes. Therein he argues that "all cultures are involved in one another; none is simple and pure, all are hybrid, heterogeneous ... and unmonolithic."[7] Similarly, Homi Bhabha posits that there indeed exists among interfacing groups a melding together of discourses that ironically unsettles as it attempts to work out cultural identities. He writes that decolonizing rhetoric, in particular, becomes the moment in which a discourse's "univocal grip on meaning" is loosened so that "it finds itself open to the trace of the language of the other."[8] Thus, episodes like the debate over removal and allotment bring into amalgamation numerous identities; it also deforms the structures of the identities involved in the exchange.

The double-voiced timbre of commingling discourses in a colonial milieu challenges the prevailing idea that marginalized cultures suffer a complete erasure at the hands of dominant cultures. Moreover, such overlap defies the suggestion that dominant identities are only scantily shaped, or oppositely reconfigured, by historically oppressed cultures. Rhetorical blending appears less deterministic in understandings of cultural contact and transformation; there is more a spectrum than a dichotomy in play, a both/and that colonization stimulates as it meanders between inclusion and exclusion (identity duality). These transformations exist within the "network of relations" as the period of interaction lengthens.[9]

An analysis of this "network of relations" throughout the removal and allotment eras reveals a number of entailments about the colonial rhetorical relationship between the US government and American Indians. First, the relationship was cultivated by both governmental and Native discourses. Both commingled and helped construct the identities of the US government and American Indian communities. At the same time, the voices influenced the debates over Native-US policies. Sure, the US government worked through colonial ideologies damaging to Native communities. But, American Indians were able to defy and détourn the rhetorical structures employed by the government in their decolonial rebukes of such policies.

A second entailment involves the US government working through the ideology of *republican fatherhood*—a colonial mechanism—to assimilate Natives. The government endorsed and predicated Natives' civic preparedness on their cultivation of the soil. Seemingly inclusive, this construct actually limited the involvement of American Indians as childlike wards. As the analysis has shown, no matter how closely they followed the government's republican tenets, Native communities were considered "perpetually under aged" and incapable of participation within the US civis.[10]

The analysis also reveals, however, that American Indian communities did not accept this construct without compunction. Natives called into question republican fatherhood, demonstrating how the US government violated the tenets of its own paternalism. Moreover, American Indians turned-around the familial relationship imbricated by republican fatherhood to illustrate the amicable characteristics of Native nations. Such conciliation to republican fatherhood became fodder for American Indians to challenge how the US government's paternalism actually failed to uplift indigenous groups. The way that the government and American Indians worked through republican fatherhood exemplifies the clash of their discourses—it was interactive and flexible, rather than one-sided and deterministic. Such Native "back talk" to the policies and identity formations bolstered by the US government spotlighted how they enacted decolonially resistive rhetorical tactics. That is, American Indians reworked time and again such institutional language to resist policy and resituate Native and governmental identities.

Third, the government's tendency to concurrently assimilate American Indians to the US citizenry while also segregating them on secluded reservations points to the identity duality of US nationalism. The endeavor to amalgamate Native communities to republicanism spoke to a pledge of inclusion. In the end, though, the implementation of Native segregation contradicted the US government's assimilationist ideals, as American Indians were moved to the farthest stretches of the frontier (removal era) and to the corners of their reservations (allotment era). This, no doubt, speaks to colonization in that indigenous land, labor, symbols, and bodies were controlled and Native spaces and lifeways were threatened to the aggrandizement of the US government and the nation writ large.[11] American Indians gave voice to this identity duality by exposing the hypocrisies of assimilation and segregation. The US government's efforts to account for such hypocrisies by offering citizenship and sovereignty to Natives in the twentieth century points to the power of American Indian voices, as the latter contributed to the relationship. We will soon see how this citizenship and sovereignty played out for Native communities.

Fourth, throughout the removal and allotment eras, land functioned as a pivotal colonizing space of contestation over American Indian rights and identities. During the removal era, the US government viewed territory as a central criterion for citizenship; prospective citizens were to cultivate the land in order to qualify for citizenship. American Indians were considered by the government, therein, too uncivilized or childish to cultivate their territories. Hence, Native communities were dismissed from land ownership and citizenship and were instead granted only tenancy under the government's watchful eye. This process emerged through the colonial doctrine of discovery that assumed territory was something to be conquered and civilized. In the process, the doctrine linked expansion and progress to US identities.

Conversely, American Indians utilized the rhetoric of moral inheritance to decolonize the Indian Removal Act and to justify connections to their homelands. Standing in stark contrast to the government's imperial exceptionalism, Native moral inheritance was channeled into an insistence on land rights—a key construction of indigenous civic and spiritual identities. Moral inheritance allowed Natives some rights to territories west of the Mississippi, though it did not protect their homelands in the East. At the same time, moral inheritance provided them with a foray into a separate sovereignty, where they constituted themselves as rightful owners, while characterizing the US government as thievish. They flipped the master narrative on Native-US relations.

By the time of allotment, the US government moved from the doctrine of discovery to the commodification of land that required productive citizens. Such cultivation of land functioned as a pathway to citizenship. The government shifted its viewpoint to images of productivity and citizenship for American Indians if they worked their allotments successfully, thus contributing to the US economy. This shift underpinned the conflation of citizenship and territory resonant during the removal era. Native moral inheritance came to bear with the Dawes Act as American Indians were offered some tie to territories. American Indians then came to view territory as a rationale to pursue either US citizenship or sovereignty outside the aegis of citizenship. Overall, land for Native communities was framed as a constitutive force of indigenous identity.

Fifth, the government offered American Indians a middle-road identity between citizenship and separatist sovereignty. Here, the government's granting of a *controlled citizenship*—promised in the Dawes Act and continued with the Indian Citizenship Act of 1924—allowed Natives limited access to citizenship. The government's management of Native lands functioned as a colonial synecdoche of this controlled citizenship. American Indians were occasionally able to vote and file lawsuits in US courts. Still, such rights and privileges were often ignored or abridged. The allowance of a *controlled sovereignty* comprised the second half of the middle-road subjectivity of American Indians. Controlled sovereignty—promised in the Indian Removal Act and continued with the Indian New Deal of 1934—sought to allow Native communities to govern themselves. Such guarantees were problematized as the government reified its own paternal identity in conjunction with Native identities as dependent, replicating earlier colonizing ideologies. American Indians experienced a double status that existed between tribalism and Americanism.

Ostensibly, the government abbreviated these autonomous rights if a case could be made that such encroachment benefited the United States, Native communities, or both. American Indians' limited access to US citizenship and tribal sovereignty buttressed the US government's self-professed control over Native communities. Territory figured in here, too, as land became a space to manage American Indians; predicating the pathway to citizenship and land rights on productivity, the government buttressed its control over Native groups. In the process, Native identities were totalized as monolithic; individual Native nations were reduced to an essentialized identity of "Indian" that occluded the histories, cultures, and territories of particular indigenous communities. But, Natives were not vulnerable and powerless within this colonial rhetorical relationship.

In fact, the ways American Indians structured their responses to policies, along with the identity constructions that the government helped constitute, contributed to the relationship. One such tactic channeled the government's monolithic identity constructions of American Indians into an empowered unity. Here, Natives gathered strength in numbers to rebuke the US government's policies. This pan-Indianism, an absolute centerpiece of tearing down colonialism, drew together previously disparate Native nations, which helped demonstrate their mass opposition to diminutive Native constructions. While still holding onto their individual tribal identities, these groups viewed a relational connection in their statuses as governmental wards. Pan-Indian groups were able to motivate the Indian Citizenship Act and the Indian New Deal, perhaps exhibiting the symbolic power of Native agency.

As the following analysis demonstrates, these clashes of colonization and decolonization inundated the acts. This conclusion addresses the clash in the co-construction of US governmental and Native identities within the Indian Citizenship Act, the Indian New Deal, and the discourses surrounding them. The acts granted US citizenship to American Indians and repealed the Dawes Act, respectively. They featured American Indian and governmental arguments from the removal and allotment eras, and punctuated how these discourses made visible the power dimensions underscoring the Native-US relationship.

The acts indicate how American Indian agency influenced Native-US relations by exposing the mythos of identity duality and by calling into question the benevolent and republican identities of the US government. Such decolonial tactics were relicts of Native discourses during the removal and allotment periods.[12] They also worked through moral inheritance that, in the end, provided them some link to territorial occupation, but concurrently failed to protect their ownership rights to homelands. American Indian rhetoric from the removal and allotment eras affected Native-US relations in the early twentieth century by urging US citizenship for Natives and helping to repeal the Dawes Act. Hence, writes Hoxie, passage of the two acts is a testament "to the success of Native talking back" over the decades.[13]

Along with the acts' empowering effects came signs of governmental dominance. That is, the Indian Citizenship Act granted American Indians a controlled citizenship as part of the US nation, while the Indian New Deal concurrently offered Natives a controlled sovereignty as members of their own tribal cultures. Notice that *controlled* is the common denominator here. These proscribed statuses developed from the influences of removal and allotment era ideologies and manifested through the identity duality of US nationalism. American Indians could not fully enjoy citizenship in the US civis as segregation worked to thwart the enactment of citizenship rights. Yet, they also could not fully enjoy separatist sovereignty because assimilation functioned to stymie their autonomy. This multi-layered subjectivity, this liminal space, amounted to an anomalous bi-cultural *Native Duality*.

The Dawes Act produced a number of legacies involving the Native-US relationship, ranging from Native empowerment to the US government's enhanced control over indigenous nations. For instance, the introduction of US citizenship for American Indian veterans of World War I revealed the agency of American Indians in demanding equal citizenship rights. But, military service as a prerequisite to citizenship also pointed to the government's colonial control over American Indians as they first had to serve. The partial malfunctions of the Dawes Act, too, precipitated changes to the government's Native policy in the form of the Indian New Deal. However, the malfunctions of the allotment policy were simultaneously linked to Native identities as pitifully unsuccessful, which further buttressed the government's call for assimilation. Finally, the Merriam Report of 1928—a scathing governmental study that prompted a repeal of the Dawes Act—uncovered the power of Native agency in motivating the Indian New Deal. At the same time, though, the report constituted American Indians as needful of increased assimilation efforts. The Dawes Act spawned many colonizing downs and decolonizing ups for Native communities.

American Indians demonstrated their empowerment as *citizen-dependents* during the throes of World War I. To integrationist Natives, full citizenship could not be had through allotment, but perhaps it could be gained by participating in US war efforts. In 1917, American Indian men were given the opportunity to join the US military during World War I in exchange for US citizenship. (Separatists typically opposed sending American Indians to the war as, what they deemed, "hired wards.")[14] The US government codified citizenship for Native war veterans in 1919, noting that an American Indian, "if he so desires, shall, on proof of discharge and after proper identification before a court of competent jurisdiction . . . be granted full citizenship."[15] The government's commitment to including these Native veterans exhibited the power of nineteenth century American Indian discourses in support of US citizenship.

Native troops—unlike African Americans—were integrated with white troops during the Great War.[16] This was so, reported Indian Commissioner Cato Sells in 1917, because segregation involving Natives was "not in harmony with . . . plans for developing Indian citizenship." Instead, Natives fought in integrated units, "side by side with the white man, not as Indians, but as Americans."[17] Of this the *New York Times* declared in 1917 that "it may seem strange to see an Apache in a sailor's blue uniform . . . but it merely shows that he has become an American and has passed the tribal stage."[18] So robust was the notion of Native inclusion in this effort that, even in the midst of Jim Crow segregation, steps were taken to incorporate them as citizen-soldiers.

At the same time, such a militaristic connection to citizenship highlighted the notion that Native dependents had to fulfill the republican father's mandates for inclusion by fighting for the nation. In this way, military service replicated the US government's Dawes era colonizing control over American Indians as commodities. According to Rogers Smith, military participation prepared dependent persons for citizenship by "affirming a supreme loyalty"; such civic education would then help "shape who and what future American citizens would be."[19]

While citizenship brought American Indian veterans one step closer toward the assimilation side of the identity duality of US nationalism, it did not completely emancipate them. Inclusion for Native veterans equated to a controlled citizenship that classified them as veritable second-class citizens.

They received territorial privileges and voting rights on paper, but there existed a disconnect between theories and practices. With the allotment policy's dictates, the US government continued to interfere in Native affairs by holding onto allotments, per the trust clause in the Dawes Act. To this contradiction, veteran Joseph Claymore (Sioux) argued that "I thought as a citizen of the United States I could manage my own affairs . . . but I found that the Indian Bureau still held on to seven sections of land I had by inheritance."[20] Here, he conveyed a sense of the inconsistency of US citizenship.

Moreover, the Interior Department and Bureau of Indian Affairs, who sanctioned the granting of Native citizenship, could deny voting rights based on American Indians' "mere" occupancy of their allotments. Of this governmental control, Red Fox Skiuhushu (Blackfoot) wrote in a 1918 *Literary Digest* editorial that "If the red man can fight, why can't he vote? . . . The Indian's grand and noble" contribution to both the war effort and the American economy through allotment "ought to cause every [white person] to reciprocate . . . by urging a bill in Congress to have the Indian free, and bestow upon them full citizenship."[21] This iteration evidences how Native veterans were offered a citizenship that typically and ironically curbed their freedom.

The Dawes Act's difficulties in converting American Indians as capitalistic agrarians also evidenced Native empowerment. The apparent collapse of allotment was linked to the US government's identities as corrupt and overzealous. Or, as progressive Indian Commissioner John Collier put it, the government was "unjust" and greedy and had passed "the Allotment Law—the agony and ruin of the Indians."[22] Collier's characterization indicates how American Indians' renderings of governmental identities transcended internal Native discourse to affect the government's self-identities as well. The government's failure with the Dawes Act spawned from two crucial factors. First, as Native lands were allotted, the government sold the surpluses to migrating settlers who homesteaded in former American Indian territories, thus ensuring that the territory had "passed into white hands."[23] This was one of the justifications for the allotment policy—to guarantee that white settlers would get the lands they desired without committing violence. Second, a number of bureaucrats and private white interests convinced American Indians to sell their territories to make some semblance of money from the land. The trade-off was, of course, that American Indians had to give up rights to their allotments. Speaking to Commissioner Collier about the inveigling of white interests in Native allotments, Antonio Luhan (Taos Pueblo) lamented that "our white neighbors are all around the edge of us, they always *look*. . . . And, maybe they see gold. They might see coal. . . . They might begin to loan money . . . or buy acres. . . . And [Indians] will lose their land in a few years because they have borrowed on it. That is enough to finish the Indians."[24] Here, Luhan spoke of the fashion in which

Natives were cajoled and in some ways forced into selling their lands in order to survive in the wake of the Dawes Act. These malfunctions allowed Native protestors like Luhan an entrée to decolonize governmental identities as fraudulent.

Separatist American Indians wishing sovereignty outside US citizenship found empowerment through a loophole in the policy. The Dawes Act required Native communities to vote on allotments. Separatist Natives put off the decision, claiming a need for further tribal deliberation, thus hampering the allotment process. Clinton Rickard (Tuscarora) and some in his nation were able to postpone allotment, claiming that it left Natives in a "strange limbo" wherein they were neither autonomous nor integrated. They needed more time to discuss allotment among themselves as sovereigns. In a rebuke of the Dawes Act, he contended, "We had a great attachment to our style of government. . . . We wished to . . . preserve our ancient rights. There was no rush among my people to go out and vote in the white man's elections."[25] Many in the Tuscarora Nation did not vote; by the time allotment ended as a policy in 1934, the nation had managed to avoid signing an agreement with the Interior Department. Even if American Indians could attain US citizenship through the Dawes Act, separatists such as Rickard were adamant about controlling their own communities as sovereign nations.

Granted, Natives were also materially harmed as the Dawes Act faltered. Ostensibly, American Indians were constructed as pitiful dependents, which were residual identity constructions from both the removal and allotment eras. They were caught in a complex web of reliance. Unable to transition from communal living to individual farming, they "had not learned to preserve and exploit their individual property in the white man's world as assimilated citizens."[26] Worse still, nearly three-quarters of the lands allotted were taken from their possession. Collier asserted in his 1935 annual report that the reduction of "Indian land holdings from 138,000,000 acres to 47,000,000" signaled a loss of "dignity in private property." He claimed that the allotment policy "had rendered whole tribes totally landless" and "had thrown more than a hundred thousand Indians virtually into the bread-line."[27] American Indians found it difficult to assimilate through republican attachments to the land while their identities were characterized as undignified.

Because of its failures to assimilate and to bestow citizenship on Natives, the Dawes Act came under heavy scrutiny from American Indians and reformers. The reform efforts leading to the allotment policy's collapse represent one of the pinnacles of American Indian empowerment and influences on US policies. To Luther Standing Bear (Ponca), the "Indian Problem" of unsuccessful integration and citizenship was created by the Dawes Act, which "caused a reaction more destructive than the war. . . . Tyranny, stupidity and a lack of vision have brought about the situation."[28] Utah Senator William King agreed with the gist of Standing Bear's assessment. In a speech to Congress, King wrote that "No system . . . could be more cynically devised to strip [Natives] of their property under the shadowy form of law than the allotment system." He condemned the government's republican fatherhood. King surmised, "Unless fundamental changes are instituted at once, the Indians are a doomed race."[29] Here, Native constructions of US governmental identities were visible within the government's own discourse, perhaps illustrating a constitutive impact of Native voice.

As a result of these Native remonstrations, Interior Secretary Hubert Work requested in 1916 that the Brookings Institute undertake a study "in a thoroughly impartial and scientific spirit with the object of making the result of its work a constructive contribution in this difficult field of government administration."[30] The time had come to investigate the Dawes Act's shortcomings partly because of requests from American Indians. The executive branch's pursuit of such a study accentuated the decolonial power of Native agency in the early twentieth century. For as Commissioner Collier noted of his meetings with scores of Native nations in the late 1920s, "These [gatherings] were palpable proof that the Indians . . . was [sic] ready to receive a voice in the management of their own affairs, and that the period of arbitrary autocratic rule over the tribes by the Indian Service had come to an end."[31]

The 1928 study was called the Merriam Report, or *The Problem of Indian Administration*, and recommended that the Dawes Act be phased out. Its goals had not been met, mostly because the General Allotment Act had weakened the communal and family basis of Indian life, thus leading to deleterious adjustments to capitalism and integration into the US civis. The report asserted that the US government "had assumed that some magic in individual ownership of property would in itself prove an educational civilizing factor, but unfortunately this policy has for the most part operated in the opposite direction."[32] In the end, the report claimed that allotment caused unacceptable conditions in health, economics, and education.

The Merriam Report signified enlivening opportunities for American Indians that reflected Natives' past decolonizing protests. Natives were characterized positively as having "much to contribute to the dominant civilization" through their "potential" inclusion as US citizens. Also, the Merriam Report called into question the imposingly insensitive language of the Dawes Act. For instance, it contended that forced assimilation would continue to backfire:

> The view . . . would not recommend the disastrous attempt to force individual Indians or groups of Indians to be what they do not want to be, to break their pride in themselves or their Indian race, or to deprive

> them of their Indian culture. Such efforts may break down the good in the old without replacing it with compensating good from new.[33]

Here, American Indians would be given the choice to hold onto vestiges of their traditional cultures. The report suggested that "he who wants to remain an Indian and live according to his old culture should be aided in doing so."[34]

However, the Merriam Report also retained some oppressive Native identity characterizations as dependents that carried over from the removal and allotment eras. And the report crystallized a controlled sovereignty for American Indians as a result of such dependency. For instance, it demanded that Natives "be absorbed into the prevailing civilization or be fitted to live in that civilization" in order "to survive." It also recommended a new policy that would monolithically "merge all [Natives] into the general population"—even as so-called sovereigns.[35] This lack of certainty regarding American Indian sovereignty and/or US citizenship reinforced the identity duality of US nationalism. How could the Merriam Report suggest sovereignty as a framework based on "depriv[ing] them of . . . Indian culture," while also recommending a merging of "all Indians" into US culture as citizen-dependents, a merging that suppressed "Indian culture"? Even the Merriam Report, an outwardly emancipatory document for American Indians, seemed to conflate Native assimilation and sovereignty.

Changes in the US government's "Indian" policy came in the first third of the twentieth century, beginning with the passage of the Indian Citizenship Act of 1924, which granted American Indians limited inclusion in the US civis. The Interior Department also crafted the Indian New Deal of 1934, which dismantled the allotment policy and began introducing tribal governance back onto the reservations. These two efforts sought a break from the detrimental impact of the Dawes Act and illustrated the vitality of American Indian agency that developed from Native resistance to the US government in the nineteenth century.

The 1920s was a decade of unprecedented affluence and comfort for many American communities, though few American Indians shared in this as allotment had diminished their progress. But with the wave of change motivated by veteran citizenship, the Merriam Report, and especially Native resistance, the US government took a turn toward emancipation for American Indians through the Indian Citizenship Act of 1924.

American Indian discourses certainly influenced the ratification of the Indian Citizenship Act, regardless of the shortcomings as policy. That the Interior Department even entertained revising Native policy is proof that the US government listened to what Native communities had to say. The discursive remnants of Native decolonial discourse during the removal and allotment debates are visible in the passage of and the rhetoric surrounding this change in Native policy. The act provided that "all non-citizen Indians born within the territorial limits of the United States be, and they are hereby declared to be, citizens of the United States"—an action that "would not impair or otherwise affect the right of any Indian to tribal or other property."[36] Here, American Indians appeared to be assimilated enough to enter the US civis. Seemingly, their moral inheritance tactic bore-out as they were seen as potential property owners.

Integrationist American Indians had sought US citizenship throughout the four decades preceding the Indian Citizenship Act of 1924 (and even earlier, as well). As the previous chapter indicates, some Natives through memorials, petitions, biographies, and oratory insisted on equal inclusion by appealing to the government's republican sensibilities and by appropriating its familial and economic language. According to Rose Stremlau, these integrationist sentiments were not enacted as policy during the height of the Dawes era.[37] However, their rhetoric functioned to decolonize the inconsistencies of identity duality by tearing down the Dawes Act's shortcomings. Relicts of their call for inclusion are visible within the discourse of governmental officials. For instance, New York Representative Homer Snyder noted in 1920 that he was angered by past office holders for failing to take into account Native opinions on US citizenship. He said that "citizenship was the only way to salvation" and that (integrationist) Native "nations wanted to rid [themselves] of dependents" especially as how "more virile" Native-US relations were becoming by not considering what Natives said.[38] The existence of a citizenship act stands as a tribute to these earlier efforts of integrationist American Indians.

Such integrationist rhetoric, like that of activist Arthur Parker (Seneca), worked through earlier forms of Native protest and emerged as the citizenship bill was being discussed. Utilizing familial and republican lines of argument, Parker noted that "we have proven our worth as children" and "have done all we can" to assimilate to agricultural subsistence.[39] In this quotation, Parker détourned the government's paternal language as a way to empower Natives as worthy US citizens. The worth that Parker championed hinged on the fulfillment of assimilation as republican agriculturalists. Also, Parker's use of the pan-Indian "we" and the elision of his own arm of the Seneca Nation signify that Parker maneuvered through the government's homogenization of American Indians under the removal and allotments acts—a move that undergirds the legacies of Native decolonial discourse.

Not all American Indians supported US citizenship for indigenous groups, however, as Native communities seeking a separatist autonomy were not always satisfied. But these separatists found an opening in the

Indian Citizenship Act's claim that it "would not impair . . . the right of any Indian" to tribalism. This clause constituted American Indians as capable in their "rights." Moreover, the clause reflected the separatists' pro-tribal viewpoints, hence punctuating the agency of their nineteenth century voices.[40] Organizing under the act's homogenous "any Indian" moniker, these separatists refused to accede to US citizenship because they still held onto the hope that they could gain independence outside the scope of governmental influence. Of this, a Mohawk chief exhorted a Bureau of Indian Affairs agent: "The law of 1924 cannot . . . apply to Indians since we are independent nations."[41] Unmistakably, American Indian identity was constituted, here, as autonomous and unified, a reflection of pan-Indianism.

Some resisted integration based on memories of pre-removal Native-US relations. This rhetorical tactic was part of decolonial American Indian rebuttals to the removal and allotment acts. Some in the Oneida and Seneca nations, for example, claimed sovereignty apart from the purview of the Indian Citizenship Act by noting we "firmly adhere to the terms of the Treaty of Canandaigua between our nations . . . and the US as of November 11, 1794" and that "any acts thereafter . . . through officers, courts, or legislature contrary to the above are without sanction of law and repugnant to the nation of Oneida Indians."[42] They referenced a time when their identities were amicable in granting the US government the treaties it desired. In the least, writes Hoxie, such remonstrances to US citizenship likely fed into the Indian Citizenship Act's clause that protected tribal rights.[43]

Outwardly channeling the identity duality of republican appeals from the anti-citizenship discourse of allotment era Natives, other American Indian separatists questioned how the Indian Citizenship Act would work. Emma D. Johnson (Mohawk) asked a group of white reformers if the act did anything to clear up the confusion of Native citizenship: "I live upon a reservation now. I know nothing whatever about my rights as a citizen. . . . My people do not know when they are citizens or when they are not."[44] Her words spoke wisdom to the havoc that the identity duality of US citizenship wrecked on American Indians. Johnson's discourse simultaneously pointed to how the Dawes Act's republicanism had failed by continuing to deny Native rights. For instance, she said: "The Department sends word back 'You are citizens of the United States. We can't [help] you'" and then "The word sometimes comes back, 'Why you are wards of the government, we cannot grant you that.'" In the end, she queried what the republican "father" actually expected of the so-called "Indian citizens": "Where are we now?" She asked for "clarity" on her status as either a US citizen or a member of a sovereign Native nation.[45]

As demonstrated, both integrationist and separatist Native rhetoric was visible with the passage of the Indian Citizenship Act. American Indian nations were granted US citizenship and also a connection to their tribalism on paper. But, the legislation left much to be desired in terms of granting wholesale equal citizenship to American Indians.

The Indian Citizenship Act, though trumpeting Native inclusion, also merged the languages of assimilation and segregation, thus calling on the colonizing ideologies of paternalism, republican fatherhood, territoriality, and citizenship that diminished Native identities during the removal and allotment eras. Of this, Francis Paul Prucha affirms that because the act made Natives "both citizens of the United States and persons with tribal relations . . . the complete transition from tribal status to individualized citizenship . . . did not occur."[46] As a result, the government furthered the ambiguities of American Indian identities as Natives were both included within US communities and excluded, having tribal relations that cordoned them off away from the US nation's epicenters. The Indian Citizenship Act offered only a controlled citizenship—one represented by governmental possession of Native land.

Governmental discourse in support of the act exhibited the inconsistencies of identity duality and injurious colonizing ideologies. According to Pennsylvania Representative Clyde Kelly who spoke on the House floor during the debate, the act confirmed "our belief that all men are equally entitled to life, liberty and the pursuit of happiness and that such equality of opportunity will best promote American civilization." Despite this emancipatory sentiment, he then said that these opportunities would best serve the US nation, not American Indians: "[Indian citizenship] means the development of the individual through liberty . . . and work . . . so that he may promote the common good of the Nation."[47] Here, Kelly masked the promotion of US welfare in a benevolent protection of Native rights to citizenship. He also alluded to Native identities as commodified laborers on their allotments, colluded the notions of citizenship and territory that was a predictable result of expansion in the late nineteenth century.

Such governmental discourse also reified the paternal and territorial ideologies that undergirded Indian policies. That is, the government was identified as a republican father in charge of a dependent Native population. Kelly continued, for instance, that "the Indian Bureau insists that it is better fitted to guard the life, liberty and pursuit of happiness of the Indian than he himself . . . it compels him [Indians] to bow to its bureaucratic will by demanding that our American civilization will be advanced by such sacrifice" of American Indians. Here, the government paternally controlled the granting of citizenship. Natives, whose identities were fashioned here as ward-like and subservient, would remain open to the influences of the republican father. American Indians were asked to "sacrifice" their independence in the service of the nation—reminiscent of ties between citizenship/inclusion and contributions to the greater good visible in both the removal and allotment eras. Such incongruity divulged the identity duality of citizenship, consequently co-constructing governmental and indigenous identities as paternal and ward-like in a way that echoed the discourse of the nineteenth century.

The government's ideology of territoriality also entered into this identity duality. Citizenship should have granted American Indians full ownership—not occupancy—of their lands. Conversely, the act's denial of Native land rights clarified the unequal status of their positionalities within the US nation, even though their inclusion was codified with the Act's passage. Rogers Smith argues that "the retreat from full and equal citizenship for Native Americans was virtually complete" with the passage of the Indian Citizenship Act.[48] Kelly's supporting speech on behalf of the act argued that American Indians would remain "wards of the courts just as are other incompetents . . . permitted to dispose of their property only upon approval from the executive [the Interior Department] with proper protection for dependents."[49] Following from the trust clause of the Dawes Act, Native citizenship did not include a mandate for the ownership of land. The government's doctrine of discovery and demands for Native toil precluded fulsome citizenship. Instead, the paternal executive controlled land use and provided the proper protection of American Indians as citizen-dependents of the government. The constitution of the government as an administrative father did not stray far from other constructions surrounding the Indian Removal and Dawes acts.

The Indian Citizenship Act forced Natives into a controlled citizenship that placed them in the discomfited position of remaining a part of the US nation as dependent wards and, yet, held them to a tribal identity that was severely weakened by the limits of the Dawes and Indian Citizenship acts. The Indian New Deal of 1934 would only slightly ameliorate this limbo-like identity duality.

As Native appeals for change in Indian policy intensified, the government considered ways to promote assimilation that were less vigorous than allotment. American Indians' economic and political conditions worsened during the Great Depression as a scarcity of funds was available. Of course, the government's attention was focused on the nation's overall economy. In the midst of this dire situation, President Franklin D. Roosevelt received urgent requests from reformers worried about the tragic condition of American Indians under allotment. Perhaps the president took the requests to heart; for, as Roosevelt crafted his New Deal he included a provision to uplift American Indian communities from the doldrums of the Dawes Act.

Roosevelt appointed Collier, an advocate for indigenous rights, as his Commissioner for Indian Affairs in 1933 to help salve the wounds of Native affairs. Heading up the Bureau of Indian Affairs, Collier started work on the Indian New Deal of 1934 to end allotment and to fulfill the following three goals for American Indian communities: "Economic reorganization of the Indians, principally on the land. Organization of the Indian tribes for managing their own affairs. [And] civil and cultural freedom and opportunity for the Indians."[50] Summarily, he hoped that Natives would play a more active role in organizing their affairs by running their own tribal governments.

The Indian New Deal was an amalgam of empowerment and oppression for American Indians. On the one hand, Natives (especially separatists) were being given what they had demanded for so many years—sovereignty. And combined with the Indian Citizenship Act, which satisfied integrationist Natives, the new policy signaled a sea change for American Indian emancipation by satisfying both demands at once. Here, Natives' use of moral inheritant links to homelands (in the service of achieving citizenship or sovereignty) garnered success.

However, the Indian New Deal also proved that juggling both US citizenship and Native sovereignty could only perpetuate more the identity duality of US nationalism. As Colin Calloway contends, the act was "another paternalistic promise to bring a 'new era' in Indian affairs . . . mandating one policy for all Indians, and making little allowance for the tremendous diversity of Indian America."[51] Such an inconsistency left American Indians with only a controlled sovereignty that was empowered and simultaneously suppressed, especially as full independence could not be achieved. Controlled sovereignty also reified the identity constructions of previous decades, including the monolithic characterizations tendered by the US government.

Native communities affected the ratification of the Indian New Deal by calling into question the Dawes Act. And one of the most reverberating signs of indigenous agency was the way in which the Bureau of Indian Affairs actually consulted with Native leaders before making decisions on Native-US policy. For instance, in 1934 as Collier was studying the Indian New Deal, he spoke with scores of Native nations. They desired "to be understood" and, hence, Collier suggested to Roosevelt, "We may be helped through knowing them and even through trying to help them in their desperately unequal struggle for continued existence."[52] Overall, Collier and his representatives met with some 200 Native nations.

Due to the self-governance promised in the Indian New Deal, American Indians seeking a separate sovereignty tended to agree with Collier's plan to reinstate tribal governments. And as with Native voices in the midst of the citizenship act discussion, they successfully urged the Bureau of Indian Affairs to listen. Sociologist Donald Young suggested to Collier that the Bureau could learn something from the separatist voice: "No culture is so perfect that it will not bear improvement by borrowing from almost any other culture."[53] Collier then reported to Roosevelt that "we should examine with a wondering and tender concern, and with some awe, these Indian communities" and what they "desire from" the US government.[54] Collier's words seem to highlight the importance of previous American Indian remonstrations to the US government's Indian policies, particularly those of separatist American Indians.

Separatists had always urged for a repeal of the Dawes Act, and Collier came into contact with these discourses.[55] One such anti-allotment viewpoint was held by Luther Standing Bear (Sioux) who told Collier that forced assimilation through the Dawes Act had produced disastrous consequences for Native nations. Speaking "for all" American Indians—a pan-Indian tactic—he explained, "True, the white man brought great change. But the varied fruits of his civilization, though highly colored and inviting, were sickening and deadening. And, if it be the part of civilization to maim, rob, and thwart, then what is the process?"[56] Constructing the US government as thievish (a relict of earlier Native protest), Standing Bear urged for a return to self-sovereignty for Native nations and heralded Collier's idea for reorganization as "what we want."[57]

Other separatists opined that the Indian New Deal would improve economic and cultural conditions for American Indians. In the process, they took a page from their Native forebears and empowered their identities as self-sustaining. Their unified stature was buttressed as individual rhetors referred to a general "us," "we" or "Indians"—an outward sign of pan-Indianism. The government's monolithic image of Natives was appropriated as way to assert the potency of American Indian unification. Ralph Fredenberg (Menominee) told the Senate Committee on Indian Affairs in 1934: "If we were to get the benefit of the [Indian New Deal] that provides that the Indians might set up their own form of organization, might form their own self-government, that would secure for us in the future the thing that we now enjoy . . . [we would] be in responsible positions."[58] In this instantiation, the Indian New Deal was described as uplifting Native communities. Fredenberg's call for self-sustenance was fortified by the Indian New Deal, which allowed American Indians "to organize for their common welfare" and granted "certain rights of home rule to Indians."[59] Here, Native identity was positioned as amenable to autonomy.

The nineteenth century argument that American Indians needed protection from the Dawes Act also appeared in Native discourse in support of the Indian New Deal. Antonio Luhan (Taos Pueblo), for example, said that allotment "nearly destroy[ed] us; call[ed] our ways bad or immoral or something, and put in the paper that they [US government] are going to stop us."[60] And, reflecting such Native sentiment, Collier employed similar reasoning in his justification of the Indian New Deal: "The allotment system with its train of evil consequences should be definitely abandoned. . . . It is a complete failure."[61]

Subsequently, the Indian New Deal predicated the end of allotment on the need to "conserve and develop" American Indians and their "rights and powers."[62] In the twentieth century, continued Luhan, Natives "look[ed] far ahead and the [Indian New Deal] is like putting a wall around us to protect us—and this [bill] is this wall. And no white man or grafter can come inside and take away our land." Co-opting the paternal and republican fatherhood ideologies of the US government, Luhan assured Collier that the Indian New Deal "would be" desired by "all of us."[63] Fredenberg similarly enacted this sentiment of pan-Indianism as he assented to the new policy: "This is the thing we want. This is what we would like to accomplish . . . the self-government title, I understand, will give us the authority to organize and submit a charter."[64] American Indian identities were shown here to be emboldened with the authority to manage their own affairs. At the same time, they were not fully independent as the US government re-enacted dependence as a part of the Indian New Deal. In both of these iterations, though, the separatist Native voice demanded a break from the forced assimilative entailments of the Dawes Act. The passage of the Indian New Deal in part reflected these Native demands.

Perhaps the most intriguing stipulation of the Indian New Deal came in the form of restoring tribal order and self-sufficiency to American Indian nations. With the Dawes Act, Native cultures were disdained in favor of all-out assimilation. With the Indian New Deal the government tried to reverse this and "rejuvenate tribal governments, preserve native languages, and revive tribal cultures."[65] Such efforts would be accomplished by allowing American Indians the right to adopt "an appropriate constitution and by-laws, which shall be authorized by a majority of the adult members of the tribe."[66] Seemingly, separatist Natives would achieve the self-governance they had demanded through their memorials, petitions, publications and many speeches of the nineteenth century.

Separatists détourned this rupture that the Indian New Deal offered in terms of organizing self-governments through constitutional documents. Here, Natives acquiesced in the form of a constitutional document to motivate sovereignty. According to activist Ben Reifel (Brule Sioux), Collier's policy appeared acceptable because it gave Natives political agency: "It was always up to the people to amend those constitutions and make them useful."[67] Republicanism was even channeled as separatists attempted to illustrate their self-sufficiency to produce on their reservations. Fredenberg urged Collier to move forward with the policy, noting that a number of Native nations "live very much as any other community does. We have our own schools. We operate everything on our reservation out of our own funds . . . We have our own milling industry . . . We have farms, dairy herds and modern machinery."[68] Fredenberg's arguments came very close to the appeals of the five southeastern nations in the nineteenth century who expressed similar assimilation. He also showed how territory as a vital component of Native identity resonated in the early twentieth century.

The passage of the Indian New Deal pointed to how, indeed, American Indians had proven themselves as self-reliant. Native leader Alfred Dubray (Rosebud Sioux) reminded Collier of the same semblance of American Indian republicanism: "[W]e are really quite politically minded."[69] Dubray, here, spoke of "Indians" in general, revealing that the residue of pan-Indianism still existed in the twentieth century. Of these reshaped Native identities of unity and stability, Collier justified the Indian New Deal by noting "they have real power and authority over their own affairs."[70] Thus, ripples of nineteenth century separatist American Indians were present in this governmental discourse.

The Native integrationist voice also influenced the Indian New Deal by prompting an "opt-out" clause. That is, if an American Indian nation did not want to participate in the Indian New Deal, they could still retain their individual allotments and remain US citizens, per the Indian Citizenship Act of 1924. According to Brian Dippie, "the opt-out clause . . . [was] the first time in the history of federal Indian affairs that Indians themselves would have the unusual privilege of accepting or rejecting a government policy initiative by referendum."[71] This clause came from Collier's many meetings with Native nations during 1934. As a result, Section 18 of the Indian New Deal mandated that "This Act shall not apply to any reservation wherein a majority of the adult Indians . . . shall vote against the application."[72] Such a choice was driven by American Indian opinions on the new policy and was simultaneously emancipating for integrationists who wanted to exercise their US citizenship on their allotments.

The integration position additionally called into question the identity duality of the Indian New Deal. Of the separation side of the duality, pro-citizenship Natives like Vera Connolly (unknown)[73] noted that the act violated the republican ideals of inclusion in the US civis: "It perpetuates segregation under the guise of self-government . . . and shifts the incentive which the authors of the Allotment Act had in mind for individual ownership of property leading toward citizenship. The policy is a reversal of the past." Connolly decolonized the alleged self-sovereignty promised in Collier's plan and called into question the limits of American Indian representation due to an empowered executive as "the Great Father."[74]

At the same time, some integrationists challenged the new legislation by hearkening to memories of past policies. Rupert Costo (Cahuilla) was suspicious because sovereignty in varying forms had been promised in the removal era. He averred that "in history . . . this has not worked."[75] Linking the negative impact of Jacksonian autonomy for American Indians to the Indian New Deal he continued, "the Indian is now being led to believe" in the same way "that they, for the first time in history, would have self-government. But . . . any plans the Indians might have for such self-government would have to be first submitted to the interior secretary or the commissioner of Indian affairs for supervision and approval." Costo, speaking here to a Collier representative, cynically interrogated the benevolent aims in recommending passage of the Indian New Deal: "I suppose you would call all this maneuvering self-rule. I call it fraud."[76] Ramon Roubideaux (Sioux) echoed Costo's sentiments that republican fatherhood was a façade. Here, he worked through paternal language to show the negative impact of a familial relationship: "It's not self-government, because self-government by permission is no self-government at all . . . it's just like the rich kid with the rich father. Everything was planned for him, he never develops this mind of his."[77] To the above viewpoints, Collier argued that Natives should "manage their own affairs effectively" free from "white interference."[78] Whether integrationists textured the Indian New Deal is difficult to say. However, after meeting with such groups, Collier addressed these critiques and identity constructions in his rhetoric.

For all the emancipatory promise of the Indian New Deal, the act and its attendant governmental discourse also reflected nineteenth century colonizing ideologies and identities. The government had dismantled allotment by transferring lands from individual American Indians back to communal Native nations. But, the Interior Department colonially possessed the ultimate role in administrating this process—a re-treading of the doctrine of discovery from the removal era. The US government's focus in the policy, first and foremost, on land occupancy alluded to the importance of territory for both US national and Native communities. Simultaneously, since land was linked to power, the paternal sentiments that were resonant in the government's allotment discourse also wound their way into the Indian New Deal. Section Three noted that "the Secretary of the Interior, if he shall find it to be in the public interest, is hereby authorized to restore to tribal ownership the . . . lands of any Indian reservation heretofore opened, or authorized to be opened, to sale, or any other form by Presidential proclamation." Here, the government was unquestionably charged with restoring and protecting tribal culture.[79]

American Indian representation in the government was minimized as a result of direct and exclusive dealings with the executive branch. Without representatives of their own within the executive, American Indians were left to the whims of the Interior Department and Bureau of Indian Affairs. Robert Burnette and John Koster argue that a lack of Native management over the transferal process disparaged a proper "system of checks and balances—no procedure through which inequities could be righted." They suggest that there was no way to "gauge" whether all of indigenous lands "were being returned."[80] Moreover, the Bureau of Indian Affairs held the deeds to the transferred lands "in trust for the Indian tribe . . . for which the land is acquired."[81] There was little difference between this provision in Section Five and the Dawes Act's paternal trust clause. This controlled sovereignty replicated identity duality and the ways that assimilation and cooperation could also involve exclusionary measures. The "trust" relationship also reified governmental and Native identities as dominant and subservient, respectively.

The colonizing ideology of territoriality and the inconsistencies of identity duality also carried into the management of reservation resources. Though Native nations were supposedly "to return their individual land holdings to the protection of tribal status" and "control them" outside of governmental influence, as Collier noted in a 1935 report, they apparently did not possess the right to use their natural resources as they pleased.[82] Instead, the Indian New Deal mandated that "the Secretary of the Interior is directed to make rules and regulations for the operation and management of Indian forestry units . . . to limit the number of livestock grazed on Indian range units." The Interior Department was authorized to "acquire . . . any interest in . . . water rights or surface rights to lands."[83] In sum, American Indians did not possess autonomous rights over their forests, cattle ranges, water sources or mineral collieries. Instead the act, working through paternalism, justified its influence over tribal lands on a benevolent protection of Natives in ways reminiscent of the Dawes Act. The Interior Department could "promulgate such rules and regulations as may be necessary to protect the range . . . to prevent soil erosion [and] to assure full utilization of the range."[84] Though American Indians were not overtly labeled as unworthy, that the government retained the right to intercede showed a continued hierarchical relationship. In a sense, this additionally alluded to the government's conflation of territory and citizenship made resonant during both the removal and allotment eras.

The US government's colonial republican fatherhood and paternal identities perpetuated this unbalanced hierarchy. The referenda for Native constitutions, for example, promised in the Dawes Act could only be "authorized and called by the Secretary of the Interior under such rules and regulations as he may prescribe."[85] Here, Native empowerment through the adoption of constitutions was impeded. This was so especially because the constitutions had to first be drafted with the aid of the Bureau of Indian Affairs and only then could they be "subject to the approval of the Secretary of the Interior" as an administrative force.[86] It remained clear that the executive controlled the trajectory of these alleged Native governments. This controlled sovereignty situated in the Indian New Deal "set up puppet governments" and "mysteriously govern[ed] all aspects of tribal life by remote control."[87] Governmental colonization was changed in form only, representing a shift in strategy rather than a substantive policy change.

Moreover, that American Indian governments had to be founded with "constitutions" demonstrated the act's support of republican structures as vital to American Indian uplift and the insistence on assimilating Native communities to these structures. Collier's boast that "personal government of the tribes by the Secretary of the Interior and the Indian Commissioner is brought to an end" remains questionable given the republican fatherhood ideology circulating throughout the early twentieth century.[88]

Ostensibly, the Indian New Deal forced Native communities into a controlled sovereignty that promised them independence as restructured tribal nations, but really only supplanted tribal governance with governmental paternalism. The latter was a ripple of nineteenth century colonizing ideologies from Jacksonian discourse in the 1830s through to the rhetoric of Senator Henry Dawes in the 1880s. The identity duality of segregating American Indians under promises of autonomy while continuing to assimilate them remains stark in the Indian New Deal. Of this controlled sovereignty, Stephen Cornell claims that "the Indian New Deal set out to grant to Indians a limited but enlarged degree of control over their affairs and destinies but did so in the service of the ends pre-selected by the dominant society."[89] The Native life-ways that Collier guaranteed would "rebuild the shattered morale of a subjugated people" continued to be eclipsed by governmental influence.[90]

The Indian Citizenship Act and the Indian Reorganization Act contained empowering and decolonizing ruptures for American Indians. Native communities were able to exploit these entreés, reshaping in the process their identities as US citizens and/or separate sovereigns of a Native nation. An assessment of the way American Indians added to the colonial relationship with the US government exemplifies the way that their agencies can be seen as vital and resonant. While nineteenth century Native protest may have achieved small in-roads during the 1830s and 1880s, the resonance of these arguments was magnified in the passage of the Indian Citizenship Act and the Indian New Deal. These two pieces of legislation stood as symbolic bookends of Native empowerment.

While the Indian Citizenship Act forced a controlled citizenship and the Indian New Deal cemented a controlled sovereignty, American Indian rhetoric was not ignored during the early twentieth century. And the combination of Native integrationist and Native separatist arguments, oftentimes crafted by pan-Indian gatherings, blended into the US government's twin policies of citizenship and self-determination. Natives' success in motivating the Indian Citizenship Act signifies the efforts of nineteenth century integrationist American Indians who sought US citizenship. These American Indians' "culturetypal" discourses, or those that "successfully rearrange the culturally established public vocabulary to produce social change," came to bear in the 1924 act.[91] In contrast, the tribalism supported by the Indian New

Deal, though far from establishing complete Native autonomy, stressed the efforts of nineteenth century separatist American Indians. These Natives engaged in a "counter-cultural" rhetoric that challenged "existing characterizations and narratives" (i.e., assimilation) by seeking separatism versus conciliation to US citizenship. As John Louis Lucaites and Celeste Michele Condit emphasize, when these culturetypal and counter-cultural discourses are combined "they can produce radical changes" in public culture.[92]

These 1924 and 1934 acts are emblematic of the colonial rhetorical relationship between the US governmental and American Indian voices. This relationship at once constructed governmental and Native identities as it proceeded to organize the ways of administrating policies among the cultures. When the US government and American Indians interacted they were not inexorably seeking union or division, but rather were making sense of their public lives together.

Analysis of this colonial governmental language and Native decolonial rhetoric implies that identities transform and merge—they change together, not in isolation or in a unidirectional fashion. Because contact among cultures involves transformations on the part of dominant and marginalized groups, power is complicated among competing agents. Hoxie is correct when he writes that the interactions of the US government and Native communities during the nineteenth and early twentieth centuries made it possible for them "to communicate . . . with each other in new ways."[93]

Notes

INTRODUCTION

1. Though the designations of "tribe" and "nation" are both correct when attributed to distinct American Indian communities, this book employs the term "nation" (lower case when discussing groups in general; upper case when speaking of a particular indigenous group). "Tribe" as a descriptor has sometimes come to represent a diminutive, less powerful "group of people united by ties of common descent from a common ancestor, community of customs and traditions, adhering to the same leaders" (Newcomb). "Tribes" *may* exist with limited negotiating power and sovereignty. Alternatively, a "nation" is "a body of people, associated with a particular territory, that is sufficiently conscious of its unity to seek or to possess a government peculiarly its own" (Newcomb). According to Steven Newcomb (Shawnee/Lenape), referring to American Indian groups as "tribes" connotes passivity, elevating their U.S. counterparts to decision-makers and sovereigns. Using the word "nation," then, identifies American Indian groups with "the most powerful terms in the English language to express . . . political identity." Steven Newcomb, "On the Words 'Tribe' and 'Nation,'" *Indian Country Today* 24, no. 26 (8 December 2004), A3.

2. Black Hawk, *Black Hawk's Autobiography* (Ames: Iowa State University Press, 1999), 9.

3. Black Elk, "The Spider's Web," in *Black Elk Speaks*, ed. John G. Neihardt (Lincoln: University of Nebraska Press, 1931), 35–36.

4. This book refers to Native populations in North America as American Indian, Indigenous, and Natives, per more current trends in American Indian cultural studies. These designations, in particular, are welcome identity signifiers according to Eva Marie Garroutte, *Real Indians: Identity and the Survival of Native America* (Berkeley: University of California Press, 2003); Devon Mihesuah, ed., *Natives and Academics: Writing About American Indians* (Lincoln: University of Nebraska Press, 1998); and Russell Thornton, ed., *Studying Native America: Problems and Prospects* (Madison: University of Wisconsin Press, 1998). Readers are encouraged to bear two precepts in mind. First, the proper designation of Native populations in North America remains controversial. Differences exist and divide sociologists, anthropologists, historians, and—most importantly—Natives themselves. Second, due to the variant descriptors, I am dedicated to integrating all three primary labels. Whenever possible, I will designate populations based on their national affiliation (e.g., Seminole Nation). Also, in the primary discourses, American Indians are sometimes referred to as "tribes," "tribal," "children," "heathen," and "savage," among other dubious terms. Such labels arise from the texts and contexts under investigation.

5. Vine Deloria, *Custer Died for Your Sins: An Indian Manifesto* (Norman: University of Oklahoma Press, 1988), 14.

6. David Leverenz, *Paternalism Incorporated: Fables of American Fatherhood, 1865–1940* (Ithaca, NY: Cornell University Press, 2003), 6.

7. Black Hawk, *Black Hawk's Autobiography*, 9–10.

8. Priscilla Wald, *Constituting Americans: Cultural Anxiety and Narrative Form* (Durham, NC: Duke University Press, 1995), 16–17.

9. Throughout this book, the terms "U.S. identities" and "Native identities" (or "American Indian identities") are used. This pluralizing takes into account Hobsbawm's argument that a national or group identity is never monolithic or uniform. That is, a nation or group is made up of a "myriad of voices" that come together to form a mosaic of identities. See E. J. Hobsbawm, *Nations and Nationalism Since 1780: Programme, Myth, Reality* (Cambridge: Cambridge University Press, 1990), 110. In terms of U.S. identities, dominant nineteenth-century voices range from English and German to Scottish and Irish ancestry, among numerous others. See Rogan Kersh, *Dreams of a More Perfect Union* (Ithaca, NY: Cornell University Press, 2001). Nineteenth-century American Indian identities worked through—and alongside—some five hundred nations and three hundred languages. See Donna Hightower Langston, *The Native American World* (Hoboken, NJ: Wiley and Sons, 2003), 103.

10. Jason Edward Black, "Native Authenticity, Rhetorical Circulation, and Neocolonial Decay: The Case of Chief Seattle's Controversial Speech," *Rhetoric & Public Affairs* 15, no. 4 (2012): 638.

11. Walter Russell Mead, *Special Providence: American Foreign Policy and How it Changed the World* (London: Routledge, 2002), 3.

12. Naturalization Act of 1790 1 Stat. 103–104 (March 26, 1790).

13. Andrew Jackson, "Second Annual Message to Congress, 1830," *U.S. House Journal*, 6 December 1830, 25.

14. William Story, "Indian Destiny," *Cherokee Phoenix* 1, no. 45 (21 January 1829): 1–2.

15. Thomas Haltburton, "Removal of the Indians," *The North American Review* 30, no. 66 (January 1830), 66.

16. Guy Gibbon, *The Sioux: The Dakota and Lakota Nations* (Malden, MA: Blackwell Publishing, 2003), 135.

17. Deloria, *Custer Died for Your Sins*, 47.

18. Thomas Morgan, "Annual Report of the Commissioner of Indian Affairs, 1889," in *House Executive Document* no. 1, 51st Congress, 1st session, serial 2725, 3–4. During the nineteenth century the Commissioner of Indian Affairs oversaw the federal government's relationship with American Indian nations. The position was created by Secretary of War John Calhoun in 1824 and placed atop the newly conceived Bureau of Indian Affairs (BIA) within the War Department. The BIA worked throughout the 1830s and 1840s to engage in Indian removal. As the enterprises of reservationism, assimilation, and allotment gained steam—and bureaucratic complexity—the BIA (also called the Indian Office, the Office of Indian Affairs, the Indian Service, and the Indian Desk) was moved under the auspices of the Department of the Interior in 1849 to administer Native-U.S. affairs.

19. Dewitt Duncan, "How Allotment Impoverishes the Indians: Testimony Before a Senate Committee Investigating Conditions in the Indian Territory," in *Senate Report* No. 5013, 59th Congress, 2d Session, Part 1, Nov. 1906. 180–190.

20. Peter Nabokov, *Native American Testimony: A Chronicle of Indian-White Relations From Prophecy to the Present, 1492–2000* (New York: Penguin Books, 1999), 259.

21. Indian Rights Association, "Statement of Objectives," in *Second Annual Report of the Executive Committee on the Indian Rights Association* (1885), 5–7.

22. Ibid. The Indian Rights Association was one of many "Friends of the Indians" reform groups that sought to bring Native populations into the U.S. fold following decades of war (especially the 1850s–1880s) between the United States and American Indian nations. Broadly, these reform organizations' "solution to the Indian problem was that the Indians were to be 'civilized,' assimilated into the economy through land ownership and education." As Hans Konig puts it, "This was a notion not only accepted by those who wanted to promote the Indian cause," but even more eagerly by the federal government. Hans Konig, *The Conquest of America: How the*

Indian Nations Lost Their Continent (New York: Cornerstone, 1993), 103–104. Thus, "Friends of the Indians" groups acted as independent mediators of the government's will toward American Indians. The Indian Rights Association in particular hoped to elevate Native nations to civilization by cutting off the federal rations program, allotting reservation land, converting Natives to productive capitalist farmers, and educating both adults and children in the English language, Christianity, and American customs and culture. William T. Hagan, *The Indian Rights Association: The Herbert Walsh Years, 1882–1904* (Tucson: University of Arizona Press, 1985), ix.

23. Frederick E. Hoxie, ed., *Talking Back to Civilization: Indian Voices from the Progressive Era* (Boston: Bedford/St. Martin's, 2001), viii.

24. Jason Edward Black, "Native Resistive Rhetoric and the Decolonization of American Indian Removal Discourse," *Quarterly Journal of Speech* 95, no. 1 (2009): 71.

25. Karlyn Kohrs Campbell, "Agency: Promiscuous and Protean," *Communication and Cultural/Critical Studies* 2 (2005): 3.

26. Benedict Anderson, *Imagined Communities: Reflections on the Origins and Spread of Nationalism* (London: Verso, 1983), 15.

27. Hobsbawm, *Nations and Nationalism*, 110.

28. Vanessa Beasley, *You, the People: American National Identity in Presidential Rhetoric* (College Station: Texas A&M University Press, 2004), 45.

29. Anderson, *Imagined Communities*; M. Lane Bruner, *Strategies of Remembrance: The Rhetorical Dimensions of National Identity* (University of South Carolina Press, 2002); Ernest Gellner, *Encounters with Nationalism* (Oxford, UK: Blackwell, 1994); Gary Gerstle, *American Crucible: Race and Nation in the Twentieth Century* (Princeton: Princeton University Press, 2001); and Ronald Takaki, *Iron Cages: Race and Culture in 19th Century America* (New York: Oxford University Press, 1990).

30. Hobsbawm, *Nations and Nationalism*, 10.

31. Raka Shome, "Postcolonial Interventions in the Rhetorical Canon: An 'Other' View," *Communication Theory* 6 (1996): 41.

32. Derek Buescher and Kent Ono, "Civilized Colonialism: *Pocahontas* as Neocolonial Rhetoric," *Women's Studies in Communication* 19 (1996): 131.

33. Stuart Hall, "Cultural Identity and Diaspora," in *Identity: Community, Culture, Difference*, ed. John Rutherford (London: Lawrence and Wishart, 1990), 222–37; Gayatri Spivak, *In Other Worlds* (New York: Routledge, 1988); Gayatri Spivak, "Can the Subaltern Speak?," in *Marxism and the Interpretation of Culture*, ed. Lawrence Grossberg and Cary Nelson (Urbana: University of Illinois Press, 1988), 271–313; Homi Bhabha, "The Other Question: Difference, Discrimination, and the Discourse of Colonialism," in *Literature, Politics, and Theory: Papers from the Essex Conference, 1976–1984*, ed. Francis Barker (London: Metheun, 1986), 148–72; Homi Bhabha, *The Location of Culture* (New York: Routledge, 1994); Edward Said, *Orientalism* (New York: Random House, 1978); and Edward Said, *Culture and Imperialism* (New York: Knopf, 1993).

34. Susan Silbey, "'Let Them Eat Cake': Globalization, Postmodern Colonialism, and the Possibilities of Justice," *Law and Society Review* 31 (1997): 210.

35. Said, *Orientalism*, 44.

36. According to Delaney, place is the physical location of boundaries and terrain, whereas space is "about social relations of power" within these physical locations. He says when we speak of these social spaces we refer to "the complex ensemble of lines" and "territorial configurations" that give meaning to "actual lived-in landscapes." Geography then involves "the shifting approximations of social space, the creation and transformation of real places, and the differing experiential geographies of real people." David Delaney, *Race, Place and the Law, 1836–1948* (Austin: University of Texas Press, 1998), vii, 13, 14.

37. William G. Robbins, "In Search of Western Lands," in *Land in the American West: Private Claims and the Common Good*, ed. William G. Robbins and James C. Foster (Seattle: University of Washington Press, 2000), 7.

38. R. Douglas Hurt, *The Indian Frontier, 1763–1846* (Albuquerque: University of New Mexico Press, 2002), xiv.

39. Ronald Niezen, *The Origins of Indigenism: Human Rights and the Politics of Identity* (Berkeley: University of California Press, 2003), 150.

40. David Rich Lewis, *Neither Wolf Nor Dog: American Indians, Environment and Agrarian Change* (New York: Oxford University Press, 1994), 10.

41. William M. Strickland, "The Rhetoric of Removal and the Trail of Tears: Cherokee Speaking Against Jackson's Indian Removal Policy, 1828–1832," *Southern Speech Communication Journal* 47 (1982): 294.

42. Robbins, "In Search of Western Lands," 5.

43. Rogers Smith, *Civic Ideals: Conflicting Visions of Citizenship in U.S. History* (New Haven, CT: Yale University Press, 1997), 30.

44. David M. Ricci, *Good Citizenship in America* (Cambridge: Cambridge University Press, 2004), 75.

45. James Madison, "The Federalist Number Ten" in *A Documentary History of the United States*, 7d., ed. Richard D. Heffner (New York: Signet, 2002), 40–43.

46. Kersh, *Dreams of a More Perfect Union*, 74–75.

47. Michael Schudson, *The Good Citizen: A History of American Civic Life* (New York: The Free Press, 1998), 28.

48. Robert E. Shalhope, *The Roots of Democracy: American Thought and Culture, 1760–1800* (Boston: Twayne, 1990), 24.

49. Celeste Michelle Condit and John Louis Lucaites, *Crafting Equality: America's Anglo-African Word* (Chicago: University of Chicago Press, 1993), 69–74

50. "Declaration of Independence," in *A Documentary History of the United States*, 7d., ed. Richard D. Heffner (New York: Signet, 2002), 12.

51. Takaki, *Iron Cages*, 63.

52. Smith, *Civic Ideals*, 14.

53. Beasley, *You, the People*, 45.

54. Raka Shome and Radha S. Hegde, "Postcolonial Approaches to Communication: Charting the Terrain, Engaging the Intersections," *Communication Theory* 12 (2002): 258.

55. Garroutte, *Real Indians*, 113.

56. Elizabeth Rich, "Remember Wounded Knee: AIM's Use of Metonymy in 20th Century Protest," *College Literature* 31, no. 3 (2004): 73.

57. For more on the process of decolonization, especially as a scholarly program, see Jason Edward Black, "A Clash of Native Space and Institutional Place in a Local Choctaw-Upper Creek Memory Site—Decolonizing Critiques and Scholar-Activist Interventions," *American Indian Culture & Research Journal* 36, no. 3 (2012): 19–44.

58. See, for instance, Richard Morris, "Educating Savages," *Quarterly Journal of Speech* 83 (1997): 152–171.

59. Garroutte, *Real Indians*, 99–139. See also Alexandra Harmon, "Wanted: More Histories of Indian Identity," in *A Companion to American Indian History*, ed. Philip Deloria and Neal Salisbury (New York: Blackwell, 2002), 259.

60. Sovereignty, here, is defined as the agency to control one's own destiny; remain close to ancestral, linguistic, familial and spiritual roots; self-identify as an independent political entity holding land; and cultivate and maintain a sense of group nationalism, oftentimes despite

oppression (i.e., U.S. Indian policies considered detrimental to Native nations). See Garroutte, *Real Indians*, 88–89 and 95–96.

61. I use the term "strategy" to mean an overarching plan of action on the part of powerful interests, governments, or institutions. In this case, colonization is a strategy of control that functioned to suppress the movement, rights, and agencies of Native nations. I use the term "tactic" to indicate particular ways that resistance ultimately worked to unveil the dominance functioning in the U.S. government's removal rhetoric. As de Certeau writes, a tactic "is a calculated action" that operates "blow by blow" to confront strategies of control. Michel de Certeau, *The Practice of Everyday Life* (Berkeley: University of California Press, 1984), 36–37. In the case of Native resistive rhetoric in the nineteenth century, tactics of decolonization involve détourning dominant discourses.

62. Patricia Bizzell, "(Native) American Jeremiad: The 'Mixedblood' Rhetoric of William Apess," in *American Indian Rhetorics of Survivance: Word Medicine, Word Magic*, ed. Ernest Stromberg (Pittsburgh, PA: University of Pittsburgh Press, 2006), 46.

63. Arnold Krupat, *Ethnocriticism: Ethnography, History, Literature* (Berkeley: University of California Press, 1992), 156.

64. For more, see Guy Debord, *The Society of the Spectacle* (New York: Zone Books, 1994).

65. Quoted in Sean McCloud, *Making the American Religious Fringe: Exotics, Subversives, and Journalists, 1955–1993* (Chapel Hill: University of North Carolina Press, 2004), 74–75.

66. Brian W. Dippie, *The Vanishing American: White Attitudes and U.S. Indian Policy* (Lawrence: University of Kansas Press, 1982), 4.

67. Black, "Native Resistive Rhetoric," 67.

68. Hoxie, *Talking Back*, viii.

69. Wayne Moquin and Charles Van Doren, *Great Documents in American Indian History* (New York: De Capo, 1995), xvi–xvii.

70. Devon Mihesuah, *So You Want to Write About American Indians? A Research Guide for Scholars, Students and Writers* (Lincoln: University of Nebraska Press, 2005), 15.

71. Nabokov, *Native American Testimony*, 426.

72. Susan Hegeman, "Native American 'Texts' and the Problem of Authenticity,'" *American Quarterly* 41 (1989): 271.

73. Arnold Krupat, *Ethnocriticism*, 157.

74. Arnold Krupat, "An Approach to Native American Texts," *Critical Inquiry* 9 (1982): 323–338.

75. Morris, "Educating Savages," 154.

76. Robert Yagelski, "A Rhetoric of Contact: Tecumseh and the Native American Confederacy," *Rhetoric Review* 14 (1995): 71.

77. Linda Tuhiwai Smith, *Decolonizing Methodologies: Research and Indigenous Peoples* (London: Zed Books, 2007), 31.

78. Smith, *Decolonizing Methodologies*, 30.

79. Shome, "Postcolonial Interventions," 46

80. Gayatri Spivak, *In Other Worlds: Essays in Cultural Politics* (New York: Routledge, 1988), 205.

81. Gayatri Spivak, "Interview," in *The Postcolonial Critic: Interviews, Strategies, Dialogues*, ed. Sarah Harasym (New York: Routledge, 1990), 51.

82. Shome, "Postcolonial Interventions," 47

83. Robbie Ethridge, *Creek Country: The Creek Indians and Their World* (Chapel Hill: University of North Carolina Press, 2003), 3.

84. Emma LaRocque, *When the Other is Me: Native Resistance Discourse, 1850–1990* (Winnipeg: University of Manitoba Press, 2010), 12.

CHAPTER ONE

1. Jill Lepore, *The Name of War: King Philip's War and the Origins of American Identity* (New York: Vintage, 1999), xiv.

2. John Smith, quoted in Roy Harvey Pearce, *Savagism and Civilization: A Study of the Indian and the American Mind* (Baltimore: Johns Hopkins University Press, 1967), 18–19.

3. Francis Paul Prucha, *The Great Father: The United States Government and the American Indians*, 1 (Lincoln: University of Nebraska Press, 1984), 11.

4. Wahunsonacock (Powhatan), "1622 Speech to John Smith," in *Travels and Works of Captain John Smith*, ed. Edward Arber (Edinburgh, 1910), 137.

5. Hans Koning, *The Conquest of America: How the Indian Nations Lost Their Continent* (New York: Cornerstone, 1993), 57–59.

6. Prucha, *The Great Father*, 11. For a comprehensive examination of colonial Indian wars, see Douglas Edward Leach, *Arms for Empire: A Military History of the British Colonies in North America, 1607–1730* (New York: MacMillan, 1973).

7. Several smaller wars between the European American colonists and American Indians took place before King Philip's War. For instance, the Pequot War of 1636 also challenged the paternal and expansionist character of European American settlers. Members of the Mahican, Mohawk, and Algonquin fought Christian church groups, the English and the French, and the Dutch trading companies during the era of 1600 to 1670. For more on these skirmishes, see Lepore, *The Name of War*; Prucha, *The Great Father*; Francis Paul Prucha, *The Indians in American Society: From the Revolutionary War to the Present* (Berkeley: University of California Press, 1988); and Neal Salisbury, "Native People and European Settlers in Eastern North America, 1600–1783," in *The Cambridge History of the Native Peoples in the Americas*, vol. 1, part 1, ed. Bruce Trigger and Wilcomb E. Washburn (London: Cambridge University Press, 1996).

8. Increase Mather, "A Brief History of the War with the Indians in New England," in *So Dreadful a Judgment: Puritan Responses to King Philip's War, 1676–1677*, ed. Richard Slotkin and James K. Folsom (Middletown, CT: Wesleyan University Press, 1978), 138–139.

9. Ward Churchill, *Indians Are Us? Culture and Genocide in North America* (Monroe, ME: Common Courage Press, 1994), 308.

10. Cotton Mather, "Decennium Luctuosum," in *Narratives of the Indian Wars, 1675–1699*, ed. Charles Lincoln (New York: Scribner's Sons, 1913), 116.

11. William Blackstone, *Commentaries on the Laws of England, 1765–1769*, vol. 1 (Chicago: University of Chicago Press, 1979), 156.

12. For some early Native resistance context, see Gregory Evans Dowd, *A Spirited Resistance: The North American Indian Struggle for Unity, 1745–1815* (Baltimore: Johns Hopkins University Press, 1992).

13. King Philip, "Speech," in *Eulogy on King Philip, as Pronounced at the Odeon*, ed. William Apes (Boston: Apes, 1836), 27.

14. For an extended discussion of the French and Indian War, see William Fowler, *Empires at War: The French and Indian War and the Struggle for North America, 1754–1763* (New York: Walker and Company, 2004).

15. Proclamation of 1763, in *The American Indian and the United States: A Documentary History*, vol. 3, ed. Wilcomb E. Washburn (New York: Random House, 1973), 2135.

16. Proclamation of 1763, 2133.

17. Proclamation of 1763, 2136.

18. Bernard Romans quoted in Pearce, *Savagism and Civilization*, 47.

19. Canassatego (Onondaga), "We Now Speak," in *Minutes of the Provincial Council of Pennsylvania*, vol. 5, ed. Samuel Hazard (Harrisburg, PA: T. Fenn & Co., 1851–53), 401–2.

20. Pontiac (Ottawa), "You Must Lift the Hatchet Against Them," in *The Conspiracy of Pontiac*, ed. Francis Parkman (New York: Champlain, 1898), 5.

21. Ibid.

22. Mihnehwehna (Ojibway), "Englishman!" in *Travels and Adventures in Canada and the Indian Territories Between the Years 1760 and 1776*, ed. Alexander Henry (New York: I. Riley, 1809), 44.

23. Prucha, *The Indians in American Society*, 30.

24. See Churchill, *Indians Are Us?*; Richard Drinnon, *Facing West: The Metaphysics of Indian Hating and Empire Building* (Norman: University of Oklahoma Press, 1997; and Anthony F. C. Wallace, *The Long, Bitter Trail: Andrew Jackson and the Indians* (New York: Hill and Wang, 1993).

25. Salisbury, "Native People and European Settlers," 446–450.

26. Hazel Hertzberg, *The Search for an American Indian Identity* (Syracuse, NY: Syracuse University Press, 1971), 31–134.

27. Francis Paul Prucha, *The Great Father: The United States Government and the American Indians, Abridged* (Lincoln: University of Nebraska Press, 1988), 195–196.

28. Antiwaneto (Cowasuck), "We Hear on All Sides," in *Documents Relative to the Colonial History of New York*, vol. 10, ed. E. B. O'Callaghan (Albany: Weed, Parsons, 1858), 252–254.

29. Kent Ono and John Sloop, "A Critique of Vernacular Discourse," *Communication Monographs* 62 (1995): 24.

30. Sidney Lens, *The Forging of the American Empire—From the Revolution to Vietnam: A History of U.S. Imperialism* (Chicago: Haymarket Press, 2003), 41.

31. Joy Porter, "Native Americans: The Assertion of Sovereignty and the Negotiation of Citizenship and Identities," in *Federalism, Citizenship and Collective Identities in U.S. History*, ed. Cornelius A. Van Minnen and Sylvia Hilton (Amsterdam: VU Boekhandel University Press, 2000), 183.

32. Treaty of McIntosh, in *The American Indian and the United States: A Documentary History*, vol. 4, ed. Wilcomb E. Washburn (New York: Random House, 1973), 2269.

33. Treaty of Hopewell, in *The American Indian and the United States: A Documentary History*, vol. 4, ed. Wilcomb E. Washburn (New York: Random House, 1973), 2275.

34. Lewis notes how the freedom to engage in economic trade and production supported Native communities' sense of nationhood, or separate sovereignty. In turn, such sovereignty allowed a "sense of place and identity." See David Rich Lewis, *Neither Wolf Nor Dog: American Indians, Environment, and Agrarian Change* (New York: Oxford University Press, 1994), 3.

35. Robert E. Shalhope, *The Roots of Democracy: American Thought and Culture, 1760–1800* (Boston: Twayne, 1990), 24.

36. Continental Congress, "Report of Committee on Indian Affairs, October 15, 1783," *Journals of the Continental Congress* 25: 681–683, 693.

37. Constitution of the United States of America, in *A Documentary History of the United States*, 7d., ed. Richard D. Heffner (New York: Signet, 2002), 22.

38. Constitution of the United States of America, 33.

39. Ibid.

40. Peter Hitchcock, *Dialogics of the Oppressed* (Minneapolis: University of Minnesota Press, 1993), 4.

41. Joseph Brant (Mohawk), "We Have Borne Everything Patiently for This Long Time," in *Indian Oratory: Famous Speeches by Noted Indian Chieftains*, ed. W. C. Vanderwerth (Norman: University of Oklahoma Press, 1989), 50–53.

42. Ohnawiio, Oteatohatongwan, and Teholagwanegen (Mohawk), "Formerly, We Enjoyed the Privilege," in *American State Papers: Indian Affairs*, vol. 7 (Washington: Office of Indian Affairs, 1903), 617.

43. Emma LaRocque, *When the Other is Me: Native Resistance Discourse, 1850–1990* (Winnipeg: University of Manitoba Press, 2010), 21

44. Thomas Jefferson, Presidential Message, 1803, Record Group 233, Records of the U.S. House of Representatives, File HR7A-D1 at the National Archives II.

45. Wallace, *The Long, Bitter Trail*, 38.

46. The Northwest Ordinance of 1787 was considered one of the most significant achievements of the early Republic, as it allowed for the opening of land in exchange for goods with Natives. The Ordinance codified the process for northern land acquisition in states like Ohio, Indiana, Illinois, Michigan, and Wisconsin, and as a result it hastened expansion. The Ordinance stated, "that the utmost good faith shall always be observed towards the Indians; their lands and property shall never be taken from them without their consent; and in their property, rights, and liberty they shall never be invaded or disturbed." Northwest Ordinance, in *The American Indian and the United States: A Documentary History*, vol. 3, ed. Wilcomb E. Washburn (New York: Random House, 1973), 2144. Notice that the Ordinance allowed for the negotiations of both U.S. and American Indian voices for further expansion.

47. Quoted in Wallace, *The Long Bitter Trail*, 38.

48. Wallace, *The Long Bitter Trail*, 32.

49. George Washington, "Third Annual Message to Congress, October 25, 1791," in *A Compilation of the Messages and Papers of the Presidents, Vol. 1*, comp., James D. Richardson (New York: Bureau of National Literature, 1897), 96–97.

50. George Washington, "Fifth Message to Congress, October 25, 1793," in *A Compilation of the Messages and Papers of the Presidents, Vol. 1*, comp., James D. Richardson (New York: Bureau of National Literature, 1897), 133.

51. Corn Tassel (Cherokee), "Let Us Examine the Facts," in T*atham's Characters Among the North American Indians* (London: Annual of Biography and Obituary, 1820).

52. Trade and Intercourse Act, March 30, 1802, *U.S. Statutes at Large*, 2: 139–46.

53. Thomas Jefferson, "Message to Congress on Indian Trading Houses, January 18, 1803," in *A Compilation of the Messages and Papers of the Presidents, Vol. 1*, comp., James D. Richardson (New York: Bureau of National Literature, 1897), 340–41.

54. Prucha, *The Indians in American Society*, 12.

55. Records of the Office of the Secretary of War, Indian Affairs, *Letters Sent*, vol A, p.143, Record Group 75, National Archives. Also found in *The American Indian and the United States: A Documentary History*, vol. 1, ed. Wilcomb E. Washburn (New York: Random House, 1973).

56. "Message of January 18, 1803," in *A Compilation of the Messages and Papers of the Presidents, Vol. 1*, comp., James D. Richardson (New York: Bureau of National Literature, 1897), 352. Also found in *The Papers of Thomas Jefferson*, vol. 10, ed. Julian Boyd, (Princeton, NJ: Princeton University Press, 1950).

57. Thomas Jefferson, "First Inaugural, March 4, 1801," in *The Inaugural Addresses of the Presidents*, ed. John Gabriel Hunt (New York: Gramercy, 1997), 24.

58. James H. Kettner, *The Development of American Citizenship*, 1608–1870 (Chapel Hill: University of North Carolina Press, 1978), 245–246.

59. Thomas Jefferson, Presidential Message 1803, Record Group 233.

60. Ibid.

61. Ibid.

62. Ibid.

63. Wallace, *The Long Bitter Trail*, 39.

64. Thomas Jefferson to William Henry Harrison, February 27, 1803, *The Writings of Thomas Jefferson*, vol. 9, ed. Albert E. Berghe (Washington: Thomas Jefferson Memorial Foundation, 1907), 370–71.

65. Wallace, *Long Bitter Trail*, 39.

66. James Monroe, "Second Annual Message, December 1818," in *A Compilation of the Messages and Papers of the Presidents, Vol. 2*, comp., James D. Richardson (New York: Bureau of National Literature, 1897), 46.

67. James Monroe, "Message on Indian Removal, January 27, 1825," in *Documents of United States Indian Policy, 2d.*, ed. Francis Paul Prucha (Lincoln: University of Nebraska Press, 1990), 40.

68. For more on Tecumseh's resistance, see Alvin Josephy, Jr., *The Patriot Chief's: A Chronicle of American Indian Resistance* (New York: Penguin, 1989), 29–173. A classic treatment of Tecumseh's life and times can found in R. David Edmunds, *The Shawnee Prophet* (Lincoln: University of Nebraska Press, 1985).

69. Tecumseh, "Sleep No Longer," in *Indian Oratory: Famous Speeches by Great Chieftains*, ed. W.C. Vanderwerth (Norman: University of Oklahoma Press, 1979): 54.

70. For more on the Fort Mims conflict, see Gregory A. Waselkov, *A Conquering Spirit: Fort Mims and the Redstick War of 1813–1814* (Tuscaloosa: University of Alabama Press, 2006).

71. Jason Edward Black, "Memories of the Alabama Creek War, 1813–1814: U.S. Governmental and Native Identities at the Horseshoe Bend National Military Park," *American Indian Quarterly* 33, no. 2 (2009), 204.

72. Andrew Jackson, "Talk with Indian Chieftains, September 20, 1821," in *Correspondence of Andrew Jackson*, vol. 3, ed. John Spencer Bassett (Washington, DC: Carnegie Institute, 1928), 118–21.

73. See Jason Edward Black, "Authoritarian Fatherhood: Andrew Jackson's Early Familial Lectures to America's 'Red Children,'" *Journal of Family History* 30, no. 3 (2005): 257.

74. Andrew Jackson, "To Choctaw Indians, October 3, 1820," *The Papers of Andrew Jackson IV*, ed. Harold D. Moser, David R. Hoth, and George H. Hoemann (Knoxville: University of Tennessee Press, 1996), 391–392.

75. Michael Paul Rogin, *Fathers and Children: Andrew Jackson and The Subjugation of the American Indian* (New York: Knopf, 1975), 43.

76. 21 U.S. 543 (1823), *Johnson and Graham v. McIntosh*, 568–569.

77. Ibid.

78. Eric Cheyfitz, "Doctrines of Discovery," *Common-Place* 2, no. 1 (2001): 4.

79. Vine Deloria and Clifford M. Lytle, *American Indians, American Justice* (Austin: University of Texas Press, 1983), 26–27.

80. James Monroe, "Message on Voluntary Indian Removal, January 27, 1825."

81. Black Thunder (Fox), "Speech to American Commissioners, 1815," in *Biography and History of the Indians of North America*, ed. Samuel G. Drake (Boston, 1841), 632.

82. Petalesharo (Pawnee), "It Is Too Soon, My Great Father, to Send Those Good Men Among Us," in *Red Men Calling on the Great White Father*, ed. Katharine C. Turner (Norman: University of Oklahoma Press, 1951).

83. James Monroe, "Second Annual Message, December 1818."

84. Ibid.

CHAPTER TWO

1. Mary E. Stuckey, *Defining Americans: The Presidency and National Identity* (Lawrence: University of Kansas Press, 2004), 22.

2. Andrew Jackson, "To James Monroe," March 4, 1817, in *Correspondence of Andrew Jackson*, vol. 2, ed. John Spencer Bassett (Washington, DC: Carnegie Institute, 1928), 278–79.

3. Andrew Jackson, "Talk with George Colbert and the Chickasaw," February 13, 1816, in *The Papers of Andrew Jackson*, vol. 4, ed. Harold D. Moser. David R. Hoth and George H. Hoemann (Knoxville: University of Tennessee Press, 1996), 13.

4. James Monroe, "Annual Message," in Richardson, 830.

5. John Forsyth, Speech, found in Ronald Satz, *American Indian Policy in the Jacksonian Era* (Lincoln: University of Nebraska Press, 1975), 24.

6. John Eaton, To the Cherokee Nation on Removal, April 18, 1829," in Office of Indian Affairs, *Letter Book* no. 5, Record Group 75, 408–412, National Archives.

7. Thomas McKinney, "Letter," in *Magazine of the Reformed Dutch Church* 4 (August 1829):118.

8. Proclamation of the Continental Congress, September 22, 1783, *Journals of the Continental Congress*, vol. 25, 602.

9. Emma LaRocque, *When the Other is Me: Native Resistance Discourse, 1850–1990* (Winnipeg: University of Manitoba Press, 2010), 41.

10. David G. Gutierrez, "Significant to Whom?: Mexican Americans and the History of the American West," in *A New Significance: Re-Envisioning the History of the American West*, ed. Clyde A. Milner III. (New York: Oxford University Press, 1996), 68.

11. See Lyon Rathbun, "The Debate Over Annexing Texas and the Emergence of Manifest Destiny," *Rhetoric and Public Affairs* 4, no. 3 (2001): 459–93.

12. John O'Sullivan, "Annexation," *The United States and Democratic Review*, Vol. 17, July/August (New York: O'Sullivan & Gardner Publishers, 1845), 5.

13. Samuel Danforth, "A Brief Recognition of New England's Errand Into the Wilderness," in *American Rhetorical Discourse*, 3d, ed. James F. Klumpp and Ronald Reid (Prospect Heights, IL: Waveland Press, 2004), 37–51.

14. Sidney Lens, *The Forging of American Empire: From the Revolution to Vietnam—A History of U.S. Imperialism* (Chicago: Haymarket Press, 2003), 2.

15. Ronald Takaki, *Iron Cages: Race and Culture in Nineteenth-Century America.* (Boston: Little, Brown, 1979), 173.

16. Rogan Kersh, *Dreams of a More Perfect Union* (New York, Cornell U P, 2005), 74

17. John William Ward, *Andrew Jackson: Symbol for an Age* (London: Oxford University Press, 1955), 168.

18. The Era of Good Feelings, the period following the War of 1812, has been so-named due to a number of optimistic changes in the U.S. nation. For one, the Federalist-Republican debate had come to an end with the 1816 election of James Monroe; political partisanship was said, then, to have loosened (see Edward Pessen, *Jacksonian America: Society, Personality, and Politics* [Urbana: University of Illinois Press, 1985], 34). Also, though, industrialization in the North and the ascendance of a "cotton culture" in the South, in addition to the lifting of British and French blockades resulting from the War of 1812, invigorated the U.S. economy. And the advent of national roads, canals, and steamboats contributed to an improved infrastructure.

19. Rogers Smith, *Civic Ideals: Conflicting Visions of Citizenship in U.S. History* (New Haven, CT: Yale University Press, 1997), 183.

20. Andrew Jackson, "Draft of First Annual Message, December 8, 1829" in *The Correspondence of Andrew Jackson*, vol. 4, ed. John Spencer Bassett (Washington, DC: Carnegie, 1928), 103.

21. Smith, *Civic Ideals*, 183

22. David Wilkins, *American Indian Sovereignty and the U.S. Supreme Court: The Masking of Justice* (Austin: University of Texas Press, 1999), 9.

23. Francis Paul Prucha, *The Indians in American Society: from the Revolutionary War to the Present* (Berkeley: University of California Press, 1988), 11.

24. Neil Fotion, "Paternalism." *Ethics* 89 (1979): 191.

25. J. Kleinig, *Paternalism* (New York: Rowan and Allenheld, 1983), 171.

26. Prucha, *The Indians in American Society*, 11.

27. Francis Paul Prucha, *Documents of United States Indian Policy*, 2d. (Lincoln: University of Nebraska Press, 1990), 10.

28. Committee Report on the Southern Department, August 3, 1787, *Journals of the Continental Congress*, vol. 33, 456, 459.

29. The Constitution of the United States, Art. 1, sec.8 and Art I, sec 10 in *A Documentary History of the United States*, ed. Richard Heffner (New York: Signet, 2002), 22.

30. David M. Ricci, *Good Citizenship in America* (Cambridge, UK: Cambridge University Press, 2004), 70.

31. 17 U.S. 316, *McCulloch v. Maryland* (1819).

32. H.W. Brands, *Andrew Jackson: His Life and Times* (New York, Doubleday, 2005), 345–55.

33. John Calhoun, "South Carolina Exposition, December 19, 1828" in *The Papers of John C. Calhoun*, vol. 10, 1825–1829, ed. Clyde N. Wilson and W. Edwin Hemphill (Columbia: University of South Carolina Press, 1977), 461.

34. John Buchanan, *Jackson's Way: Andrew Jackson and the People of the Western Waters* (New York: Wiley, 2001), 366–68.

35. Andrew Jackson, "Letter to Rachel Jackson," October 21, 1814, in *The Correspondence of Andrew Jackson*, vol. 1, ed. John Spencer Bassett (Washington, DC: Carnegie, 1928), 365–66.

36. For more on Jackson's personal political life—especially concerning issues of Native relations—see Andrew Burstein, *The Passions of Andrew Jackson* (New York: Vintage, 2004) and Jon Meacham, *American Lion: Andrew Jackson in the White House* (New York: Random House, 2009)

37. Andrew Jackson, "Letter to John Williams," May 18, 1815, in *The Papers of Andrew Jackson*, vol. 3, ed. Harold D. Moser. David R. Hoth and George H. Hoemann (Knoxville: University of Tennessee Press, 1996), 74–75.

38. Ibid.

39. Ibid.

40. Ibid.

41. Andrew Jackson, "To Choctaw Indians, October 17, 1820," *The Papers of Andrew Jackson* vol. 4, ed. Mozer, Hoth, Hoemann (Knoxville: University of Tennessee Press, 1996), 393–96.

42. Mary R. Jackman, *The Velvet Glove: Paternalism and Conflict in Gender, Class and Race Relations* (Berkeley: University of California Press, 1993), 14–15.

43. Andrew Jackson, "First Inaugural," March 4, 1829, in *A Compilation of the Messages and Papers of the Presidents*, vol. 2, comp., James D. Richardson (Washington, DC: Bureau of National Literature and Art, 1937), 438.

44. Jackson, "To James Monroe," 278–79.

45. Ibid.

46. Andrew Jackson, "Letter to James Gadsen," October 12, 1829, in *Correspondence of Andrew Jackson*, vol. 4, ed. John Spencer Bassett (Washington, DC: Carnegie Institute, 1928), 81.

47. Andrew Jackson, "First Annual Message," December 7, 1829, in *A Compilation of the Messages and Papers of the Presidents*, vol. 2, comp., James D. Richardson (Washington, DC: Bureau of National Literature and Art, 1937), 457–59.

48. For instance, see Brands, *Andrew Jackson*, 435; and Satz, *American Indian Policy*, 9–12

49. "Report of the Joint Committee in the Legislature of Georgia on Cherokee Lands," *Cherokee Phoenix* 1, no. 3 (March 6, 1828): 1, col. 4B.

50. Ibid.

51. Jackson, "First Annual Message," 459.

52. The Constitution of the United States, 22–23.

53. Trade and Intercourse Act of 1802, *U.S. Statutes at Large*, vol. 2, 145.

54. Concerning issues related to the state, the Jacksonian era witnessed notable Southern antagonisms toward the renewal of the U.S. Bank and over the Nullification issue. Jackson worked within this political and sectional milieu as he considered Indian removal and reasoned for its implementation. For more on Jacksonian contexts, see Edward Pessen, *Jacksonian America*.

55. Andrew Jackson, "Letter to John Pitchlynn, August 5, 1830," in *Correspondence of Andrew Jackson*, vol. 4, ed. John Spencer Bassett (Washington, DC: Carnegie Institution, 1929), 169.

56. Quoted in Albert K. Weinberg, *Manifest Destiny: A Study of Nationalistic Expansionism in American History* (Baltimore: Johns Hopkins University Press, 1935), 83.

57. *House Report* no. 237, 21:1, serial 200, 6–7

58. I am indebted to the outlines developed by Prucha, *Great Father* [unabridged], Robert V. Remini, *Andrew Jackson and His Indian Wars* (New York: Penguin, 2001), and Satz, *American Indian Policy* concerning the unfolding of Congressional debates on the Indian Removal Act. Satz's work, in particular, is worthy for its narrative chronology of the events of the twenty-first Congress.

59. Satz, *American Indian Policy*, 26.

60. John Forsyth, Remarks, April 15, 1830, *Gales & Seaton's Register of Debates in Congress*, Senate (April 14, 15, 1830), 326.

61. John Forsyth, Remarks, 327

62. Ibid.

63. Ibid.

64. John Forsyth, Remarks, 333

65. Robert Adams, Remarks, April 20, 1830, *Gales & Seaton's Register of Debates in Congress*, Senate (April 20, 1830), 359.

66. Robert Adams, Remarks, 364.

67. Ibid.

68. Robert Adams, Remarks, 359.

69. Theodore Frelinghuysen, Remarks, April 9, 1830, *Gales & Seaton's Register of Debates in Congress*, Senate (April 9, 1830), 312.

70. Theodore Frelinghuysen, Remarks, 312.

71. Theodore Frelinghuysen, Remarks, 381.

72. Related to the jeremiad, moral inheritance charges society with fulfilling the promises and values set up, and fought for, by its ancestry. See Michael W. Casey and Douglas A. Foster, "The Moral Inheritance of a President," in *The Stone-Campbell Movement: An International Religious Tradition*, ed. Michael W. Casey and Douglas A. Foster (Knoxville: University of Tennessee Press, 2001), 109–127.

73. Theodore Frelinghuysen, Remarks, 381.

74. Theodore Frelinghuysen, Remarks, 320.

75. Peleg Sprague, Remarks, April 17, 1830, *Gales & Seaton's Register of Debates in Congress*, Senate (April 17, 1830), 356.

76. Ibid.

77. Indian Removal Act (1830), *U.S. Statutes at Large*, vol. 4: 411–12.

78. Kendall R. Phillips, "Spaces Of Invention: Dissension, Freedom, And Thought In Foucault," *Philosophy & Rhetoric* 34, no. 4 (2002): 328–44.

79. Indian Removal Act (1830), *U.S. Statutes at Large*, vol. 4: 411–12.

80. Ibid.

81. Patricia Wald, "Terms of Assimilation: Legislating Subjectivity in the Emerging Nation," *Cultures of United States Imperialism*, ed. Amy Kaplan and Donald Pease (Durham: Duke University Press, 2000), 59.

82. Phillip Frickey, "Marshalling Past and Present: Colonialism, Constitutionalism, and Interpretation in Federal Indian Law," 107 *Harv. L.Rev.* 381 (December 1993). See also Kent Newmeyer, "Law and Character: John Marshall as an American Original—Some Thoughts on Personality and Judicial Statesmanship," 71 *U. Colo. L.Rev.* 1365 (2000); and Samuel Olken, "Chief Justice John

Marshall and the Course of American Constitutional History." 33 J. *Marshall L.Rev.* 743 (Summer 2000).

83. A cipher is a conduit, channel, or "type of empty [cultural] container" that the powerful uses to fill with whatever values, images and meaning it wishes" in order to achieve a desired end. A cipher acts as a commodified vessel that assists a dominant culture in achieving its goals (see Jason Edward Black, "Sacagawea as Commodity, Currency and Cipher: Consequences of the U.S. Mint's Gold Dollar for American Indian Women," *International Journal of Media and Cultural Politics* 1, no. 2 [2005]: 227–28). For instance, the Supreme Court "channeled" its desire to overshadow states' rights through the issue of American Indian sovereignty in *Cherokee Nation v. Georgia*.

84. Andrew Jackson, "Annual Message," December 7, 1835, in *A Compilation of the Messages and Papers of the Presidents*, vol. 3, comp., James D. Richardson (Washington, DC: Bureau of National Literature and Art, 1937), 172–73.

85. See Gloria Jahoda, *The Trail of Tears: The Story of the American Indian Removal, 1813–1855* (New York: Wings Books, 1995), 48–49.

86. Andrew Jackson, Talk to Cherokee," March 1835, in Remini, *Indian Wars*, 266.

87. Jackson disdained the Supreme Court—and particularly Chief Justice Marshall—and considered it a "fortress of conservatism." He was often fond of "colliding with the court" over issues of presidential authority. Arthur M. Schlesinger, Jr., *The Age of Jackson* (New York: Book Find Club, 1945), 322–23.

88. Andrew Jackson, "Letter to Colonel Anthony Butler, March 6, 1832," *Correspondence of Andrew Jackson*, vol. 4, ed. John Spencer Bassett (Washington, DC: Carnegie Institution of Washington, 1929), 415.

89. John Marshall, "To Joseph Story, May 1, 1828," *Papers of John Marshall*, vol. 11, ed. Charles F. Hobson (Chapel Hill: University of North Carolina Press, 2002), 94.

90. See Tadd M. Johnson and James Hamilton, "Sovereignty and the Native American Nation: Self-Governance for Indian Tribes—From Paternalism to Empowerment." *Conn. L.Rev.* 27 1253 (1995): 166–67.; and Olken, "Chief Justice John Marshall."

91. The legal question at stake in *Johnson v. McIntosh* was whether American Indians held land rights and could subsequently sell land, or whether the United States' encroachment into and annexation of the land superceded any former Native title. The Court "found that such a sale [of land by Natives] was not legal, precisely because, in the opinion of the Court, the United States held absolute title to Indian lands." Eric Cheyfitz, "Doctrines of Discovery," *Common-Place* 2, no. 1 (2001): 3. The primary legal consequence of *Johnson* was the transfer of Indian land ownership from tribal authority to the United States. The Court admitted Natives were "occupants" of land, but with the caveat that "their rights to complete sovereignty, as independent nations, were necessarily diminished, and their power to dispose of the soil at their own will, to whomsoever they pleased, was denied "by the fundamental principle of discovery." Cheyfitz, "Doctrines of Discovery," 1. Marshall's rhetoric pointed to a paternalism that blocked American Indian empowerment. His insistence on the doctrine of discovery as law solidified the European narrative of the conquest of America.

92. "Report of the Joint Committee in the Legislature of Georgia on Cherokee Lands," *Cherokee Phoenix* 1, no. 3 (March 6, 1828): 1, col. 4b. See also n. 74 and n. 75 above.

93. 30 U.S. 1 (1831), *Cherokee Nation v. State of Georgia*.

94. Ibid.

95. The Constitution of the United States, 28.

96. 30 U.S. 1 (1831), *Cherokee Nation v. State of Georgia*.

97. Ibid.

98. Ibid.

99. James Monroe, "Monroe Doctrine—Annual Message of 1823," in *A Documentary History of the United States*, 7d., ed. Richard D. Heffner (New York: Signet, 2002), 96–98.

100. 30 U.S. 1 (1831), *Cherokee Nation v. State of Georgia.*

101. Ibid.

102. James Boyd White quoted in Jody Freeman, "Constitutive Rhetoric: Law as a Literary Activity," *Harvard Woman's Law Journal* 14 (1991): 307.

103. Wilkins, *American Indian Sovereignty and the U.S. Supreme Court*, 44–45.

104. Olken, "Chief Justice John Marshall," 746.

105. 31 U.S. 515 (1832), *Worcester v. State of Georgia.*

106. Johnson and Hamilton, "Sovereignty and the Native American Nation," 1253.

107. Prucha, *Great Father* [abridged], 31–40.

108. Remini, *Andrew Jackson and His Indian Wars*, 257.

109. Haig A. Bosmajian, "Defining the 'American Indian': A Case Study in the Language of Suppression," *The Speech Teacher* 21 (March 1973): 92.

CHAPTER THREE

1. Francis Paul Prucha, *American Indian Treaties: The History of a Political Anomaly* (Berkeley: University of California Press, 1994), 24–27. Readers should bear in mind that treaties and Native reactions to land cessions also occurred prior to the colonies' movement for independence. Since this study focuses on Native-U.S. relations, though, it traces the "first" treaty between the United States and American Indian nations to the Delaware Treaty of 1778. For more information on North American Native treaties with the English, French and the Dutch, see Wilcomb E. Washburn, ed., *The American Indian and the United States: A Documentary History*, vol. 4 (New York: Random House, 1973).

2. William Unrau, *The Kaw People* (Phoenix: Indian Tribal Series, 1975), 116.

3. The Treaty of Hopewell in 1785 represents the quintessential example of such promises of moratoria on Native removals. "Treaty of Hopewell (1785)" in *The American Indian and the United States: A Documentary History*, vol. 4, ed. Wilcomb E. Washburn (New York: Random House, 1973), 2275.

4. Frederick Hoxie, ed., *Talking Back to Civilization: Indian Voices from the Progressive Era* (Boston: Bedford/St. Martin's, 2001), vii.

5. See Jason Edward Black, "Native Resistive Rhetoric and the Decolonization of American Indian Removal Discourse," *Quarterly Journal of Speech* 95, no. 1 (2009): 70–71.

6. Alisse Portnoy, *Their Right to Speak: Women's Activism in the Indian and Slave Debates* (Cambridge: Harvard University Press, 2005), 63–64.

7. Andrew Jackson, "Second Annual Message," December 6, 1830, in *U.S. House Journal* (6 Dec. 1830), 25.

8. Siobhan Senier, *Voices of American Indian Assimilation and Resistance* (Norman: University of Oklahoma Press, 2001), 19; 21.

9. The Cherokee Nation is separated into an independent analytical section because it presented "the most controversial episode in the actual emigration to the West" (Prucha, *The Great* Father, 85). This was so because the Cherokee Nation had assimilated the most to United States standards and demands; they had—for instance—formulated a constitution, a written syllabary, a republican government, and likewise boasted high populations of literate, agrarian and Christian citizens, many of whom identified as at least partially Anglo. Donna Hightower, *The Native American World* (Hoboken, NJ: Wiley and Sons, 2003), 147.

10. Indian Removal Act (1830), *U.S. Statutes at Large*, vol. 4, 411–12.

11. Ronald Satz, *American Indian Policy in the Jacksonian Era* (Lincoln: University of Nebraska Press, 1975), 78–79.

12. Recall that one of the primary removal opponents in the Senate, Theodore Frelinghuysen, argued that such imperialism over American Indians was detrimental to U.S. governmental ideals of equality and trust. He noted, "The time has come when this unbought treasure shall be plucked from dishonor" and made better by leaving Native communities to their homelands. Theodore Frelinghuysen, Remarks, April 9, 1830, *Gales & Seaton's Register of Debates in Congress*, Senate (April 9, 1830), 312.

13. Andrew Jackson, "Second Annual Message," December 6, 1830, in *U.S. House Journal* (6 Dec. 1830), 25.

14. Francis Paul Prucha, *American Indian Treaties: The History of a Political Anomaly* (Berkeley: University of California Press, 1994), 2.

15. For a classic study of Choctaw culture and politics during this time period, see the staple Angie Debo, *The Rise and Fall of the Choctaw Republic* (Norman: University of Oklahoma Press, 1934). Another good account of Choctaw politics leading into removal is Greg O'Brien, *Choctaws in a Revolutionary Age, 1750–1830* (Lincoln: University of Oklahoma Press, 2002). Readers seeking more on Choctaw spirituality are encouraged to access Tom Mould, *Choctaw Prophecy: A Legacy for the Future* (Tuscaloosa: University of Alabama Press, 2003).

16. John Eaton, "Secretary of War Annual Report (1830)" in *American State Papers*, vol. 4, serial 458, 286.

17. "Treaty of Dancing Rabbit Creek (1830)" in *The American Indian and the United States: A Documentary History*, vol. 4, ed. Wilcomb E. Washburn (New York: Random House, 1973), 2423–2436.

18. *American Creeds* refers to "the set of great democratic, legal and individualist beliefs and principles on which the American state and constitution is founded." These principles are said to be providential and nearly "natural" in the American experience. Furthermore, such principles are held to be exceptional and helps raise the United States as a model of/to the free world. See Anatol Lieven, *American Right or Wrong: An Anatomy of American Nationalism* (New York: Oxford University Press, 2004), 5.

19. Ames was a member of the Choctaw Nation of Mississippi and was an occasional contributor to the *Cherokee Phoenix*. Though no record of him exists in the academic literature, the coincidence of his name with Edward Raymond Ames (a white Methodist Episcopal reverend who lived in Mississippi and married a Choctaw woman), indicates that he may have been related to this family in some way. "Mixed blood" among the "five civilized tribes" and Europeans was not uncommon by the early nineteenth century. See Theda Perdue, *Mixed Blood Indians: Racial Construction in the Early South* (Athens: University of Georgia Press, 2002).

20. Ames, "The Choctaws," *Cherokee Phoenix* 2, no. 37 (December 23, 1830): 2, col. 2a–4b.

21. "The Constitution of the United States," Art. 1, sec.8 and Art I, sec 10 in *A Documentary History of the United States*, ed. Richard Heffner (New York: Signet, 2002), 22–23.

22. Ames, "The Choctaws."

23. Ibid.

24. Pushmataha was a major chief of the Choctaw Nation from the 1810s to the 1820s. He fought on the side of the United States during the War of 1812 and opposed Tecumseh's quest for pan-Indianism in 1811. Eckert discusses the two leaders' debate in depth, as does Lincecum. See Allan Eckert, A *Sorrow in Our Heart: The Life of Tecumseh* (New York: Bantam, 1993) and Gideon Lincecum, *Pushmataha: A Choctaw Leader and His People* (Tuscaloosa: University of Alabama Press, 2004). Pushmataha thus began his relationship with the U.S. government amicably, but

he began challenging the government to engage in removal more responsibly. Puckshunnubbee appears as a co-author with Pushmataha in at least one more editorial in the *Cherokee Phoenix*. Pushmataha and Puckshunnubbee's open letter is a plea for sovereignty in the face of continued efforts on the part of the U.S. government to motivate a voluntary removal of the Choctaw Nation.

25. Pushmataha and Puckshunnubbee, "For the Cherokee Phoenix," *Cherokee Phoenix* 2, no. 29 (September 22, 1829): 2, col. 2b

25. For instance, Jefferson declared to Congress his desire to assimilate Native nations by "leading them thus to agriculture, to manufactures, and civilization . . . and preparing them ultimately to participate in the benefits of our Government." Thomas Jefferson, "Letter on Indian Trading Houses, January 18, 1803," in *A Compilation of the Messages and Papers of the Presidents*, vol. 1, comp., James D. Richardson (Washington, DC: Bureau of National Literature and Art, 1937), 341.

27. Pushmataha and Puckshunnubbee, "For the Cherokee Phoenix," 2, col. 2b

28. George Harkins, "Farewell Letter to the American People (1832)," *The American Indian* 1, no. 3 (December 1926), 7, 12.

29. Ibid.

30. Edward Pessen, *Jacksonian America: Society, Personality, and Politics* (Urbana: University of Illinois Press, 1985), 297.

31. Theodore Frelinghuysen, Remarks, April 9, 1830, *Gales & Seaton's Register of Debates in Congress*, Senate (April 9, 1830), 312.

32. Homi Bhabha, *Nations and Narration* (London: Routledge, 1990), 145.

33. William Storr, Remarks, May 15, 1830, *Gales & Seaton's Register of Debates in Congress*, House (May 15, 1830), 998.

34. U.S. Congress, 23d, 1st session, *Senate Document* 512, vol. 1, 240.

35. Ibid.

36. "Treaty of Doak's Stand (1828)" in *The American Indian and the United States: A Documentary History*, vol. 4, ed. Wilcomb E. Washburn (New York: Random House, 1973), 2377.

37. For more on Creek history and politics, see Angie Debo, *The Road to Disappearance: A History of the Creek Indians* (Norman: University of Oklahoma Press, 1941); Michael D. Green, *The Creeks: A Critical Bibliography* (Bloomington: Indiana University Press, 1979); Michael D. Green, *The Politics of Indian Removal: Creek Government and Society in Crisis* (Lincoln: University of Nebraska Press, 1982); Harvey H. Jackson, III., *Rivers of History: Life on the Coosa, Tallapoosa, Cahaba, and Alabama* (Tuscaloosa: University of Alabama Press, 1995); and Robbie Ethridge, *Creek Country: The Creek Indians and Their World* (Chapel Hill: University of North Carolina Press, 2003).

38. Robert V. Remini, *Andrew Jackson and His Indian Wars* (New York: Penguin, 2001), 84–86.

39. John Coffee, "Talk to the Creek and Chickasaw (September 18, 1830)," quoted in Arrell Gibson, *The Chickasaws* (Norman: University of Oklahoma Press, 1971), 154.

40. Wilcomb E. Washburn, "Introduction," in *The American Indian and the United States: A Documentary History*, vol. 4, ed. Wilcomb E. Washburn (New York: Random House, 1973), 2448.

41. "Pontitock Creek Treaty (March 24, 1832)" in *The American Indian and the United States: A Documentary History*, vol. 4, ed. Wilcomb E. Washburn (New York: Random House, 1973), 2449.

42. Black, "Native Resistive Rhetoric," 73.

43. Levi Colbert was a half-blood chief of the Chickasaw Nation throughout the 1820s and 1830s and was one of the principle figures in negotiating the Treaty of Ponticock Creek in 1832. Apparently, Colbert fought for tribal separatism, but later moved toward conciliation with the U.S. government as removal seemed in inevitable in 1829. See H.B. Cushman, *History of the*

Choctaw, Chickasaw, and Natchez Indians (Norman: University of Oklahoma Press, 1999), 17. Colbert spoke English, based on his assimilation with settlers along the upper Mississippi and Alabama borders (Fulsom Charles Scrivner, *Early Chickasaws: Profile in Courage* (New York: Vantage Press, 2006). Colbert's "Plea" was a response to the government's early efforts to remove the Chickasaw Nation through a voluntary removal process. Mention of this text was first found in Anne Kelley Hoyt, *Bibliography of the Chickasaw* (Lanham, MD: Rowman and Littlefield, 1987).

44. Levi Colbert, "Plea from the Chickasaw," in *Native American Testimony: A Chronicle of Indian-White Relations from Prophecy to the Present, 1492–2000*, ed. Peter Nabokov (New York: Penguin, 1999), 151–52.

45. Peleg Sprague, Remarks, April 17, 1830, *Gales & Seaton's Register of Debates in Congress*, Senate (April 17, 1830), 356.

46. Levi Colbert, "Plea from the Chickasaw," 151–52.

47. The Constitution of the United States, 18.

48. Tuske-Ne-Hau (Creek), Hopithle-Ho-Lo (Creek) and others, "To the Citizens of Alabama and Georgia," *Cherokee Phoenix* 2, no. 22 (September 2, 1829): 2, col. 1b.

49. David Rich Lewis, *Neither Wolf Nor Dog: American Indians, Environment and Agrarian Change* (New York: Oxford University Press, 1994), 10.

50. R. Douglas Hurt, *The Indian Frontier, 1763–1846* (Albuquerque: University of New Mexico Press, 2002), xiv.

51. Lumpkin's Remarks, May 17, 1830, *Gales & Seaton's Register of Debates in Congress*, House (May 17, 1830), 1016.

52. Tisho Mingo, William M'Gilvery and Stimoluet, "Indian Emigration," in *Cherokee Phoenix* 1, no. 16 (June 11, 1828): 2, col. 1–2.

53. Mingo, McGilvery and Stimoluet were colleagues of Levi Colbert, all of whom engaged in a letter writing campaign against the U.S. government's removal policy. Mingo et al. wrote their open letter in the *Cherokee Phoenix* seemingly as a response to U.S. Indian agents demanding a voluntary removal treaty prior to the election of Andrew Jackson. No mention of these names in particular are noted in Cushman, *History of the Choctaw, Chickasaw and Natchez Indians*, though the book does discuss Colbert having confederates in his anti-removal campaigns.

54. Shullushoma, "It's Been a Great Many Years," in U.S. Congress, 23d, 1st session, *Senate Document* 512, vol.1, 240.

55. Yoholo, Tuckaubatchie Hajo, Tustenuggee, Smut Eye, et. al., "Memorial of the Creek Nation of Indians," in *Cherokee Phoenix* 2, no. 48 (March 17, 1830): 4, col. 1a–4b.

56. Ibid.

57. J. Leitch Wright, *Creeks and Seminoles: The Destruction and Regeneration of the Muscogugle People* (Lincoln: University of Nebraska Press, 1986), 245.

58. Lewis Cass to the President of the United States, Department of War, January 23, 1832. National Archives, Record Group 75, Ratified Indian Treaty File No. 178, Item 2-T, Secretary of War, Letters Sent, vol. 9.

59. Prucha, *The Great Father*, abridged, 84.

60. "Treaty of Payne's Landing (May 9, 1832)" in *The American Indian and the United States: A Documentary History*, vol. 4, ed. Wilcomb E. Washburn (New York: Random House, 1973), 2443.

61. John K. Mahon and Brent R. Weisman, "Florida's Seminole and Miccosukee People," in *The New History of Florida*, ed. Michael Gannon (Gainesville: University of Florida Press, 1996), 192–93.

62. There is evidence to suggest that the U.S. government persuaded a desolate minority of the Seminole Nation's leadership to sign the treaty in exchange for food, clothing and money.

"Treaty of Fort Gibson (March 28, 1833)" in *The American Indian and the United States: A Documentary History*, vol. 4, ed. Wilcomb E. Washburn (New York: Random House, 1973), 2446.

63. Ter Ellington, *The Myth of the Noble Savage* (Berkeley: University of California Press, 2001), 64–65.

64. Coacoochee was a war chief of the Seminole Nation known mostly for his "prowess in battle," particularly during the Second Seminole War of 1835–1842. John Missall and Mary Lou Missall, *Seminole Wars: America's Longest Indian Conflict* (Gainesville: University Press of Florida, 2004), 41–69. During that time period, he also emerged as an outspoken and crafty leader whose railings against removal became legendary within Seminole and Creek circles. For more on Coacoochee's legacy, see Susan A. Miller, *Coacoochee's Bones: A Seminole Saga* (Lawrence: University Press of Kansas, 2003).

65. Coacoochee, "Speech to Removal Council," in John T. Sprague, *The Origin, Progress and Conclusion of the Florida War* (New York: D. Appleton and Company, 1847), 259–60.

66. Ibid.

67. Ibid.

68. Ibid.

69. Osceola, "To Thompson (October 23, 1834)," in Charles Coe, *Red Patriots: The Story of the Seminoles* (Cincinnati, OH: Editor Publishing, 1898), 91.

70. For more on Osceola's life and politics, see Alvin Josephy, *The Patriot Chiefs: A Chronicle of American Indian Resistance* (New York: Penguin, 1989), 197–207 (for his role in the Seminole Wars in particular); and Patricia Riles Wickman, *Osceola's Legacy* (Tuscaloosa: University of Alabama Press, 2006).

71. For a thorough, longitudinal story of Cherokee removal politics, see John Ehle, *Trail of Tears: The Rise and Fall of the Cherokee Nation* (New York: Anchor Books, 1988). See also the best and quintessential study of Cherokee Nation documents with headnotes, Theda Perdue and Michael D. Green, *The Cherokee Removal: A Brief History with Documents* (Boston: Bedford Books, 1995).

72. To this effect, the Cherokee Nation did the following: formed a national council with executive and legislative branches in 1794; adopted the English language into their internal laws in 1808; declared themselves a "republic" in 1817; implemented an alphabet in 1821; founded a Washington-style capital city at New Echota, Georgia in 1826; drafted a constitution (replete with the holding of a constitutional convention) in 1827; and supported a national newspaper in 1828. I am indebted to Konkle for compiling a concise list of the Cherokee Nation's republican efforts. See Maureen Konkle, *Writing Indian Nations: Native Intellectuals and Politics of Historiography, 1827–1863* (Chapel Hill: University of North Carolina Press, 2004). To get a sense of diplomatic historical evidence on this subject, see Civilization Fund Act, March 3, 1819, *U.S. Statutes at Large*, 3:516–517.

73. Gloria Jahoda, *The Trail of Tears: The Story of the American Indian Removals, 1813–1855* (New York: Wings Books, 1975), 42–45.

74. Andrew Jackson, "Talk to the Cherokees," March 6, 1835, in *The Correspondence of Andrew Jackson*, vol. 1, ed. John Spencer Bassett (Washington, DC: Carnegie, 1928), 86.

75. John Ross and William Hicks, "The Cherokees," in *Cherokee Phoenix*, vol 1: 44 (January 14, 1829): 1, col. 4b–5a.

76. John Ross, "Letter to Lewis Cass, March 9, 1835," in Gary Moulton, ed., *The Papers of Chief John Ross*, vol. 1 (Norman: University of Oklahoma Press, 1985), 332–333.

77. James Monroe, "Special Message to Congress," January 27, 1825, in *A Compilation of the Messages and Papers of the Presidents*, vol. 2, comp., James D. Richardson Washington, DC: Bureau of National Literature and Art, 1937, 280.

78. Cherokee Council, "The Cherokees," in *Cherokee Phoenix* 1, no. 44 (January 14, 1829): 1, col. 4b–5a.

79. Wood Pecker, Roman Nose, Locust, Timson, Samuel Ward, Situagee and Ball Town George, "To Aquohee District," in *Cherokee Phoenix* 1, no. 30 (September 24, 1838): 2, col. 4a.

80. The *Cherokee Phoenix* was founded in 1828 by Elias Boudinot, a Cherokee leader and expert in English and the Cherokee syllabary, in part to protest the impending removal controversy. The paper represented the anti-removal positions of the other "four tribes" in addition to the Cherokee Nation in Georgia. According to Grace Steele Woodward, the newspaper was sent to the U.S. Congress on a regular basis as well as "the four corners of the United States," thus prompting newspaper editors in New Orleans, New York, Washington City, Philadelphia, Boston, and Baltimore to reprint its editorials. Grace Steele Woodward, *The Cherokees* (Norman: University of Oklahoma Press, 1963), 168. The newspaper's reach to white Americans therefore may have been somewhat widespread. For more on the *Cherokee Phoenix* and its influence on the U.S. government and public, see Theda Perdue, *Cherokee Editor: The Writings of Elias Boudinot* (Athens: University of Georgia Press, 1996), which in addition to providing background details about the paper, includes most of its vital anti-removal editorials.

81. Elias Boudinot, "To the Publics," in *Cherokee Phoenix* 1, no. 1 (February 21, 1828): 3, col. 2b–4.

82. Ibid.

83. John Ridge, quoted in John Ehle, *Trail of Tears: The Rise and Fall of the Cherokee Nation* (New York: Doubleday, 1988), 254.

84. Elias Bouinot, "New Echota Editorial," in *Cherokee Phoenix* 1, no. 6 (March 27, 1828): 3, col. 1b.

85. T. Hartley Crawford, "Report of the Commissioner of Indian Affairs (November 25, 1838)" in *The American Indian and the United States: A Documentary History*, vol. 1, ed. Wilcomb E. Washburn (New York: Random House, 1973), 31.

86. Elias Boudinot, "Editorial (November 12, 1831)" in Perdue, *Cherokee Editor*, 142.

87. See Gary Moulton, *John Ross, Cherokee Chief* (Athens: University of Georgia Press, 1978).

88. John Ross, "Annual Message, October 14, 1829," in Gary Moulton, ed., *The Papers of Chief John Ross*, vol. 1 (Norman: University of Oklahoma Press, 1985), 169. There is evidence to suggest that Ross sent his annual messages to both the U.S. Congress and the Executive. Regardless, given the U.S. government's interest in obtaining Cherokee territory, it is highly likely that federal Indian agents monitored closely the Cherokee president's discourse (Moulton, *John Ross, Cherokee Chief*).

89. Prucha, *American Indian Treaties*, 2.

90. *Cherokee Nation v. Georgia* (1831), 5 Peters 15–20.

91. John Ross, "Annual Message, November 11, 1831," in Gary Moulton, ed., *The Papers of Chief John Ross*, vol. 1 (Norman: University of Oklahoma Press, 1985), 169.

92. Theodore Frelinghuysen, Remarks, April 9, 1830, *Gales & Seaton's Register of Debates in Congress*, Senate (April 9, 1830), 312.

93. Moral suasion is an appeal "to the moral vision of the people" that includes pathos, natural law, and Christianity. William E. Cain, ed., *William Lloyd Garrison and the Fight Against Slavery—Selections from* The Liberator (Boston: Bedford, 1995), 28.

94. John Ross, "Letter to Andrew Jackson, March 12, 1834," in Gary Moulton, ed., *The Papers of Chief John Ross*, vol. 1 (Norman: University of Oklahoma Press, 1985), 279.

95. Ibid.

96. Ibid.

97. John Ross, "Letter to Lewis Cass, February 29, 1836," in Gary Moulton, ed., *The Papers of Chief John Ross*, vol. 1 (Norman: University of Oklahoma Press, 1985), 388.

98. Amy Kaplan, *Anarchy of Empire in the Making of U.S. Culture* (Cambridge, MA: Harvard University Press, 2002), 16.

99. Ross, "Letter to Lewis Cass, February 29, 1836," 388.

100. William Medill, "Annual Report of the Commissioner of Indian Affairs (November 30, 1848)," in *House Executive Document*, no. 1, 30th Congress, 2d session, serial 537, 387.

101. See Treaty of Fort Stanwix (October 22, 1784), 7 Stat. 15.; and Northwest Ordinance (July 13, 1787), National Archives Microfilm Publication, M332, roll 9.

102. Chippewa Removal Song, in John Trent Irving, Jr., *Indian Sketches Taken During an Expedition to the Pawnee Tribes* [1833] (Norman: University of Oklahoma Press, 1955), 27.

103. Brian W. Dippie, *The Vanishing American: White Attitudes and U.S. Indian Policy* (Lawrence: University of Kansas Press, 1982), 73.

104. Organization of the Department of Indian Affairs (June 30, 1834), *U.S. Statutes at Large*, 4: 735–38.

105. Ohio Wyandot Council, "Speech on Removal," in U.S. Congress, 23d, 1st session, *Senate Document* 512, vol. 2, 597.

106. Indian Affairs had been housed in the War Department; when the Department of the Interior was formulated in 1849 the Taylor Administration dismantled the War Department. See Prucha, *American Indian Treaties*, 15; and the "Transfer of Indian Affairs to the Department of the Interior" (March 3, 1849), *U.S. Statutes at Large*, 9:395.

107. According to social critic Kenneth Burke, with mortification, we find "'the subjection of the passions and appetites, by penance, abstinence or painful severities inflicted on the body,' mortification as a kind of governance, an extreme form of 'self-control,' the deliberate, disciplinary 'slaying' of any motive that, for 'doctrinal' reasons, one thinks of as unruly." Kenneth Burke, *The Rhetoric of Religion: Studies in Logology* (Berkeley: University of California Press, 1970), 289.

108. See Cecil Eby, "*That Disgraceful Affair*"—*The Black Hawk War* (New York: Norton, 1972); Miriam Gurko, *Indian America: The Black Hawk War* (New York: Crowell, 1970); and William T. Hagan, *The Sac and Fox Indians* (Norman: University of Oklahoma Press, 1988).

109. Autobiographies of Native leaders in the nineteenth century can offer problems, as they are typically ghost-written or co-written. Unfortunately, sometimes the only accounts we have extant and available are these sources. Readers will note that I do not make arguments about Black Hawk's intent here. Rather, as discussed in this book's Introduction, I treat discourses like Black Hawk's autobiography as a relict of the Native and U.S. governmental voices mingling during this context and time period. For more on the difficulties of reporting such histories, see Linda Tuhiwai Smith, *Decolonizing Methodologies: Research and Indigenous Peoples* (London: Zed Books, 2007), 30–31.

110. Donald Jackson, "Introduction," *Black Hawk: An Autobiography*, ed. Donald Jackson (Urbana-Champaign: University of Illinois Press, 1964), 15.

111. Black Hawk, *Black Hawk: An Autobiography*, ed. Donald Jackson (Urbana-Champaign: University of Illinois Press, 1964), 112.

112. See Hightower-Langston, *The Native American*, 335–37; Jackson, "Introduction"; Remini, *Andrew Jackson*, 258–61; Satz, *American Indian Policy*, 113–14; and W.C. Vanderwerth (ed.), *Indian Oratory: Famous Speeches by Noted Indian Chieftains* (Norman: University of Oklahoma Press, 1989), 90.

113. Jason Edward Black, "Native Authenticity, Rhetorical Circulation, and Neocolonial Decay: The Case of Chief Seattle's Controversial Speech," *Rhetoric & Public Affairs* 15, no. 4 (2012): 639.

114. Black Hawk, *Black Hawk's Autobiography*, ed. Roger L. Nichols (Ames: Iowa State University Press, 1999), 7.

115. For more, see Jason Edward Black, "Symbolic Suicide as Mortification, Transformation, and Counterstatement: The Conciliatory (Yet) Resistant Surrender of Maka-tai-mesh-ekia-kiak," *Kenneth Burke Journal* 2, no. 1 (2005): 3.

116. Homi Bhabha, *Location of Culture* (London: Routledge, 1994), 154.

117. Black Hawk, *Autobiography*, 52.

118. Ibid.

119. Black Hawk, *Autobiography*, 88.

120. Black Hawk, *Autobiography*, 52.

121. Black Hawk, *Autobiography*, 79.

122. Mikhail Bakhtin, *The Dialogic Imagination: Four Essays*, ed. Michael Holquist, trans. Caryl Emerson and Michael Holquist (Austin: University of Texas Press, 1981), 344.

123. Maureen Konkle, *Writing Indian Nations: Native Intellectuals and the Politics of Historiography, 1827–1863* (Chapel Hill: University of North Carolina Press, 2004), 5.

124. Jana Sequoya Magdaleno, "How (!) Is An Indian? A Contest of Stories, Round 2," *Postcolonial Theory and the United States: Race, Ethnicity and Literature*, ed. Amritjit Singh and Peter Schmidt (Jackson: University Press of Mississippi, 2000), 286–87.

125. Arnold Krupat, *Red Matters: Native American Studies* (Philadelphia: University of Pennsylvania Press, 2002), 215.

126. Joy Harjo and Gloria Bird, "Introduction," in *Reinventing the Enemy's Language: Contemporary Native Women's Writings of North America*, ed. Joy Harjo and Gloria Bird (New York: W.W. Norton, 1997), 25.

127. The implications of many of these issues are discussed in Duane Champagne, *Social Order and Political Change: Constitutional Governments among the Cherokee, the Choctaw, the Chickasaw, and the Creek* (Stanford, CA: Stanford University Press, 1992).

CHAPTER FOUR

1. Frederick Hoxie, *A Final Promise: The Campaign to Assimilate the Indians, 1880–1920* (Lincoln: University of Nebraska Press, 1984), xviii.

2. Grover Cleveland, "Second Annual Message," December 6, 1886 in *A Compilation of the Messages and Papers of the Presidents*, vol. 8, comp., James D. Richardson (Washington, DC: Bureau of National Literature and Art, 1937), 519.

3. Ibid.

4. Frederick Jackson Turner, *The Significance of the Frontier in American History*, ed. S. P. Langley, Annual Report of the American Historical Association for the Year 1893 (Washington, DC: Government Printing Office, 1894): 200.

5. William T. Sherman, "End of the Indian Problem" in *House Executive Document* no. 1, 48th Congress, 1st session, serial 2182, 45–46. It is not my intention to report on the history of the "Indian Wars" between the 1850s and the 1880s. Historians have done a great deal of thorough research in this area. For more information on such military confrontations, see Dee Brown, *Bury My Heart at Wounded Knee: An Indian History of the America West* (New York: Henry Holt, 2000); William Osborn, *The Wild Frontier* (New York: Random House 2000); Robert M. Utley, *The Indian Frontier of the American West, 1846–1890* (Albuquerque: University of New Mexico Press, 1984); and Bill Yenne, *Indian Wars: The Campaign for the American West* (Yardley, PA: Westholme, 2005).

6. Ibid.

7. Brian W. Dippie, *The Vanishing American: White Attitudes and U.S. Indian Policy* (Lawrence: University of Kansas Press, 1982), 141.

8. Henry Dawes, "Solving the Indian Problem," in Fifteenth Annual Report of the Board of Indian Commissioners (1883), 69–70.

9. Thomas Skinner, Debate on Bill to Provide Lands in Severalty, December 15–16 and January 18, 25, 1887, in *The American Indian and the United States: A Documentary History*, vol. 4, ed. Wilcomb E. Washburn (New York: Random House, 1973), 1849.

10. General Allotment Act (1887), *U.S. Statutes at Large*, vol. 24, 388–91.

11. Speaking of such inconsistencies of U.S. citizenship, Mary Stuckey has argued that Progressive Era presidents, like Woodrow Wilson, issued "seemingly inclusive" constructions of citizenship, even going so far as to demand a "universalizing" of the U.S. citizenry regardless of ethnically hyphenated identities. In the end, though, this institutional discourse "served as a means for silencing" people of color and immigrants, thereby demonstrating how a "universal" conception of U.S. citizenship could "nonetheless be an exclusionary one." Mary Stuckey, "'The Domain of Public Conscience': Woodrow Wilson and the Establishment of a Transcendent Political Order," *Rhetoric and Public Affairs* 6, no. 1 (2005) 2.

12. The population west of the Mississippi grew substantially from seven to eleven million in the 1870s alone; these numbers increased four-fold by the dawn the twentieth century (Hoxie, *A Final Promise*, 43). See also, D.S. Otis, *The Dawes Act and the Allotment of Indian Lands* (Norman: University of Oklahoma Press, 1973).

13. Turner, *The Significance of the Frontier*, 3.

14. Francis Paul Prucha, *The Great Father: The United States Government and the American Indians*, abd. (Lincoln: University of Nebraska Press, 1986), 118.

15. William Medill, "Annual Report of the Commissioner of Indian Affairs," November 30 1848, *House Executive Document* no. 1, 30th Congress, 2d session, serial 537, 386.

16. Report of the Doolittle Commission, January 26, 1867, in *Senate Report* no. 156, 39th Congress, 2d session, serial 1279, 3–10.

17. Ibid.

18. Report of the Indian Peace Commission, January 7, 1868, in *House Executive Document* no. 97, 40th Congress, 2d session, serial 1337, 15–17.

19. The Homestead Act, May 20, 1862, 37th Congress, 2d session, Chapter 75.

20. Columbus Delano, "Report of the Secretary of the Interior, November 23, 1874, *House Executive Document* no. 1, part 5, 43-2, serial 1639, v, vii.

21. Found in Brad Agnew, "Voices from the Land Run of 1889," *The Chronicles of Oklahoma* 67 (1989): 4

22. Alisse Portnoy, *Their Right to Speak: Women's Activism in the Indian and Slave Debates* (Cambridge: Harvard University Press, 2005), 132–33.

23. For more on this construct, see Jason Edward Black, "Authoritarian Fatherhood: Andrew Jackson's Early Familial Lectures to America's 'Red Children,'" *Journal of Family History* 30, no. 3 (2005): 248.

24. John Demos, "The Changing Faces of Fatherhood: A New Exploration in family History," in *Father and Child: Developmental and Clinical Perspectives*, ed. Stanley Cath, Alan Gurwitt and John Munder Ross (Boston: Little and Brown, 1982), 427.

25. Linda Kerber, "The Republican Mother: Women and the Enlightenment—An American Perspective," *American Quarterly* 28, no. 2 (1976): 205.

26. Shawn Parry-Giles and Diane M. Blair, "The Rise of the Rhetorical First Lady: Politics, Gender Ideology and Women's Voice, 1789–2002," *Rhetoric and Public Affairs* 5, no. 4 (2002): 565.

27. Mary R. Jackman, *The Velvet Glove: Paternalism and Conflict in Gender, Class and Race Relations* (Berkeley: University of California Press, 1993), 13.

28. David Wilkins, *American Indian Sovereignty and the U.S. Supreme Court: The Masking of Justice* (Austin: University of Texas Press, 1999), 64.

29. Ivan Musicant, *Empire By Default: The Spanish-American War and the Dawn of the American Century* (New York: Henry Holt), 656.

30. General James Rusling, "Interview with President William McKinley," *The Christian Advocate* 22 (January 1903): 17.

31. Kristin L. Hoganson, *Fighting for American Manhood: How Gender Politics Provoked the Spanish-American and Philippine American Wars* (New Haven, CT: Yale University Press, 1998), 201.

32. George Manypenny, "Annual Report of the Commissioner of Indian Affairs," November 22 1856, *Senate Executive Document* no. 5, 34th Congress, 3d session, serial 875, 571–75.

33. John Q. Smith, "Annual Report of the Commissioner of Indian Affairs," October 30, 1876, *House Executive Document* no. 1, 44th Congress, 2d session, serial 1749, vii–xi.

34. Ezra Hayt, "To Secretary of the Interior Carl Schurz, January 24, 1879," in *That the People Might Live: Native American Literatures and Native American Community*, ed. Jace Weaver. London: Oxford University Press, 1997, 87.

35. Ibid.

36. Rutherford B. Hayes, "Third Annual Message, December 1, 1879," in *Great Debates in American History, Civil Rights*, part two, volume VIII., ed. Marion Mills Miller (New York: Little and Ives, 1913), 287.

37. Hayt, "To Secretary of the Interior Carl Schurz," 2–3.

38. Carl Schurz, "Annual Report of the Secretary of the Interior," December 7, 1879, *House Executive Document* no. 1, part 5, 46th Congress, 2d session, serial 1910, 5–6.

39. Ibid.

40. Ibid.

41. Carl Schurz, "Present Aspects of the Indian Problem," *North American Review CXXXIII* (July 1881): 6.

42. Carl Schurz, "Annual Report of the Secretary of the Interior," November 1, 1880, *House Executive Document* no. 1, 46th Congress, 3d session, serial 1959, 3–4; 11–13.

43. Chester A. Arthur, "Annual Message to Congress," December 6, 1881, in *A Compilation of the Messages and Papers of the Presidents*, vol. 8, comp., James D. Richardson (New York: Bureau of National Literature and Art, 1937), 54. Emphasis mine.

44. According to Prucha, by the 1870s and 1880s, the executive branch, through the Interior and its bureaus, overwhelmingly administrated the Native-U.S. relationship and Native policies (Prucha, *Great Father* abd., 224–28).

45. Francis Paul Prucha, *The Great Father: The United States Government and the American Indians*, unabd. (Lincoln: University of Nebraska Press, 1986), 664.

46. Coke Bill of 1881, in Henry S. Pancoast, *Indian Land in Severalty As Provided For By the Coke Bill*, 46th Congress,1st session, S. 48 (Philadelphia, 1884), 3–7.

47. Ibid.

48. Coke Bill of 1881, 3–7.

49. Ibid.

50. Richard Coke, in U.S. Congress, Senate, Debate on Bill to provide Lands in Severalty, January 20, 1881 from Congressional Record, 46th Congress, 3d session, as reprinted in *The American Indian and the United States: A Documentary History*, vol. 4, ed. Wilcomb E. Washburn (New York: Random House, 1973), 1700–1704.

51. George Vest, in U.S. Congress, Senate, Debate on Bill to provide Lands in Severalty, January 20, 1881 from Congressional Record, 46th Congress, 3d session, as reprinted in *The American Indian and the United States: A Documentary History*, vol. 4, ed. Wilcomb E. Washburn (New York: Random House, 1973), 1700–1704.

52. Alvin Saunders, in U.S. Congress, Senate, Debate on Bill to provide Lands in Severalty, January 20, 1881 from Congressional Record, 46th Congress, 3d session, as reprinted in *The*

American Indian and the United States: A Documentary History, vol. 4, ed. Wilcomb E. Washburn (New York: Random House, 1973), 1700–1704.

53. Ibid.

54. Richard Coke, in U.S. Congress, Senate, Debate on Bill to provide Lands in Severalty, January 20, 1881 from Congressional Record, 46th Congress, 3d session, as reprinted in *The American Indian and the United States: A Documentary History,* vol. 4, ed. Wilcomb E. Washburn (New York: Random House, 1973), 1700–1704.

55. Ibid.

56. Henry Teller, in U.S. Congress, Senate, Debate on Bill to provide Lands in Severalty, January 20, 1881 from Congressional Record, 46th Congress, 3d session, as reprinted in *The American Indian and the United States: A Documentary History,* vol. 4, ed. Wilcomb E. Washburn (New York: Random House, 1973), 1700–1704.

57. Ibid.

58. John Morgan, in U.S. Congress, Senate, Debate on Bill to provide Lands in Severalty, January 20, 1881 from Congressional Record, 46th Congress, 3d session, as reprinted in *The American Indian and the United States: A Documentary History,* vol. 4, ed. Wilcomb E. Washburn (New York: Random House, 1973), 1700–1704.

59. Morgan, in U.S. Congress, 1700–1704.

60. Grover Cleveland, "First Inaugural Address," March 4, 1885 in *The Inaugural Addresses of the Presidents,*" ed. John Gabriel Hunt (New York: Gramercy, 1997), 247.

61. J. D. C. Atkins, "Report of the Commissioner of Indian Affairs," October 5, 1885, in *The American Indian and the United States: A Documentary History,* vol. 3, ed. Wilcomb E. Washburn (New York: Random House, 1973), 357

62. Utley, *The Indian Frontier of the American West,* 213.

63. General Allotment Act (1887), *United States Statutes at Large,* 24, 388–91.

64. Henry L. Dawes, "Senate Arguments, December 15, 1886" reprinted in *Proceedings of the Fifth Annual Meeting of the Lake Mohonk Conference of the Friends of the Indian,* 1887 (Philadelphia, 1887), 12–13; 63–69.

65. Ibid.

66. Ibid.

67. Dawes, "Senate Arguments, December 15, 1886," 63–69.

68. Hoxie, *A Final Promise,* 71.

69. Thomas Skinner, Debate on Bill to Provide Lands in Severalty, December 15–16 and January 18, 25, 1887, in *The American Indian and the United States: A Documentary History,* vol. 4, ed. Wilcomb E. Washburn (New York: Random House, 1973), 1849.

70. Skinner, Debate on Bill, 1852.

71. Ibid.

72. Bishop Perkins, Debate on Bill to Provide Lands in Severalty, December 15, 1886, in *Congressional Record,* 49th Congress, 2d session, 191.

73. Prucha, *Great Father,* abd., 226.

74. Skinner, Debate on Bill, 1851.

75. William Springer, Debate on Bill to Provide Lands in Severalty, December 15–16 and January 18, 25, 1887, in *The American Indian and the United States: A Documentary History,* vol. 4, ed. Wilcomb E. Washburn (New York: Random House, 1973), 1863.

76. The Dawes Act of 1887, initially, did not extend allotment "to the territory occupied by the Cherokees, Creeks, Choctaws, Chickasaws . . . or Seminoles" (General Allotment Act [1887], *United States Statutes at Large,* 24, 388–91). This was so because they were already on their way toward agricultural assimilation. Over time, however, the government sought to "draw up rolls and allot lands to Indians on the rolls" to speed up assimilation among the five southeastern

nations (Prucha, *Documents of United States Indian Policy*, 197). This extension of the Dawes Act—the Curtis Act of 1898—provided that expediting allotment would grant "protection of the people of the Indian Territory." (Curtis Act [1898], 174 *U.S. Reports*, 445, 488–89).

77. Wilcomb E. Washburn, *The Assault on Indian Tribalism: The General Allotment Law (Dawes Act) of 1887* (Philadelphia: J. P. Lippincott, 1975), 68.

78. General Allotment Act (1887), *United States Statutes at Large*, 24, 388–391.

79. Ibid.

80. Demos, "The Changing Faces of Fatherhood," 427.

81. Ibid.

82. General Allotment Act (1887), *United States Statutes at Large*, 24, 388–91.

83. Ibid.

84. Dawes, Senate Arguments, 63–69.

85. Skinner, Debate on Bill, 1850.

86. Thomas J. Morgan, Report of the Commissioner of Indian Affairs, October 1, 1889, in *The American Indian and the United States: A Documentary History*, vol. 1, ed. Wilcomb E. Washburn (New York: Random House, 1973), 429.

87. Theodore Roosevelt, "A Proclamation: June 23, 1902," in *Indian Affairs: Laws and Treaties*, vol. 1, ed. Charles J. Kappler (Washington, DC: Government Printing Office, 1904).

88. John H. Oberly, Report of the Commissioner of Indian Affairs, December 3, 1888, in *The American Indian and the United States: A Documentary History*, vol. 1, ed. Wilcomb E. Washburn (New York: Random House, 1973), 422–23.

89. Ibid.

90. Ibid.

91. Morgan, Report of the Commissioner of Indian Affairs, October 1, 1889, 429.

92. Ethan Allen Hitchcock, Annual Report of the Department of the Interior, June 30, 1903, in *Indian Affairs: Laws and Treaties*, vol. 18, ed. Charles J. Kappler (Washington, DC: Government Printing Office, 1904), 2–3.

93. Ibid.

94. Thomas J. Morgan, Annual Report of the Commissioner of Indian Affairs, September 5, 1890 in *The American Indian and the United States: A Documentary History*, vol. 1, ed. Wilcomb E. Washburn (New York: Random House, 1973), 435.

95. Thomas J. Morgan, Annual Report of the Commissioner of Indian Affairs, October 1, 1891 in *The American Indian and the United States: A Documentary History*, vol. 1, ed. Wilcomb E. Washburn (New York: Random House, 1973), 529.

96. Dawes, Senate Arguments, 63–69.

97. 112 U.S. Reports, 98–99, 102, 109, *Elk v. Wilkins*. The Fourteenth Amendment stated that "all persons born . . . in the United States . . . are citizens of the United States" and that "no State shall make or enforce any law which shall abridge the privileges or immunities of citizens." The Constitution of the United States, in *A Documentary History of the United States*, ed. Richard Heffner (New York: Signet, 2002), 33.

98. 112 U.S. Reports, 98–99, 102, 109, *Elk v. Wilkins* (1884).

99. Major Crimes Act, *U.S. Statutes at Large*, 22, 385.

100. 118 U.S. Reports, 375, *United States v. Kagama* (1886).

101. Ibid.

102. 187 U.S. 553, *Lone Wolf v. Hitchcock* (1903). Emphasis mine.

103. Ann Laquer Estin, "*Lone Wolf v. Hitchcock*: The Long Shadow," in *The Aggressions of Civilization: Federal Indian Policy Since the 1880s*, ed. Sandra Cadwalader and Vine Deloria, Jr. (Philadelphia: Temple University Press, 1984), 216–17.

104. Jason Edward Black, "Plenary Rhetoric in Indian Country: The *Lone Wolf v. Hitchcock* Case and the Codification of a Weakened Native Character," *Advances in the History of Rhetoric* 11/12 (2008/2009): 74.

105. Senator Matthew Quay, "*Lone Wolf* Comments, 1903," in Russell L. Brash and James Y. Henderson, *The Road: Indian Tribes and Political Liberty* (Berkeley: University of California Press, 1980), 95.

106. 19 App. D.C. 315, *Lone Wolf v. Hitchcock* (1902).

107.18 App. D.C. 515, *Lone Wolf v. Hitchcock* (1901).

108. 187 U.S. 553, *Lone Wolf v. Hitchcock* (1903).

109. Ibid.

110. Blue Clark, *Lone Wolf v. Hitchcock: Treaty Rights and Indian Law at the End of the Nineteenth Century* (Lincoln: University of Nebraska Press, 1994), 6–10.

111. Ibid.

112. Ibid.

113. Wilkins *American Indian Sovereignty*, 65.

114. 187 U.S. 553, *Lone Wolf v. Hitchcock* (1903).

115. Clark contends that the commodification of American Indian labor and land was predicated on seizing more land for white settlers: "Setting a precedent, the Court held that Indian consent was no longer necessary and that Congress could unilaterally diminish Indian reservations. In effect, Congress was given a green light to force allotment in severalty upon reluctant Indian wards. Tribal property rights an tribal political authority became commodities that Congress controlled" (Blue Clark, *Lone Wolf v. Hitchcock*, 10–11).

116. 187 U.S. 553, *Lone Wolf v. Hitchcock* (1903).

CHAPTER FIVE

1. Quinney, "Fourth of July Address at Reidsville, New York, 1854" in *The American Indian* (January, 1928), n.p.

2. Ibid.

3. Red Cloud, "Speech at Cooper Union, July 16, 1870," *New York Times* (July 17, 1870): 6, col. 1.

4. Ibid.

5. Satank, "Teach Us the Road to Travel," *New York Daily Tribune* (Nov. 30, 1871), n.p.

6. Ibid.

7. Frederick Hoxie, *A Final Promise: The Campaign to Assimilate the Indians, 1880–1920* (Lincoln: University of Nebraska Press, 1984), xviii.

8. Elizabeth Rich, "Remember Wounded Knee: AIM's Use of Metonymy in 21st Century Protest," *College Literature* 31, no. 3 (2004): 73.

9. Brian W. Dippie, *The Vanishing American: White Attitudes and U.S. Indian Policy* (Lawrence: University of Kansas Press, 1982), 142.

10. Maureen Konkle, *Writing Indian Nations: Native Intellectuals and Politics of Historiography, 1827–1863* (Chapel Hill: University of North Carolina Press, 2004), 26.

11. Lucy Maddox, *Citizen Indians: Native American Intellectuals, Race and Reform* (Ithaca, NY: Cornell University Press, 2005), 9.

12. Amy Kaplan, *Anarchy of Empire in the Making of U.S. Culture* (Cambridge, MA: Harvard University Press, 2002), 12.

13. Peter Nabokov, *Native American Testimony: A Chronicle of Indian-White Relations From Prophecy to the Present, 1492–2000* (New York: Penguin Books, 1999), 216–17.

14. Hoxie, *Talking Back to Civilization*, viii.

15. Francis Paul Prucha, *The Indians in American Society: from the Revolutionary War to the Present* (Berkeley: University of California Press, 1988), 56–58.

16. William M. Clements, *Oratory in Native North America* (Tucson: University of Arizona Press, 2002), xv–xvii.

17. Susan Zaeske, *Signatures of Citizenship: Petitioning, Antislavery and Women's Political Identity* (Chapel Hill: University of North Carolina Press, 2003), 3.

18. Ibid.

19. Siobhan Senier, *Voices of American Indian Assimilation and Resistance: Helen Hunt Jackson, Sarah Winnemucca, and Victoria Howard* (Norman: University of Oklahoma Press, 2001), ix–x.

20. Carl Schurz, "Annual Report of the Secretary of the Interior," December 7, 1879, *House Executive Document* no. 1, part 5, 46th Congress, 2d session, serial 1910, 5–6.

21. John Forsyth, Remarks, April 15, 1830, *Gales & Seaton's Register of Debates in Congress*, Senate (April 14, 15, 1830), 326.

22. John E. O'Connor, "The White Man's Indian: An Institutional Approach," in *Hollywood's Indian: The Portrayal of the Native American in Film*, ed. Peter C. Rollins and John E. O'Connor (Lexington: University of Kentucky Press, 1998), 27–31.

23. Theodore Roosevelt, *An Autobiography* (New York: Macmillan, 1893), 94.

24. Siobhan Senier, "Allotment Protest and Tribal Discourse: Reading *Wynema's* Successes and Shortcomings," *American Indian Quarterly* 24, no. 3 (2000): 431.

25. Kathryn Shanley, "Writing Indian," in *Studying Native America: Problems and Prospects*, ed. Russell Thornton (Madison: University of Wisconsin Press, 1998), 146.

26. Lewis Gould, *The Tyranny of Change: America in the Progressive Era, 1890–1914* (Brunswick, NJ: Rutgers University Press, 2000), v.

27. Helen Hunt Jackson, *A Century of Dishonor: A Sketch of the United States Government's Dealings with Some of the Indian Tribes* (Norman: University of Oklahoma Press, 1995), 29.

28. Francis Paul Prucha, *Americanizing the American Indians: Writings by the Friends of the Indian, 1880–1900* (Cambridge, MA: Harvard University Press, 1973), iv.

29. Richard Henry Pratt, "Opening Comments," in *Official Report of the Nineteenth Annual Conference of Charities and Correction* (1892), 46–59. Reprinted in Richard Henry Pratt, "The Advantages of Mingling Indians with Whites," in Prucha, *Americanizing the American* Indians, 260. This move reflected the larger integration of immigrants, who were encouraged by Presidents Woodrow Wilson and Theodore Roosevelt to "lose their hyphens" and become "Americans" (Leroy G. Dorsey and Rachel Harlow, "'We Want Americans Pure and Simple': Theodore Roosevelt and the Myth of Americanism," *Rhetoric and Public Affairs* 6, no. 1 (2003): 55–78.

30. Maddox, *Citizen Indians*, 8.

31. Konkle, *Writing Indian Nations*, 5.

32. General Allotment Act (1887), *United States Statutes at Large*, 24, 388–91.

33. Ibid.

34. Howard Zinn, *A People's History of the United States: 1492–Present* (New York: HarperCollins, 2005), viii.

35. Curtis Act (1898), 174 *U.S. Reports*, 445, 488–89.

36. Choctaw Nation, "Congressional Memorial, February 17, 1894," Senate Committee on Indian Affairs File, RG233, HR53A-H13.3, box no. 141, Library of Congress.

37. Creek and Choctaw Indians of Oklahoma, "To the Committee on Indian Affairs—A Protest Against Allotment of Lands by the Full Blood Creek Indians, November 21, 1899," Senate Committee on Indian Affairs File, RG233, HR56A-H9.3, Library of Congress.

38. Creek and Seminole Nations, "To the Congress of the United States, 1890," Senate Committee on Indian Affairs File, RG233, HR54A-H13.1, box 193, Library of Congress.

39. Ibid.

40. Choctaw Nation. "Congressional Memorial."

41. Ibid.

42. Choctaw Nation, "Congressional Memorial."

43. Ibid.

44. Ibid.

45. Seminole Nation, "Memorial of the Seminole, February 6, 1897," Senate Committee on Indian Affairs File, RG233, HR54A-13.1, box 193, Library of Congress.

46. Cherokee Nation, "A Petition, January 29, 1897," Senate Committee on Indian Affairs File, RG233, HR54A-H13, box 192, Library of Congress.

47. Seminole Nation, "Memorial of the Seminole, February 6, 1897."

48. In discussing "western" Native nations, I refer particularly to the Sioux (Lakota, Dakota, Nakota), Leech Lake, Kiowa, Comanche, Apache, Winnebago, Ute, Nez Perce, Piute, Pottawatomie, Red Lake, Cheyenne, Crow and Pueblo nations among many, many others whose original homelands existed west of the Mississippi River.

49. George Manypenny, "Annual Report of the Commissioner of Indian Affairs," November 22 1856, *Senate Executive Document* no. 5, 34th Congress, 3d session, serial 875, 571–75.

50. Thomas Morgan, "Annual Report of the Commissioner of Indian Affairs, 1889," in *House Executive Document* no. 1, 51st Congress, 1st session, serial 2725, 3–4.

51. Dippie, *The Vanishing American*, 142.

52. Winnebago Indians, *To the Senate and House of Representatives in Congress Assembled—A Petition of the Winnebago Indians of Wisconsin* (Stevens Point, WI: Gazette Book and Job Office, 1889), 15. Emphasis mine.

53. Ibid.

54. Ibid.

55. David Wilkins, *American Indian Sovereignty and the Supreme Court: The Masking of Justice* (Austin: University of Texas Press, 1999), 64.

56. Kiowa, Comanche and Apache Nations, "Memorial of the Kiowa, Comanche, and Apache Tribes of Indians in Oklahoma Territory, 1903," Senate Committee on Indian Affairs File, RG233, HR57A-H10.1, box 93, Library of Congress.

57. See 187 U.S. 553, *Lone Wolf v. Hitchcock* (1903).

58. Kiowa, Comanche and Apache Nations, "Memorial, 1903."

59. Guy Gibbon, *The Sioux: The Dakota and Lakota Nations* (Malden, MA: Blackwell Publishing, 2003), 134.

60. Dee Brown, *Bury My Heart at Wounded Knee: An Indian History of the America West* (New York: Henry Holt, 2000), 416.

61. Rosebud Sioux, "Copy of Petition, January 15, 1897," Senate Committee on Indian Affairs File, RG233, HR54A-H13.1, box 193, Library of Congress. Emphasis mine.

62. Ibid.

63. Thomas J. Morgan, Annual Report of the Commissioner of Indian Affairs, September 5, 1890 in *The American Indian and the United States: A Documentary History*, vol. 1, ed. Wilcomb E. Washburn (New York: Random House, 1973), 435.

64. Leech Lake, "Protest of Leech Lake Indians Against the Removal of Reservation, January 12, 1898," Senate Committee on Indian Affairs File, RG233, HR55A-H8.1, box 193, Library of Congress.

65. Prucha, *The Great Father*, 109.

66. Leech Lake, "Protest, 1898."

67. Senier, *Voices of American Indian Assimilation and Resistance*, ix.

68. Louis S. Warren, *Buffalo Bill's America: William Cody and the Wild West Show* (New York: Knopf, 2005), 191.

69. Barbie Zelizer, "Reading the Past Against the Grain: The Shape of Memory Studies," *Critical Studies in Mass Communication* 12 (1995): 214.

70. Michael Kammen, *The Mystic Chords of Memory: The Transformation of Tradition in American Culture* (New York: Alfred Knopf, 1991), 11.

71. Jason Edward Black, "Remembrances of Removal: Native Resistance to Allotment and the Unmasking of Paternal Benevolence," *Southern Communication Journal* 72, no. 2 (2007): 191.

72. Randall A. Lake, "Between Myth and History: Enacting Time in Native American Protest Rhetoric," *Quarterly Journal of Speech* 77 (1991): 124.

73. With Lake, we find that American Indian discourses are also be vital for "the purposes of gathering the like-minded" and for serving "consummatory purposes prescribed by traditional Indian . . . precepts." Randall A. Lake, "Enacting Red Power: The Consummatory Function in Native American Protest Rhetoric," *Quarterly Journal of Speech* 69 (1983): 128.

74. Black, "Remembrances of Removal," 199.

75. Young Joseph, "An Indian's Views of Indian Affairs," *North American Review* 128 (April 1879), 412; 433.

76. Ibid.

77. Ibid.

78. Ibid.

79. General Allotment Act (1887), *United States Statutes at Large*, 24, 388–91.

80. D.S. Otis, *The Dawes Act and the Allotment of Indian Lands* (Norman: University of Oklahoma Press, 1973), 9.

81. Simon Pokagon, *The Red Man's Greeting at the Chicago Columbian World's Exposition of 1893* (Hartford, MI: C.H. Engle, 1893), n.p.

82. Ibid.

83. Ibid.

84. Pokagon, *The Red Man's Greeting.*

85. Carlos Montezuma, "What Indians Must Do," *Quarterly Journal* 2 (1914): 294.

86. Ibid.

87. Montezuma, "What Indians Must Do," 294.

88. Ibid.

89. According to Todd McDorman, reconstruction refers to the ways that protestors critique the discourse of institutions for flawed identity formations and, doubly, "adjust" to and "complete" the critique by reshaping these identities. See Todd McDorman, "Challenging Constitutional Authority: African American Responses to *Scott v. Sandford*," *Quarterly Journal of Speech* 83 (1997): 194; 204.

90. Montezuma, "What Indians Must Do," 294.

91. Konkle, *Writing Indian Nations*, 5.

92. David H. DeJong, *Promises of the Past: A History of Indian Education* (Golden, CO: North American Press, 1993), 107–32

93. Hoxie, *Talking Back to Civilization*, 26.

94. Nabokov, *Native American Testimony*, 276–82.

95. Bonnie J. Dow and Mari Boor Tonn, "'Feminine Style' and Political Judgment in the Rhetoric of Ann Richards," *Quarterly Journal of Speech* 79 (1993): 287.

96. Hoxie, *Talking Back to Civilization*, 26.

97. Sarah Winnemucca, *Life Among the Piutes: Their Wrongs and Claims* (Reno: University of Nevada Press, 1994), 207.

98. Senier, *Voices of American Indian Assimilation and Resistance*, ix.

99. Winnemucca, *Life Among the Piutes*, 107.

100. Rosemarie Zagarri, "Morals, Manners, and the Republican Mother," *American Quarterly* 44, no. 2 (1992): 192–94.

101. Zitkala Sa, "Impressions of an Indian Childhood," in *Atlantic Monthly* 85 (1900), 37–47.

102. Ibid.

103. S. Alice Callahan, *Wynema: A Child of the Forest* (Lincoln: University of Nebraska Press, 1997), 82.

104. Senier, *Voices of American Indian Assimilation and Resistance*, viii.

105. Callahan, *Wynema*, 1.

106. Callahan, *Wynema*, 82.

107. Ibid.

108. Winnemucca, *Life Among the Piutes*, 109.

109. Cheryl Walker, *Indian Nation: Native American Literature and Nineteenth-Century Nationalisms* (Durham, NC: Duke University Press, 1997), 10–11.

110. Richard Morris and Phillip Wander, "Native American Rhetoric: Dancing in the Shadows of the Ghost Dance," *Quarterly Journal of Speech* 76 (1990): 165.

111. Lake, "Enacting Red Power," 128.

112. Prucha, *The Great Father*, 242.

113. Hoxie, *Talking Back*, 22.

114. Washakie, "Protest to Governor John W. Hoyt," in *Washakie*, ed. Grace Raymond Hebard (Cleveland, OH: Arthur Clark, 1930), 212.

115. Ibid.

116. Wilkins, *American Indian Sovereignty*, 64.

117. Thomas L. Sloan, "The Reservation System, Report to the Interior Department" from *Proceedings of the First Annual Conference of the Society of the American Indians* (Washington, DC: Smithsonian., 1912), 112.

118. Ibid.

119. Sloan, "The Reservation System," 112.

120. Hoxie, *Talking Back*, 25–27.

121. Dewitt Duncan, "How Allotment Impoverishes the Indians: Testimony Before a Senate Investigating Conditions in Indian Country," in *Senate Report* No. 5013, 59th Congress, 2d Session, Part 1, Nov. 1906. 180–90.

122. Sloan, "The Reservation System." As this book's conclusion contends, such American Indian speeches helped simultaneously pass the Indian Citizenship Act (1924) and produce the scathing Merriam Report (1928), which recommended overturning the Dawes Act.

123. Maddox, *Citizen Indians*, 4–5.

124. John H. Oberly, Report of the Commissioner of Indian Affairs, December 3, 1888, in *The American Indian and the United States: A Documentary History*, vol. 1, ed. Wilcomb E. Washburn (New York: Random House, 1973), 422–23.

125. Albert Yava, "We Want to Tell You Something," in Nabokov, *Native American Testimony*, 246–50.

126. Ibid.

127. Mitchell Deroin, "The Chiefs, April 15, 1895" in Office of Indian Affairs, *Special Case* 147, L 1866-1895, National Archives.

128. Ibid.

129. Senier, *Voices of American Indian Resistance*, xiii.

130. Indian Commissioner Cato Sells, "Speech to the Indian Rights Association, October 2, 1920" in Prucha, *Great Father*, unab, 801.

131. For more, see Jason Edward Black, "Kicking Bear's 'I Bring You Word from Your Fathers the Ghosts' Address," *Voices of Democracy Journal* 3 (2008): 34–49.

132. John W. Bowers, Donovan J. Ochs and Richard J. Jensen, *The Rhetoric of Agitation and Control*, 2d (Prospect Heights, IL: Waveland Press, 1993), 34–35.

133. Michael Hittman, *Wovoka and the Ghost Dance* (Lincoln: University of Nebraska Press, 1997), 3–7.

134. Joe Starita, *Dull Knifes of Pine Ridge: A Lakota Odyssey* (New York: Putnam's Sons, 1995), 97.

135. Wovoka, "Promise of the Ghost Dance," in James Mooney, *The Ghost Dance Religion and the Sioux Outbreak of 1891* (Washington, DC: Bureau of Ethnology, 1896), n.p.

136. Kicking Bear, "I Bring You Word from Your Fathers the Ghosts," in *Indian Oratory: Famous Speeches by Noted Indian Chieftains*, ed. W.C. Vanderwerth (Norman: University of Oklahoma Press, 2000), 247.

137. Paul Chaat Smith and Robert Allen Warrior, *Like a Hurricane: The Indian Movement from Alcatraz to Wounded Knee* (New York: New Press, 1996), 229.

138. Kicking Bear, "I Bring You Word," 247–248.

139. Ibid.

140. Ibid.

141. Sioux Man, "The Dead Did Not Return, 1891," in Ella Deloria, *Speaking of Indians* (New York: Friendship Press, 1944), 63.

142. Wovoka, "Promise of the Ghost Dance."

143. Ibid.

144. Hoxie, *Talking Back to Civilization*, 26.

145. Colin G. Calloway, *First Peoples: A Documentary Survey of American Indian History* (Boston: Bedford/St. Martin's, 1999), 367–68.

CONCLUSION

1. Dewitt Clinton Duncan, "Conditions in Indian Territory," Senate Committee Investigation, *Senate Report* no. 5013, 59th Congress, 24th session, pt. 1, Nov. 1906.

2. Ibid.

3. Frederick Hoxie, *Talking Back to Civilization: Indian Voices from the Progressive Era* (Boston: Bedford/St. Martin's, 2001), 26–27.

4. Peter Nabokov, *Native American Testimony: A Chronicle of Indian-White Relations From Prophecy to the Present, 1492–2000* (New York: Penguin Books, 1999), 256–63.

5. Ruth Muskrat Bronson, "Life on the Checkerboard," in *Indians Are People Too*, ed. Ruth Muskrat Bronson (New York: Friendship Press, 1944), 262.

6. Bronson, "Life on the Checkerboard," 262.

7. Edward Said, *Culture and Imperialism* (London: Verso, 1993), xxv.

8. Homi Bhabha, "Signs Taken for Wonders: Questions of Ambivalence and Authority under a Tree Outside Delhi, May 1817," *Critical Inquiry* 12, no. 1 (1985): 154

9. Edouard Glissant, *Poetics of Relation* (Ann Arbor: University of Michigan Press, 1999), 144.

10. Michael Paul Rogin, *Fathers and Children: Andrew Jackson and The Subjugation of the American Indian* (New York: Knopf, 1975), 10.

11. Jason Edward Black, "Native Resistive Rhetoric and the Decolonization of American Indian Removal Discourse," *Quarterly Journal of Speech* 95, no. 1 (2009): 71.

12. This conception of Native voice conflicts with Phillip Wander's theory of the *Third Persona*, or the silhouetted audience that is "not present" and is forgotten "in history, a being whose presence, though relevant to what is said, is negated through silence." Rather, this project signifies

that American Indian agency was neither forgotten nor silent during these eras, but rather empowered and vital to Native-U.S. relations (Philip Wander, "The Third Persona: An Ideological Turn in Rhetorical Theory," *Central States Speech Journal* 35 [1984]: 210–11). Perhaps the status or classification of the *Third Persona* becomes a space of invention—and thus of dissension—for marginalized groups.

13. Hoxie, *Talking Back to Civilization*, 27.

14. Separatist American Indians were granted this same opportunity for U.S. citizenship. Most, however, "resisted . . . because they saw [military service] as an infringement of their tribal sovereignty and treaty rights." Moreover, some declared war on Germany separately to underscore the idea that "they were independent nations" and would fight "as allies, not as subjects of the United States." Colin G. Calloway, *First Peoples: A Documentary Survey of American Indian History* (Boston: Bedford/St. Martins, 1999), 374.

15. Citizenship for Native World War I Veterans, November 6, 1919, *U.S. Statutes at Large*, 41: 350.

16. President Woodrow Wilson insisted on the segregation of black and white troops during World War I, ironically at a time of increased inclusion of other immigrants as a part of the U.S. citizenry by reprobating "hyphenization." He urged segregation to quell Jim Crow-era tensions between whites and African Americans in the U.S. civis and within the military itself. See Mary Stuckey, "'The Domain of Public Conscience': Woodrow Wilson and the Establishment of a Transcendent Political Order," *Rhetoric and Public Affairs* 6, no. 1 (2005), 12–14.

17. Cato Sells, "The 'First Americans' as Loyal Citizens," *American Review of Reviews* 57 (May 1918): 523.

18. Found in Calloway, *First Peoples*, 373.

19. Rogers Smith, *Civic Ideals: Conflicting Visions of Citizenship in U.S. History* (New Haven, CT: Yale University Press, 1997), 274; 463.

20. Joseph Claymore in *Native American Testimony: A Chronicle of Indian-White Relations from Prophecy to the Present, 1492–2000*, ed. Peter Nabokov (New York: Penguin, 1999), 281.

21. Red Fox Skiuhushu, "If the Red Man Can Fight, Why Can't He Vote?" in *Literary Digest* 59 (Dec. 21, 1918): 36–37.

22. John Collier, "Radio Address, May 7, 1934," quoted in Francis Paul Prucha, *The Great Father: The United States Government and the American Indians*, abridged ed. (Lincoln: University of Nebraska Press, 1986), 323.

23. Prucha, *The Indians in American Society*, 54.

24. Antonio Luhan, "To John Collier, Feb. 1934," in Mable Dodge Luhan, *Winter in Taos* (New York: Harcourt Brace, 1935), 20.

25. Clinton Rickard, "Comments," in *Report of the Executive Council on the Proceedings of the First Annual Conference of the Society of American Indians, October 12–17, 1911, Columbus, Ohio*, ed. Arthur C. Parker (Washington, DC: Printing Office, 1912), n.p.

26. Francis Paul Prucha, *The Indians in American Society: From the Revolutionary War to the Present* (Berkeley: University of California Press, 1988), 54.

27. John Collier, "Annual Report of the Commissioner of Indian Affairs, 1935," in *The American Indian and the United States: A Documentary History*, vol. 2, ed. Wilcomb E. Washburn (Westport, CT: Greenwood Press, 1973), 921; 926.

28. Chief Standing Bear, *Land of the Spotted Eagle* (Boston: Houghton Mifflin, 1933), 90.

29. William H. King, "Speech on Allotment Reform, April 11, 1932," *Congressional Record*, 72d Congress, 1st session, 7938; 7935.

30. Hubert Work, quoted in Lewis Merriam, *The Problem of Indian Administration* (Baltimore, MD: Johns Hopkins University Press, 1928), vii.

31. John Collier, "An Indian Renaissance," in *The American Indian and the United States: A Documentary History*, vol. 2 (Westport, CT: Greenwood Press, 1973), 921–26.

32. Merriam, *The Problem of Indian Administration*, 7.

33. Ibid., 86.

34. Ibid., 87.

35. Ibid., 22.

36. Indian Citizenship Act, June 2, 1924, *U.S. Statutes at Large*, 43: 253.

37. Rose Stremlau, "'To Domesticate and Civilize Wild Indians': Allotment and the Campaign to Reform Indian Families, 1875–1887," *Journal of Family History* 30 (2005): 272.

38. Homer Snyder, quoted in Frederick Hoxie, *A Final Promise: The Campaign to Assimilate the Indians, 1880–1920* (Lincoln: University of Nebraska Press, 1984), 182.

39. Arthur C. Parker, quoted in Russel Lawrence Barsh, "American Indians in the Great War," *Ethnohistory* 38 (1991): 287–88.

40. Indian Citizenship Act, June 2, 1924, *U.S. Statutes at Large*, 43: 253.

41. Unnamed Mohawk Chief, quoted in Laurence Hauptman, *The Iroquois and the New Deal* (Syracuse, NY: Syracuse University Press, 1981), 6.

42. Unnamed Oneida and Seneca, quoted in *To Be An Indian: An Oral History*, ed. Joseph H. Cash and Herbert T. Hoover (St. Paul: Minnesota Historical Society Press, 1995), 124–25.

43. Hoxie, *Talking Back to Civilization*, 27.

44. Emma D. Johnson, "Discussion on Reservation Administration," in Nabokov, *Native American Testimony*, 286.

45. Ibid.

46. Prucha, *The Great Father*, 273.

47. Clyde Kelly, "On Behalf of Indian Citizenship," in Laurence F. Schmeckebier, *The Office of Indian Affairs: Its History, Activities and Organization* (Baltimore: Johns Hopkins University Press, 1927), 158–60.

48. Smith, *Civic Ideals*, 463.

49. Clyde Kelly, "On Behalf of Indian Citizenship," 158–60.

50. John Collier, *From Every Zenith: A Memoir and Some Essays on Life and Thought* (Denver: Sage Books, 1963), 115.

51. Colin G. Calloway, *First Peoples: A Documentary Survey of American Indian History* (Boston: Bedford/St. Martin's, 1999), 418.

52. John Collier, quoted in Richard Weiss, "Ethnicity and Reform: Minorities and the Ambience of the Depression Years," *Journal of American History* 66 (1979): 566.

53. Donald Young, *American Minority Peoples: A Study in Racial and Cultural Conflicts in the United States* (New York: Harper & Brothers, 1932), 460.

54. Weiss, "Ethnicity and Reform," 566.

55. Prucha, *The Great Father*, 319.

56. Chief Standing Bear, *Land of the Spotted Eagle*, 90.

57. Ibid.

58. Ralph Fredenberg, "Indian Self-Determination, 1934" in Hearings before the Committee on Indian Affairs, *U.S. Senate*, 73d Congress, 2d session, S. 2755 and S. 3645, Part 2, 110–13.

59. Indian Reorganization Act (Wheeler-Howard Act), June 18, 1934, *U.S. Statutes at Large*, 48: 984–88.

60. Antonio Luhan, "To John Collier, Feb. 1934,"

61. Collier, Annual Report of the Secretary of the Interior, 1934," 225.

62. Indian Reorganization Act (Wheeler-Howard Act), June 18, 1934, *U.S. Statutes at Large*, 48: 984–88.

63. Antonio Luhan, "To John Collier, Feb. 1934,"

64. Fredenberg, "Indian Self-Determination, 1934," 110–13.

65. Calloway, *First Peoples*, 417.

66. Indian Reorganization Act (Wheeler-Howard Act), June 18, 1934, *U.S. Statutes at Large*, 48: 984–88.

67. Ben Reifel, quoted in *To Be An Indian: An Oral History*, ed. Joseph H. Cash and Herbert T. Hoover (St. Paul: Minnesota Historical Society Press, 1995), 124–25.

68. Fredenberg, "Indian Self-Determination, 1934," 110–12.

69. Alfred Dubray, quoted in *To Be An Indian: An Oral History*, ed. Joseph H. Cash and Herbert T. Hoover (St. Paul: Minnesota Historical Society Press, 1995), 124–25.

70. John Collier, Annual Report of the Secretary of the Interior, 1934, 227.

71. Dippie, *The Vanishing American*, 317.

72. Indian Reorganization Act (Wheeler-Howard Act), June 18, 1934, *U.S. Statutes at Large*, 48: 984–88.

73. Though rarely occurring, sometimes a Native rhetor's nationality is not discernible from the texts under consideration. In these atypical instances, "unknown" is noted in parenthesis following their names.

74. Vera Connolly, "Washington Conference," *Indian Truth* 11 (January 1934): 3–4.

75. Rupert Costo, quoted in *Indian Self-Rule*, ed. Kenneth R. Philip (Salt Lake City, UT: Howe Brothers, 1986), 34.

76. Ibid.

77. Ramon Roubideaux, quoted in *To Be An Indian: An Oral History*, ed. Joseph H. Cash and Herbert T. Hoover (St. Paul: Minnesota Historical Society Press, 1995), 124–25.

78. John Collier, "Annual Report of the Secretary of the Interior, 1934" in *Documents of United States Indian Policy* (Lincoln: University of Nebraska Press, 1990), 227.

79. Indian Reorganization Act (Wheeler-Howard Act), June 18, 1934, *U.S. Statutes at Large*, 48: 984–88.

80. Robert Burnette and John Koster, *The Road to Wounded Knee* (New York: Bantam Doubleday, 1974), 15–16.

81. Indian Reorganization Act (Wheeler-Howard Act), June 18, 1934, *U.S. Statutes at Large*, 48: 984–88.

82. John Collier, "Annual Report of the Commissioner of Indian Affairs 1935," 921; 926.

83. Indian Reorganization Act (Wheeler-Howard Act), June 18, 1934, *U.S. Statutes at Large*, 48: 984–88.

84. Ibid.

85. Ibid.

86. Ibid.

87. Vine Deloria, *Custer Died For Your Sins: An Indian Manifesto* (Norman: University of Oklahoma Press, 1988), 145.

88. John Collier, "Annual Report of the Commissioner of Indian Affairs, 1935," in *The American Indian and the United States: A Documentary History*, vol. 2, ed. Wilcomb E. Washburn (Westport, CT: Greenwood Press, 1973), 921; 926.

89. Stephen Cornell, *The Return of the Native: American Indian Political Resurgence* (New York: Oxford University Press, 1988), 94–95.

90. John Collier, Annual Report of the Secretary of the Interior, 1934 in *Documents of United States Indian Policy* (Lincoln: University of Nebraska Press, 1990), 227.

91. John Louis Lucaites and Celeste Michelle Condit, "Reconstructing <Equality>: Culturetypal and Counter-Cultural Rhetoric in the Martyred Black Vision," in *Readings in Rhetorical Criticism*, 3d edition, ed. Carl R. Burgchardt (State College, PA: Strata, 2005), 469.

92. Lucaites and Condit, "Reconstructing <Equality>," 470.

93. Hoxie, *Talking Back to Civilization*, 27.

Bibliography

17 U.S. 316, *McCulloch v. Maryland* (1819).

18 App. D.C. 515, *Lone Wolf v. Hitchcock* (1901).

19 App. D.C. 315, *Lone Wolf v. Hitchcock* (1902).

21 U.S. 543 (1823), *Johnson and Graham v. McIntosh*, 568–69.

30 U.S. 1 (1831), *Cherokee Nation v. State of Georgia.*

31 U.S. 515 (1832), *Worcester v. State of Georgia.*

112 U.S. Reports, 98–99, 102, 109, *Elk v. Wilkins.*

118 U.S. Reports, 375, *United States v. Kagama* (1886).

187 U.S. 553, *Lone Wolf v. Hitchcock* (1903).

Adams, Robert. Remarks, April 20, 1830, *Gales & Seaton's Register of Debates in Congress*, Senate (April 20, 1830), 359.

Agnew, Brad. "Voices from the Land Run of 1889," *The Chronicles of Oklahoma* 67 (1989): 4–29.

Ames. "The Choctaws." *Cherokee Phoenix* 2, no. 37 (December 23, 1830): 2, col. 2a–4b.

Anderson, Benedict. *Imagined Communities: Reflections on the Origins and Spread of Nationalism.* London: Verso, 1983.

Arthur, Chester A. "Annual Message to Congress, December 6, 1881." In *A Compilation of the Messages and Papers of the Presidents*, vol. 8, compiled by James D. Richardson, 54. New York: Bureau of National Literature and Art, 1937.

Atkins, J. D. C. "Report of the Commissioner of Indian Affairs, October 5, 1885." In *The American Indian and the United States: A Documentary History*, vol. 3, edited by Wilcomb E. Washburn, 357. New York: Random House, 1973.

Antiwaneto. "We Hear on All Sides." In *Documents Relative to the Colonial History of New York*, vol. 10, edited by E. B. O'Callaghan, 252–54. Albany: Weed, Parsons, 1858.

Bakhtin, Mikhail. *The Dialogic Imagination: Four Essays.* Edited by Michael Holquist. Translated by Caryl Emerson and Michael Holquist. Austin: University of Texas Press, 1981.

Beasley, Vanessa. *You, the People: American National Identity in Presidential Rhetoric.* College Station: Texas A&M University Press, 2004.

Bhabha, Homi. "Signs Taken for Wonders: Questions of Ambivalence and Authority under a Tree Outside Delhi, May 1817." *Critical Inquiry* 12, no. 1 (1985): 144–65.

———. "The Other Question: Difference, Discrimination, and the Discourse of Colonialism." In *Literature, Politics, and Theory: Papers from the Essex Conference, 1976–1984*, edited by Francis Barker, 148–72. London: Metheun, 1986.

———. *Nations and Narration.* London: Routledge, 1990.

———. *Location of Culture.* London: Routledge, 1994.

Bizzell, Patricia. "(Native) American Jeremiad: The 'Mixedblood' Rhetoric of William Apess." In *American Indian Rhetorics of Survivance: Word Medicine, Word Magic*, edited by Ernest Stromberg, 34–49. Pittsburgh, PA: University of Pittsburgh Press, 2006.

Black Elk. "The Spider's Web." In *Black Elk Speaks*, edited John G. Neihardt, 35–36. Lincoln: University of Nebraska Press, 1931.

Black Hawk. *Black Hawk: An Autobiography.* Edited by Donald Jackson. Urbana-Champaign: University of Illinois Press, 1964.

Black Hawk. *Black Hawk's Autobiography*. Edited by Roger L. Nichols. Ames: Iowa State University Press, 1999.

Black Thunder (Fox). "Speech to American Commissioners, 1815." In *Biography and History of the Indians of North America*, edited by Samuel G. Drake, 632. Boston, 1841.

Black, Jason Edward. "Sacagawea as Commodity, Currency and Cipher: Consequences of the U.S. Mint's Gold Dollar for American Indian Women." *International Journal of Media and Cultural Politics* 1, no. 2 (2005): 226–30.

———. "Authoritarian Fatherhood: Andrew Jackson's Early Familial Lectures to America's 'Red Children.'" *Journal of Family History* 30, no. 3 (2005): 247–64.

———. "Symbolic Suicide as Mortification, Transformation, and Counterstatement: The Conciliatory (Yet) Resistant Surrender of Maka-tai-mesh-ekia-kiak." *Kenneth Burke Journal* 2, no. 1 (2005): 1–14.

———. "Remembrances of Removal: Native Resistance to Allotment and the Unmasking of Paternal Benevolence." *Southern Communication Journal* 72, no. 2 (2007): 185–203.

———. "Kicking Bear's 'I Bring You Word from Your Fathers the Ghosts' Address." *Voices of Democracy Journal* 3 (2008): 34–49.

———. "Memories of the Alabama Creek War, 1813–1814: U.S. Governmental and Native Identities at the Horseshoe Bend National Military Park." *American Indian Quarterly* 33, no. 2 (2009): 200–229.

———. "Native Resistive Rhetoric and the Decolonization of American Indian Removal Discourse." *Quarterly Journal of Speech* 95, no. 1 (2009): 66–88.

———. "Plenary Rhetoric in Indian Country: The *Lone Wolf v. Hitchcock* Case and the Codification of a Weakened Native Character." *Advances in the History of Rhetoric* 11/12 (2011): 59–80.

———. "Native Authenticity, Rhetorical Circulation, and Neocolonial Decay: The Case of Chief Seattle's Controversial Speech." *Rhetoric & Public Affairs* 15, no. 4 (2012): 635–46.

———. "A Clash of Native Space and Institutional Place in a Local Choctaw-Upper Creek Memory Site—Decolonizing Critiques and Scholar-Activist Interventions." *American Indian Culture & Research Journal* 36, no. 3 (2012): 19–44.

Bosmajian, Haig. "Defining the 'American Indian': A Case Study in the Language of Suppression." *The Speech Teacher* 21 (1973): 89–99.

Boudinot, Elias. "To the Publics." *Cherokee Phoenix* 1, no. 1 (February 21, 1828): 3, col. 2b–4.

———. "New Echota Editorial." *Cherokee Phoenix* 1, no. 6 (March 27, 1828): 3, col. 1b.

———. "Editorial (November 12, 1831)." In *Cherokee Editor: The Writing of Elias Boudinot*, edited by Theda Perdue, 142. Knoxville: University of Tennessee Press, 1983.

Bowers, John, Donovan J. Ochs, and Richard J. Jensen. *The Rhetoric of Agitation and Control*. Prospect Heights, IL: Waveland, 1994.

Brands, H. W. *Andrew Jackson: His Life and Times*. New York, Doubleday, 2005.

Brant, Joseph. "We Have Borne Everything Patiently for This Long Time." In *Indian Oratory: Famous Speeches by Noted Indian Chieftains*, edited by W.C. Vanderwerth, 50–53. Norman: University of Oklahoma Press, 1989.

Bronson, Ruth Muskrat. "Life on the Checkerboard." In *Native American Testimony: A Chronicle of Indian-White Relations From Prophecy to the Present, 1492–2000*, edited by Peter Nabokov, 262. New York: Penguin, 1999.

Brown, Dee. *Bury My Heart At Wounded Knee: An Indian History of the American West*. New York: Henry Holt, 2000.

Bruner, M. Lane. *Strategies of Remembrance: The Rhetorical Dimensions of National Identity*. Columbia: University of South Carolina Press, 2002.

Buchanan, John. *Jackson's Way: Andrew Jackson and the People of the Western Waters*. New York: Wiley and Sons, 2001.

Buescher, Derek, and Kent Ono. "Civilized Colonialism: *Pocahontas* as Neocolonial Rhetoric," *Women's Studies in Communication* 19 (1996): 127–53.

Burke, Kenneth. *The Rhetoric of Religion: Studies in Logology*. Berkeley: University of California Press, 1970.

Burnette, Robert, and John Koster. *The Road to Wounded Knee*. New York: Bantam Doubleday, 1974.

Burstein, Andrew. *The Passions of Andrew Jackson*. New York: Vintage, 2004.

Cain, William E., ed. *William Lloyd Garrison and the Fight Against Slavery—Selections from The Liberator*. Boston: Bedford, 1995.

Calhoun, John. "South Carolina Exposition, December 19, 1828." In *The Papers of John C. Calhoun*, vol. 10, 1825–1829, edited by Clyde N. Wilson and W. Edwin Hemphill, 444–534. Columbia: University of South Carolina Press, 1977.

Callahan, S. Alice. *Wynema: A Child of the Forest*. Lincoln: University of Nebraska Press, 1997.

Calloway, Colin G. *First Peoples: A Documentary Survey of American Indian History*. Boston: Bedford/St. Martin's, 1999.

Campbell, Karlyn Kohrs. "Agency: Promiscuous and Protean." *Communication and Critical/Cultural Studies* 2 (2005): 1–19.

Canassatego (Onondaga). "We Now Speak." In *Minutes of the Provincial Council of Pennsylvania*, vol. 5, edited by Samuel Hazard, 401–02. Harrisburg, PA: T. Fenn & Co., 1851–1853.

Casey, Michael W., and Douglas A. Foster. "The Moral Inheritance of a President." In *The Stone-Campbell Movement: An International Religious Tradition*, edited by Michael W. Casey and Douglas A. Foster, 109–127. Knoxville: University of Tennessee Press, 2001.

Cass, Lewis. "To the President of the United States, Department of War, January 23, 1832." National Archives, Record Group 75, Ratified Indian Treaty File No. 178, Item 2-T, Secretary of War, Letters Sent, vol. 9.

Champagne, Duane. *Social Order and Political Change: Constitutional Governments among the Cherokee, the Choctaw, the Chickasaw, and the Creek*. Stanford, CA: Stanford University Press, 1992.

Cherokee Council. "The Cherokees." *Cherokee Phoenix* 1, no. 44 (January 14, 1829): 1, col. 4b–5a.

Cherokee Nation. "A Petition, January 29, 1897." Senate Committee on Indian Affairs File, RG233, HR54A-H13, box 192, Library of Congress.

Cheyfitz, Eric. "Doctrines of Discovery," *Common-Place* 2, no. 1 (2001): 1–5.

Chief Standing Bear. *Land of the Spotted Eagle*. Boston: Houghton Mifflin, 1933.

Chippewa Removal Song. In *Indian Sketches Taken During an Expedition to the Pawnee Tribes* [1833], edited by John Trent Irving, Jr., 27. Norman: University of Oklahoma Press, 1955.

Choctaw Nation. "Congressional Memorial, February 17, 1894." Senate Committee on Indian Affairs File, RG233, HR53A-H13.3, box no. 141, Library of Congress.

Churchill, Ward. *Indians Are Us? Culture and Genocide in Native North America*. Monroe, ME: Common Courage Press, 1993.

Citizenship for Native World War I Veterans, November 6, 1919, *U.S. Statutes at Large*, 41: 350.

Civilization Fund Act, March 3, 1819, *U.S. Statutes at Large*, 3:516–17.

Clark, Blue. *Lone Wolf v. Hitchcock: Treaty Rights and Indian Law at the End of the Nineteenth Century*. Lincoln: University of Nebraska Press, 1994.

Claymore, Joseph. "Commentary." In *Native American Testimony: A Chronicle of Indian-White Relations From Prophecy to the Present, 1492–2000*, edited by Peter Nabokov, 281. New York: Penguin Books, 1999.

Clements, William M. *Oratory in Native North America*. Tucson: University of Arizona Press, 2002.

Cleveland, Grover. "First Inaugural Address, March 4, 1885." In *The Inaugural Addresses of the Presidents*, edited by John Gabriel Hunt, 247. New York: Gramercy, 1997.

———. "Second Annual Message, December 6, 1886." In *A Compilation of the Messages and Papers of the Presidents*, vol. 8, compiled by James D. Richardson, 519. Washington, DC: Bureau of National Literature and Art, 1937.

Coacoochee. "Speech to Removal Council." In *The Origin, Progress and Conclusion of the Florida War*, edited by John T. Sprague, 259–60. New York: Appleton and Company, 1847.

Coffee, John. "Talk to the Creek and Chickasaw (September 18, 1830)." In *The Chickasaws*, edited by Arrell Gibson, 154. Norman: University of Oklahoma Press, 1971.

Coke Bill of 1881. In *Indian Land in Severalty as Provided for By the Coke Bill*, 46th Congress, 1st session, S. 48, edited by Henry S. Pancoast, 3–7. (Philadelphia: Lippincott, 1884.

Coke, Richard. "U.S. Congress, Senate, Debate on Bill to Provide Lands in Severalty, January 20, 1881, from Congressional Record, 46th Congress, 3d session." In *The American Indian and the United States: A Documentary History*, vol. 4, edited by Wilcomb E. Washburn, 1700–1704. New York: Random House, 1973.

Colbert, Levi. "Plea from the Chickasaw." In *Native American Testimony: A Chronicle of Indian-White Relations from Prophecy to the Present, 1492–2000*, edited by Peter Nabokov, 151–52. New York: Penguin, 1999.

Collier, John. "Annual Report of the Secretary of the Interior, 1934." In *Documents of United States Indian Policy*, edited by Francis Paul Prucha, 225–29. Lincoln: University of Nebraska Press, 1990.

———. "Radio Address, May 7, 1934." In *The Great Father: The United States Government and the American Indians*, edited by Francis Paul Prucha, 323. Lincoln: University of Nebraska Press, 1984.

———. "Annual Report of the Commissioner of Indian Affairs, 1935." In *The American Indian and the United States: A Documentary History*, vol. 2, edited by Wilcomb Washburn, 921–27. Westport, CT: Greenwood Press, 1973.

———. "An Indian Renaissance." In *The American Indian and the United States: A Documentary History*, vol. 2, edited by Wilcomb E. Washburn. Westport, CT: Greenwood Press, 1973, 921–26.

———. *From Every Zenith: A Memoir and Some Essays on Life and Thought.* Denver: Sage Books, 1963.

"Committee Report on the Southern Department, August 3, 1787." *Journals of the Continental Congress*, vol. 33., 456–59.

Condit, Celeste Michelle, and John Louis Lucaites. *Crafting Equality: America's Anglo-African Word.* Chicago: University of Chicago Press, 1993.

Connolly, Vera. "Washington Conference." *Indian Truth* 11 (January 1934): 3–4.

Continental Congress. "Report of Committee on Indian Affairs, October 15, 1783." *Journals of the Continental Congress*, 25: 681–83, 693.

Constitution of the United States of America. In *A Documentary History of the United States*, 7d., edited by Richard D. Heffner, 18–38. New York: Signet, 2002.

Cornell, Stephen. *The Return of the Native: American Indian Political Resurgence.* New York: Oxford University Press, 1988.

Corn Tassel. "Let Us Examine the Facts." In T*atham's Characters Among the North American Indians.* London: Annual of Biography and Obituary, 1820.

Costo, Rupert. "Resisting the Indian New Deal." In *Indian Self-Rule*, edited by Kenneth R. Philip, 34. Salt Lake City, UT: Howe Brothers, 1986.

Crawford, T. Hartley. "Report of the Commissioner of Indian Affairs, November 25, 1838." In *The American Indian and the United States: A Documentary History*, vol. 1, edited by Wilcomb E. Washburn, 31. New York: Random House, 1973.

Creek and Choctaw Indians of Oklahoma. "To the Committee on Indian Affairs—A Protest Against Allotment of Lands by the Full Blood Creek Indians, November 21, 1899." Senate Committee on Indian Affairs File, RG233, HR56A-H9.3, Library of Congress.

Creek and Seminole Nations. "To the Congress of the United States, 1890." Senate Committee on Indian Affairs File, RG233, HR54A-H13.1, box 193, Library of Congress.

Curtis Act (1898), 174 *U.S. Reports*, 445, 488–89.

Cushman, H. B. *History of the Choctaw, Chickasaw, and Natchez Indians*. Norman: University of Oklahoma Press, 1999.

Danforth, Samuel. "A Brief Recognition of New Englands Errand Into the Wilderness." In *American Rhetorical Discourse*, edited by James F. Klumpp and Ronald Reid, 37–51. Prospect Heights, IL: Waveland Press, 2004.

Dawes, Henry. "Solving the Indian Problem." In *Fifteenth Annual Report of the Board of Indian Commissioners* (1883), 69–70.

Dawes, Henry L. "Senate Arguments, December 15, 1886." In *Proceedings of the Fifth Annual Meeting of the Lake Mohonk Conference of the Friends of the Indian*, 1887 (Philadelphia, 1887), 12–13; 63–69.

Debo, Angie. *The Rise and Fall of the Choctaw Republic*. Norman: University of Oklahoma Press, 1934.

———. *The Road to Disappearance: A History of the Creek Indians*. Norman: University of Oklahoma Press, 1941.

Debord, Guy. *The Society of the Spectacle*. New York: Zone Books, 1994.

De Certeau, Michel. *The Practice of Everyday Life*. Berkeley: University of California Press, 1984.

Declaration of Independence. In *A Documentary History of the United States*, edited by Richard D. Heffner, 9–13. New York: Signet, 2002.

DeJong, David H. *Promises of the Past: A History of Indian Education*. Golden, CO: North American Press, 1993.

Delaney, David. *Race, Place and the Law, 1836–1948*. Austin: University of Texas Press, 1998.

Deloria, Ella. *Speaking of Indians*. New York: Friendship Press, 1944.

Deloria, Vine. *Custer Died for Your Sins: An Indian Manifesto*. Norman: University of Oklahoma Press, 1988.

Deloria, Vine, and Clifford M. Lytle. *American Indians, American Justice*. Austin: University of Texas Press, 1983.

Delano, Columbus. Report of the Secretary of the Interior, November 23, 1874, *House Executive Document* no. 1, part 5, 43–42, serial 1639, v, vii.

Demos, John. "The Changing Faces of Fatherhood: A New Exploration in Family History." In *Father and Child: Developmental and Clinical Perspectives*, edited by Stanley Cath, Alan Gurwitt, and John Munder Ross, 427–33. Boston: Little and Brown, 1982.

Deroin, Mitchell. "The Chiefs, April 15, 1895." In Office of Indian Affairs, *Special Case* 147, L 1866-1895, National Archives.

Dippie, Brian. *The Vanishing American: White Attitudes and U.S. Indian Policy*. Lawrence: University of Kansas Press, 1991.

Dorsey, Leroy G., and Rachel M. Harlow. "'We Want Americans Pure and Simple': Theodore Roosevelt and the Myth of Americanism." *Rhetoric and Public Affairs* 6, no. 1 (2003): 55–78.

Dow, Bonnie J., and Mari Boor Tonn, "'Feminine Style' and Political Judgment in the Rhetoric of Ann Richards." *Quarterly Journal of Speech* 79 (1993): 286–302.

Dowd, Gregory Evans. *A Spirited Resistance: The North American Indian Struggle for Unity, 1745–1815*. Baltimore: Johns Hopkins University Press, 1992.

Drinnon, Richard. *Facing West: The Metaphsyics of Indian Hating and Empire Building*. Norman: University of Oklahoma Press, 1997.

Dubray, Alfred. In *To Be An Indian: An Oral History*, edited by Joseph H. Cash and Herbert T. Hoover. St. Paul: Minnesota Historical Society Press, 1995. 124–125

Duncan, Dewitt (D.W.). "How Allotment Impoverishes the Indians: Testimony Before a Senate Investigating Conditions in Indian Country." *Senate Report No. 5013*, 59th Congress, 2d Session, Part 1, Nov. 1906. 180–190.

Eaton, John. "To the Cherokee Nation on Removal, April 18, 1829." In Office of Indian Affairs, *Letter Book* no. 5, Record Group 75, 408–412, National Archives.

———. "Secretary of War Annual Report (1830)." In *American State Papers*, vol. 4, serial 458, 286.

Edmunds, R. David. *The Shawnee Prophet*. Lincoln: University of Nebraska Press, 1985.

Eby, Cecil. "*That Disgraceful Affair*"—*The Black Hawk War*. New York: Norton, 1972.

Eckert, Allan. A *Sorrow in Our Heart: The Life of Tecumseh* New York: Bantam, 1993.

Ehle, John. *Trail of Tears: The Rise and Fall of the Cherokee Nation*. New York: Anchor Books, 1988.

Ellington, Ter. *The Myth of the Noble Savage*. Berkeley: University of California Press, 2001.

Estin, Ann Laquer. "*Lone Wolf v. Hitchcock*: The Long Shadow." In *The Aggressions of Civilization: Federal Indian Policy Since the 1880s*, edited by Sandra Cadwalader and Vine Deloria, Jr., 215–45. Philadelphia: Temple University Press, 1984.

Ethridge, Robbie. *Creek Country: The Creek Indians and Their* World. Chapel Hill: University of North Carolina Press, 2003.

Forsyth, John. "Remarks, April 15, 1830." *Gales & Seaton's Register of Debates in Congress*, Senate (April 14, 15, 1830), 326.

———. Speech. In *American Indian Policy in the Jacksonian Era*, edited by Ronald Satz, 24. Lincoln: University of Nebraska Press, 1975.

Fotion, Neil. "Paternalism." *Ethics* 89 (1979): 191–98.

Fowler, William. *Empires at War: The French and Indian War and the Struggle for North America, 1754–1763*. New York: Walker and Company, 2004.

Fredenberg, Ralph. "Indian Self-Determination, 1934." Hearings before the Committee on Indian Affairs, *U.S. Senate*, 73d Congress, 2d session, S. 2755 and S. 3645, Part 2, 110–13.

Freeman, Jody. "Constitutive Rhetoric: Law as a Literary Activity." *Harvard Woman's Law Journal* 14 (1991): 305–325.

Frelinghuysen, Theodore. "Remarks, April 9, 1830." *Gales & Seaton's Register of Debates in Congress*, Senate (April 9, 1830), 312.

Frickey, Phillip. "Marshalling Past and Present: Colonialism, Constitutionalism, and Interpretation in Federal Indian Law." *Harvard Law Review* 107 (December 1993), 381.

Garroutte, Eva Marie. *Real Indians: Identity and the Survival of Native America*. Berkeley: University of California Press, 2003.

Gellner, Ernest. *Encounters with Nationalism*. Oxford, UK: Blackwell, 1994.

General Allotment Act (1887), *U.S. Statutes at Large*, vol. 24, 388–91.

Gerstle, Gary. *American Crucible: Race and Nation in the Twentieth Century*. Princeton: Princeton University Press, 2001.

Gibbon, Guy. *The Sioux: The Dakota and Lakota Nations*. Malden, MA: Blackwell Publishing, 2003.

Glissant, Edouard. *Poetics of Relation*. Ann Arbor: University of Michigan Press, 1999.

Gould, Lewis Gould. *The Tyranny of Change: America in the Progressive Era, 1890–1914*. Brunswick, NJ: Rutgers University Press, 2000).

Green, Michael D. *The Creeks: A Critical Bibliography*. Bloomington: Indiana University Press, 1979.

———. *The Politics of Indian Removal: Creek Government and Society in Crisis*. Lincoln: University of Nebraska Press, 1982.

Gurko, Miriam. *Indian America: The Black Hawk War*. New York: Crowell, 1970.

Gutierrez, David G. "Significant to Whom?: Mexican Americans and the History of the American West." In *A New Significance: Re-Envisioning the History of the American West*, edited by Clyde A. Milner III, 67–89. New York: Oxford University Press, 1996.

Hagan, William T. *The Indian Rights Association: The Herbert Walsh Years, 1882–1904* Tucson: University of Arizona Press, 1985.

———. *The Sac and Fox Indians*. Norman: University of Oklahoma Press, 1988.

Hall, Stuart Hall. "Cultural Identity and Diaspora." In *Identity: Community, Culture, Difference*, edited by John Rutherford, 222–37. London: Lawrence and Wishart, 1990.

Haliburton, Thomas. "Removal of the Indians," *The North American Review* 30, no. 66 (January 1830), 66.

Harjo, Joy, and Gloria Bird. "Introduction." In *Reinventing the Enemy's Language: Contemporary Native Women's Writings of North America*, edited by Joy Harjo and Gloria Bird, 19–34. New York: W.W. Norton, 1997.

Harkins, George. "Farewell Letter to the American People, 1832." *The American Indian* 1, no. 3 (December 1926), 7–12.

Harmon, Alexandra. "Wanted: More Histories of Indian Identity." In *A Companion to American Indian History*, edited by Philip Deloria and Neal Salisbury, 259–70. New York: Blackwell, 2002.

Hayes, Rutherford B. "Third Annual Message, December 1, 1879." In *Great Debates in American History, Civil Rights*, part 2, vol. 8, edited by Marion Mills Miller, 287. New York: Little and Ives, 1913.

Hayt, Ezra. "To Secretary of the Interior Carl Schurz, January 24, 1879." In *That the People Might Live: Native American Literatures and Native American Community*, edited by Jace Weaver, 87. London: Oxford University Press, 1997.

Susan Hegeman. "Native American 'Texts' and the Problem of Authenticity.'" *American Quarterly* 41 (1989): 271.

Hertzberg, Hazel. *The Search for an American Indian Identity*. Syracuse: Syracuse University Press, 1971.

Hitchcock, Ethan Allen. "Annual Report of the Department of the Interior, June 30, 1903." In *Indian Affairs: Laws and Treaties*, vol. 18, edited by Charles J. Kappler, 2–3. Washington, DC: Government Printing Office, 1904.

Hitchcock, Peter. *Dialogics of the Oppressed*. Minneapolis: University of Minnesota Press, 1993.

Hittman, Michael. *Wovoka and the Ghost Dance*. Lincoln: University of Nebraska Press, 1997.

Hobsbawm, E. J. *Nations and Nationalism Since 1780: Programme, Myth, Reality*. Cambridge, UK: Cambridge University Press, 1990.

Hoganson, Kristin L. *Fighting for American Manhood: How Gender Politics Provoked the Spanish-American and Philippine American Wars*. New Haven, CT: Yale University Press, 1998.

Homestead Act, May 20, 1862, 37th Congress, 2d session, Chapter 75.

House Report no. 237, 21:1, serial 200, 6–7

Hoxie, Frederick. *A Final Promise: The Campaign to Assimilate the Indians, 1880–1920*. Lincoln: University of Nebraska Press, 1984.

———. *Talking Back to Civilization: Indian Voices from the Progressive Era*. Boston: Bedford/St. Martin's, 2001.

Hoyt, Anne Kelley. *Bibliography of the Chickasaw*. Lanham, MD: Rowman and Littlefield, 1987.

Hurt, R. Douglas. *The Indian Frontier, 1763–1846*. Albuquerque: University of New Mexico Press, 2002.

Indian Citizenship Act, June 2, 1924, *U.S. Statutes at Large*, 43: 253.

Indian Reorganization Act (Wheeler-Howard Act), June 18, 1934, *U.S. Statutes at Large*, 48: 984–88.

Indian Removal Act (1830), *U.S. Statutes at Large*, vol. 4: 411–12.

Indian Rights Association. "Statement of Objectives." *Second Annual Report of the Executive Committee on the Indian Rights Association* (1885), 5–7.

Jackman, Mary R. *The Velvet Glove: Paternalism and Conflict in Gender, Class and Race Relations.* Berkeley: University of California Press, 1993.

Jackson, Andrew. "Letter to Rachel Jackson, October 21, 1814." In *The Correspondence of Andrew Jackson*, vol. 1, edited by John Spencer Bassett, 365–66. Washington, DC: Carnegie, 1928.

———. "Letter to John Williams, May 18, 1815." In *The Papers of Andrew Jackson*, vol. 3, edited by Harold D. Moser, David R. Hoth, and George H. Hoemann, 74–75. Knoxville: University of Tennessee Press, 1996).

———. "Talk to the Creeks, September 4, 1815." In *Correspondence of Andrew Jackson*, vol. 2, edited by John Spencer Bassett, 216–17. Washington, DC: Carnegie Institute, 1928.

———. "Talk with George Colbert and the Chickasaw, February 13, 1816." In *The Papers of Andrew Jackson*, vol. 4, edited by Harold D. Moser, David R. Hoth, and George H. Hoemann, 13. Knoxville: University of Tennessee Press, 1996.

———. "To James Monroe, March 4, 1817." In *Correspondence of Andrew Jackson*, vol. 2, edited by John Spencer Bassett, 278–79. Washington, DC: Carnegie Institute, 1928.

———. "To Choctaw Indians, October 3, 1820." In *The Papers of Andrew Jackson*, vol. 4, edited by Harold D. Moser, David R. Hoth, and George H. Hoemann, 391–92. Knoxville: University of Tennessee Press, 1996.

———. "To Choctaw Indians, October 17, 1820." In *The Papers of Andrew Jackson* vol. 4, edited by Harold D. Moser, David R. Hoth, and George H. Hoemann, 393–96. Knoxville: University of Tennessee Press, 1996.

———. "Talk with Indian Chieftains, September 20, 1821." In *Correspondence of Andrew Jackson*, vol. 3, edited by John Spencer Bassett. 118–21. (Washington, DC: Carnegie Institute, 1928).

———. "First Inaugural, March 4, 1829." In *A Compilation of the Messages and Papers of the Presidents*, vol. 2, compiled by James D. Richardson, 438. Washington, DC: Bureau of National Literature and Art, 1937.

———. "Letter to James Gadsden, October 12, 1829." In *Correspondence of Andrew Jackson*, vol. 4, edited by John Spencer Bassett, 81. Washington, DC: Carnegie Institute, 1928.

———. "Draft of First Annual Message, December 7, 1829." In *The Correspondence of Andrew Jackson*, vol. 4, edited by John Spencer Bassett, 103. Washington, DC: Carnegie, 1928.

———. "First Annual Message, December 7, 1829." In *A Compilation of the Messages and Papers of the Presidents*, vol. 2, compiled by James D. Richardson, 457–59. Washington, DC: Bureau of National Literature and Art, 1937.

———. "Letter to John Pitchlynn, August 5, 1830." In *Correspondence of Andrew Jackson*, vol. 4, edited by John Spencer Bassett, 169. Washington, DC: Carnegie Institution, 1929.

———. "Second Annual Message to Congress, 1830." *U.S. House Journal*, 6 December 1830, 25.

———. "Letter to Colonel Anthony Butler, March 6, 1832." In *Correspondence of Andrew Jackson*, vol. 4, edited by John Spencer Bassett, 415. Washington, DC: Carnegie Institution of Washington, 1929.

———. "Talk to the Cherokees, March 6, 1835." In *The Correspondence of Andrew Jackson*, vol. 1, edited by John Spencer Bassett, 86. Washington, DC: Carnegie, 1928.

———. "Annual Message, December 7, 1835." In *A Compilation of the Messages and Papers of the Presidents*, vol. 3, compiled by James D. Richardson, 172–73. Washington, DC: Bureau of National Literature and Art, 1937.

Jackson, Donald. "Introduction." *Black Hawk: An Autobiography*, edited by Donald Jackson, 1–15. Urbana-Champaign: University of Illinois Press, 1964.

Jackson, III., Harvey H. *Rivers of History: Life on the Coosa, Tallapoosa, Cahaba, and Alabama.* Tuscaloosa: University of Alabama Press, 1995.

Jackson, Helen Hunt. *A Century of Dishonor: A Sketch of the United States Government's Dealings with Some of the Indian Tribes.* Norman: University of Oklahoma Press, 1995.

Jahoda, Gloria. *The Trail of Tears: The Story of the American Indian Removal, 1813-1855.* New York: Wings Books, 1995.

Jefferson, Thomas. "First Inaugural, March 4, 1801." In *The Inaugural Addresses of the Presidents,* edited by John Gabriel Hunt, 24. New York: Gramercy, 1997.

———. "On Indian Trading Houses—Confidential Letter to Congress, January 18, 1803." In *A Compilation of the Messages and Papers of the Presidents,* vol. 1, compiled by James D. Richardson, 340-41. Washington, DC: Bureau of National Literature and Art, 1937.

———. "Presidential Message, 1803." Record Group 233, Records of the U.S. House of Representatives, File HR7A-D1, National Archives II.

———. "Message of January 18, 1803." In *A Compilation of the Messages and Papers of the Presidents, Vol. 1,* compiled by James D. Richardson, 352. New York: Bureau of National Literature, 1897.

———. "Letter to William Henry Harrison, February 27, 1803." In *The Writings of Thomas Jefferson,* vol. 9, edited by Albert E. Berghe, 370–371. Washington, DC: Thomas Jefferson Memorial Foundation, 1907.

Johnson, Emma D. "Discussion on Reservation Administration." In *Native American Testimony, Native American Testimony: A Chronicle of Indian-White Relations From Prophecy to the Present, 1492-2000,* edited by Peter Nabokov, 286. New York: Penguin Books, 1999.

Johnson, Tadd M., and James Hamilton. "Sovereignty and the Native American Nation: Self-Governance for Indian Tribes—From Paternalism to Empowerment." *Connecticut Law Review* 27, 1253 (1995): 166–67.

Josephy, Jr., Alvin. *The Patriot Chief's: A Chronicle of American Indian Resistance.* New York: Penguin, 1989.

Kammen, Michael. *The Mystic Chords of Memory: The Transformation of Tradition in American Culture.* New York: Alfred Knopf, 1991.

Kaplan, Amy. *Anarchy of Empire in the Making of U.S. Culture.* Cambridge, MA: Harvard University Press, 2002.

Kelly, Clyde. "On Behalf of Indian Citizenship." In *The Office of Indian Affairs: Its History, Activities and Organization,* edited by Laurence F. Schmeckebier, 158–60. Baltimore: Johns Hopkins University Press, 1927.

Kerber, Linda. "The Republican Mother: Women and the Enlightenment—An American Perspective." *American Quarterly* 28, no. 2 (1976): 187–205.

Kersh, Rogan. *Dreams of a More Perfect Union.* Ithaca, NY: Cornell University Press, 2001.

Kettner, James H. *The Development of American Citizenship,* 1608–1870. Chapel Hill: University of North Carolina Press, 1978.

Kicking Bear. "I Bring You Word from Your Fathers the Ghosts." In *Indian Oratory: Famous Speeches by Noted Indian Chieftains,* edited by W. C. Vanderwerth, 247. Norman: University of Oklahoma Press, 2000.

King, William H. "Speech on Allotment Reform, April 11, 1932." *Congressional Record,* 72d Congress, 1st session, 7938; 7935.

King Philip. "Speech." In *Eulogy on King Philip, As Pronounced at the Odeon,* edited by William Apes, 27. Boston: Apes, 1836.

Kiowa, Comanche, and Apache Nations. "Memorial of the Kiowa, Comanche, and Apache Tribes of Indians in Oklahoma Territory, 1903." Senate Committee on Indian Affairs File, RG233, HR57A-H10.1, box 93, Library of Congress.

Kleinig, J. *Paternalism*. New York: Rowan and Allenheld, 1983.

Konig, Hans. *The Conquest of America: How the Indian Nations Lost Their Continent*. New York: Cornerstone, 1993.

Konkle, Maureen. *Writing Indian Nations: Native Intellectuals and Politics of Historiography, 1827–1863*. Chapel Hill: University of North Carolina Press, 2004.

Krupat, Arnold. "An Approach to Native American Texts." *Critical Inquiry* 9 (1982): 323–38.

———. *Ethnocriticism: Ethnography, History, Literature*. Berkeley: University of California Press, 1992.

———. *Red Matters: Native American* Studies. Philadelphia: University Pennsylvania Press, 2002.

Hightower-Langston, Donna. *The Native American World*. Hoboken, NJ: Wiley and Sons, 2003.

LaRocque, Emma. *When the Other is Me: Native Resistance Discourse, 1850–1990*. Winnipeg: University of Manitoba Press, 2010.

Leach, Douglas Edward. *Arms for Empire: A Military History of the British Colonies in North America, 1607–1730*. New York: MacMillan, 1973.

Leech Lake. "Protest of Leech Lake Indians Against the Removal of Reservation, January 12, 1898." Senate Committee on Indian Affairs File, RG233, HR55A-H8.1, box 193, Library of Congress.

Lake, Randall. "Enacting Red Power: The Consummatory Function in Native American Protest Rhetoric." *Quarterly Journal of Speech* 69 (1983): 127–42.

———. "Between Myth and History: Enacting Time in Native American Protest Rhetoric." *Quarterly Journal of Speech* 77 (1991): 123–51.

Lens, Sidney. *The Forging of the American Empire—From the Revolution to Vietnam: A History of U.S. Imperialism*. Chicago: Haymarket Press, 2003.

Lepore, Jill. *The Name of War: King Philip's War and the Origins of American Identity*. New York: Vintage, 1999.

Levernz, David. *Paternalism Incorporated: Fables of American Fatherhood, 1865–1940*. Ithaca: Cornell University Press, 2003.

Lewis, David Rich. *Neither Wolf Nor Dog: American Indians, Environment and Agrarian Change*. New York: Oxford University Press, 1994.

Lieven, Anatol. *American Right or Wrong: An Anatomy of American Nationalism*. New York: Oxford University Press, 2004.

Lincecum, Gideon. *Pushmataha: A Choctaw Leader and His People*. Tuscaloosa: University of Alabama Press, 2004.

Lucaites, John Louis, and Celeste Michelle Condit. "Reconstructing <Equality>: Culturetypal and Counter-Cultural Rhetoric in the Martyred Black Vision." In *Readings in Rhetorical Criticism*, edited by Carl R. Burgchardt, 467–86. State College, PA: Strata, 2005.

Luhan, Antonio. "To John Collier, Feb. 1934." In *Winter in Taos*, edited by Mable Dodge Luhan, 20. New York: Harcourt Brace, 1935.

"Lumpkin's Remarks, May 17, 1830," *Gales & Seaton's Register of Debates in Congress*, House (May 17, 1830), 1016.

Maddox, Lucy. *Citizen Indians: Native American Intellectuals, Race and Reform*. Ithaca, NY: Cornell University Press, 2005.

Madison, James. "The Federalist Number Ten." In *A Documentary History of the United States*, edited by Richard D. Heffner, 40–43. New York: Signet, 2002.

Magdaleno, Jana Sequoya. "How (!) Is An Indian? A Contest of Stories, Round 2." In *Postcolonial Theory and the United States: Race, Ethnicity and Literature*, edited by Amritjit Singh and Peter Schmidt, 286–87. Jackson: University Press of Mississippi, 2000.

Mahon, John K., and Brent R. Weisman. "Florida's Seminole and Miccosukee People." In *The New History of Florida*, edited by Michael Gannon, 183–206. Gainesville: University of Florida Press, 1996.

Major Crimes Act, *U.S. Statutes at Large*, 22, 385.

Manypenny, George. "Annual Report of the Commissioner of Indian Affairs, November 22 1856." *Senate Executive Document* no. 5, 34th Congress, 3d session, serial 875, 571–75.

Marshall, John. "To Joseph Story, May 1, 1828." In *Papers of John Marshall*, vol. 11, edited by Charles F. Hobson, 94. Chapel Hill: University of North Carolina Press, 2002.

Mather, Cotton. "Decennium Luctuosum." In *Narratives of the Indian Wars, 1675–1699*, edited by Charles H. Lincoln, 242. New York: Lincoln, 1913.

Mather, Increase. "A Brief History of the War with the Indians in New England." In *So Dreadful a Judgment: Puritan Responses to King Phillip's War, 1676–1677*, edited by Richard Slotkin and James K. Folsom, 138–39. Middletown, CT: Wesleyan University Press, 1978.

McCloud, Sean. *Making the American Religious Fringe: Exotics, Subversives, and Journalists, 1955–1993*. Chapel Hill: University of North Carolina Press, 2004.

McDorman, Todd. "Challenging Constitutional Authority: African American Responses to *Scott v. Sandford*." *Quarterly Journal of Speech* 83 (1997): 194; 204.

McKinney, Thomas. "Letter." In *Magazine of the Reformed Dutch Church* 4 (August 1829): 118.

Meacham, Jon. *American Lion: Andrew Jackson in the White House*. New York: Random House, 2009.

Mead, Walter Russell. *Special Providence: American Foreign Policy and How it Changed the World*. London: Routledge, 2002.

Medill, William. "Annual Report of the Commissioner of Indian Affairs," November 30 1848, *House Executive Document* no. 1, 30th Congress, 2d session, serial 537, 385–89.

Merriam, Lewis. *The Problem of Indian Administration*. Baltimore, MD: Johns Hopkins University Press, 1928.

Mihesuah, Devon, ed. *Natives and Academics: Writing About American Indians*. Lincoln: University of Nebraska Press, 1998.

———. *So You Want to Write About American Indians? A Research Guide for Scholars, Students and Writers*. Lincoln: University of Nebraska Press, 2005.

Mihnehwehna. "Englishman!" In *Travels and Adventures in Canada and the Indian Territories Between the Years 1760 and 1776*, edited by Alexander Henry, 44. New York: I. Riley, 1809.

Miller, Susan A. *Coacoochee's Bones: A Seminole Saga*. Lawrence: University Press of Kansas, 2003.

Missall, John, and Mary Lou Missall. *Seminole Wars: America's Longest Indian Conflict*. Gainesville: University Press of Florida, 2004.

Monroe, James. "Second Annual Message, December 1818." In *A Compilation of the Messages and Papers of the Presidents, Vol. 2*, comp., James D. Richardson, 46. New York: Bureau of National Literature, 1897.

———. "Message on Indian Removal, January 27, 1825." In *Documents of United States Indian Policy*, 2d., edited by Francis Paul Prucha, 40. Lincoln: University of Nebraska Press, 1990.

———. "Monroe Doctrine—Annual Message of 1823." In *A Documentary History of the United States*, edited by Richard D. Heffner, 96–98. New York: Signet, 2002.

Montezuma, Carlos. "What Indians Must Do." *Quarterly Journal* 2 (1914): 294–99.

Moquin, Wayne, and Charles Van Doren. *Great Documents in American Indian History*. New York: De Capo, 1995.

Morgan, John. "U.S. Congress, Senate, Debate on Bill to provide Lands in Severalty, January 20, 1881 from Congressional Record, 46th Congress, 3d session." In *The American Indian and the United States: A Documentary History*, vol. 4, edited by Wilcomb E. Washburn, 1700–1704. New York: Random House, 1973.

Morgan, Thomas J. "Annual Report of the Commissioner of Indian Affairs, October 1, 1889." in *The American Indian and the United States: A Documentary History*, vol. 1, edited by Wilcomb E. Washburn, 531. New York: Random House, 1973.

———. "Annual Report of the Commissioner of Indian Affairs, September 5, 1890." In *The American Indian and the United States: A Documentary History*, vol. 1, edited by Wilcomb E. Washburn, 435. New York: Random House, 1973.

———. "Annual Report of the Commissioner of Indian Affairs, October 1, 1891." In *The American Indian and the United States: A Documentary History*, vol. 1, edited by Wilcomb E. Washburn, 529. New York: Random House, 1973.

Morris, Richard, and Phillip Wander. "Native American Rhetoric: Dancing in the Shadows of the Ghost Dance." *Quarterly Journal of Speech* 76 (1990): 164–91.

Morris, Richard. "Educating Savages." *Quarterly Journal of Speech* 83 (1997): 152–71.

Mould, Tom. *Choctaw Prophecy: A Legacy for the Future*. Tuscaloosa: University of Alabama Press, 2003.

Moulton, Gary. *John Ross, Cherokee Chief*. Athens: University of Georgia Press, 1978.

Musicant, Ivan. *Empire By Default: The Spanish-American War and the Dawn of the American Century*. New York: Henry Holt.

Nabokov, Peter. *Native American Testimony: A Chronicle of Indian-White Relations From Prophecy to the Present, 1492–2000*. New York: Penguin Books, 1999.

Naturalization Act of 1790 1 Stat. 103–104 (March 26, 1790).

Newcomb, Steven. "On the Words 'Tribe' and 'Nation.'" *Indian Country Today* 24, no. 26 (8 December 2004), A3.

Newmeyer, R. Kent. "Law and Character: John Marshall as an American Original—Some Thoughts on Personality and Judicial Statesmanship." *University of Colorado Law Review* 71, (2000), 1365.

Niezen, Ronald. *The Origins of Indigenism: Human Rights and the Politics of Identity*. Berkeley: University of California Press, 2003.

Northwest Ordnance. In *The American Indian and the United States: A Documentary History*, vol. 3, edited by Wilcomb E. Washburn, 2144. New York: Random House, 1973).

Oberly, John H. "Report of the Commissioner of Indian Affairs, December 3, 1888. In *The American Indian and the United States: A Documentary History*, vol. 1, edited by Wilcomb E. Washburn, 422–23. New York: Random House, 1973.

O'Brien, Greg. *Choctaws in a Revolutionary Age, 1750–1830*. Lincoln: University of Oklahoma Press, 2002.

O'Connor, John E. "The White Man's Indian: An Institutional Approach." In *Hollywood's Indian: The Portrayal of the Native American in Film*, edited by Peter C. Rollins and John E. O'Connor, 27–31. Lexington: University of Kentucky Press, 1998.

Ohio Wyandot Council. "Speech on Removal," in U.S. Congress, 23d, 1st session, *Senate Document* 512, vol. 2, 597.

Ohnawiio, Oteatohatongwan, and Teholagwanegen. "Formerly, We Enjoyed the Privilege." In *American State Papers: Indian Affairs*, vol. 7, 617. Washington: Office of Indian Affairs, 1903.

Olken, Samuel. "Chief Justice John Marshall and the Course of American Constitutional History." J. *Marshall Law Review*, 33 (Summer 2000), 743.

Ono, Kent, and John Sloop. "A Critique of Vernacular Discourse," *Communication Monographs* 62 (1995): 24.

Organization of the Department of Indian Affairs, June 30, 1834, *U.S. Statutes at Large*, 4:735–38.

Osborn, William. *The Wild Frontier*. New York: Random House 2000.

Osceola. "To Wiley Thompson, October 23, 1834." In *Red Patriots: The Story of the Seminoles*, edited by Charles Coe, 91. Cincinnati, OH: Editor Publishing, 1898.

O'Sullivan, John. "Annexation." *The United States and Democratic Review*, vol. 17, July/August 1845, New York: O'Sullivan & Gardner Publishers, 5.

Otis, D. S. *The Dawes Act and the Allotment of Indian Lands*. Norman: University of Oklahoma Press, 1973.

Parker, Arthur C. Quoted in Russel Lawrence Barsh, "American Indians in the Great War," *Ethnohistory* 38 (1991): 287–88.

Parry-Giles, Shawn, and Diane M. Blair. "The Rise of the Rhetorical First Lady: Politics, Gender Ideology and Women's Voice, 1789–2002." *Rhetoric and Public Affairs* 5, no. 4 (2002): 565–99.

Pearce, Roy Harvey. *Savagism and Civilization: A Study of the Indian and the American Mind*. Baltimore: Johns Hopkins University Press, 1967.

Perdue, Theda. *Cherokee Editor: The Writings of Elias Boudinot*. Athens: University of Georgia Press, 1996.

———. *Mixed Blood Indians: Racial Construction in the Early South*. Athens: University of Georgia Press, 2002.

Perdue, Theda, and Michael D. Green. *The Cherokee Removal: A Brief History with Documents*. Boston: Bedford Books, 1995.

Perkins, Bishop. "Debate on Bill to Provide Lands in Severalty, December 15, 1886." In *Congressional Record*, 49th Congress, 2d session, 191.

Pessen, Edward. *Jacksonian America: Society, Personality, and Politics*. Urbana: University of Illinois Press, 1985.

Petalesharo. "It Is Too Soon, My Great Father, to Send Those Good Men Among Us." In *Red Men Calling on the Great White Father*, edited by Katharine C. Turner. Norman: University of Oklahoma Press, 1951.

Phillips, Kendall R. "Spaces Of Invention: Dissension, Freedom, And Thought In Foucault." *Philosophy & Rhetoric* 34, no. 4 (2002): 328–44.

Pokegon, Simon. *The Red Man's Greeting at the Chicago Columbian World's Exposition of 1893*. Hartford, MI: C. H. Engle, 1893.

Pontiac. "You Must Lift the Hatchet Against Them." In *The Conspiracy of Pontiac*, edited by Francis Parkman, 5. New York: Champlain, 1898.

Pontitock Creek Treaty, March 24, 1832. In *The American Indian and the United States: A Documentary History*, vol. 4, edited by Wilcomb E. Washburn, 2449 (New York: Random House, 1973.

Porter, Joy. "Native Americans: The Assertion of Sovereignty and the Negotiation of Citizenship and Identities." In *Federalism, Citizenship and Collective Identities in U.S. History*, edited by Cornelius A. Van Minnen and Sylvia Hilton, 180–98. Amsterdam: VU Boekhandel University Press, 2000.

Portnoy, Alisse. *Their Right to Speak: Women's Activism in the Indian and Slave Debates*. Cambridge: Harvard University Press, 2005.

Pratt, Richard Henry. "Opening Comments." In *Official Report of the Nineteenth Annual Conference of Charities and Correction* (1892), 46–59.

Proclamation of 1763. In *The American Indian and the United States: A Documentary History*, vol. 3, edited by Wilcomb E. Washburn, 2135. New York: Random House, 1973.

Proclamation of the Continental Congress, September 22, 1783, *Journals of the Continental Congress*, vol. 25, 602.

Prucha, Francis Paul. *Americanizing the American Indians: Writings by the Friends of the Indian, 1880–1900*. Cambridge, MA: Harvard University Press, 1973.

———. *The Great Father: The United States Government and the American Indians*. Lincoln: University of Nebraska Press, 1986.

———. *The Indians in American Society: From the Revolutionary War to the* Present. Berkeley: University of California Press, 1988.

———. *The Great Father: The United States Government and the American Indians,* abridged. Lincoln: University of Nebraska Press, 1988.

——— *Documents of United States Indian Policy,* 2d. Lincoln: University of Nebraska Press, 1990.

———. *American Indian Treaties: The History of a Political Anomaly.* Berkeley: University of California Press, 1994.

Pushmataha and Puckshunnubbee. "For the Cherokee Phoenix." *Cherokee Phoenix* 2, no. 29 (September 22, 1829): 2, col. 2b

Quay, Matthew Quay. "*Lone Wolf* Comments, 1903." In *The Road: Indian Tribes and Political Liberty,* edited by Russell L. Brash and James Y. Henderson, 95. Berkeley: University of California Press, 1980.

Quinney. "Fourth of July Address at Reidsville, New York, 1854." *The American Indian* (January, 1928), n.p.

Rathbun, Lyon. "The Debate Over Annexing Texas and the Emergence of Manifest Destiny." *Rhetoric and Public Affairs* 4, no. 3 (2001): 459–93.

Records of the Office of the Secretary of War, Indian Affairs, *Letters Sent,* vol A, 143, Record Group 75, National Archives. Also found in *The American Indian and the United States: A Documentary History,* vol. 1, edited by Wilcomb E. Washburn. New York: Random House, 1973.

Red Cloud. "Speech at Cooper Union, July 16, 1870." *New York Times* (July 17, 1870): 6, col. 1.

Red Fox Skiuhushu. "If the Red Man Can Fight, Why Can't He Vote?" In *Literary Digest* 59 (December 21, 1918): 36–37.

Reifel, Ben. In *To Be An Indian: An Oral History,* edited by Joseph H. Cash and Herbert T. Hoover. 124–25. St. Paul: Minnesota Historical Society Press, 1995.

Remini, Robert V. *Andrew Jackson and His Indian Wars.* New York: Penguin, 2001.

Report of the Doolittle Commission, January 26, 1867, *Senate Report* no. 156, 39th Congress, 2d session, serial 1279, 3–10.

Report of the Indian Peace Commission, January 7, 1868. *House Executive Document* no. 97, 40th Congress, 2d session, serial 1337, 15–17.

"Report of the Joint Committee in the Legislature of Georgia on Cherokee Lands." *Cherokee Phoenix* 1, no. 3 (March 6, 1828): 1, col. 4B.

Ricci, David M. *Good Citizenship in America.* Cambridge, UK: Cambridge University Press, 2004.

Rich, Elizabeth. "Remember Wounded Knee: AIM's Use of Metonymy in 21st Century Protest." *College Literature* 31, no. 3 (2004): 63–73.

Rickard, Clinton. "Comments." In *Report of the Executive Council on the proceedings of the First Annual Conference of the Society of American Indians, October 12–17, 1911, Columbus, Ohio,* edited by Arthur C. Parker. Washington, DC: Printing Office, 1912.

Ridge, John. "You Asked Us." In *Trail of Tears: The Rise and Fall of the Cherokee Nation,* edited by John Ehle, 254. New York: Doubleday, 1988.

Robbins, William G. "In Search of Western Lands." In *Land in the American West: Private Claims and the Common Good,* edited by William G. Robbins and James C. Foster, 3–22. Seattle: University of Washington Press, 2000.

Rogin, Michael Paul. *Fathers and Children: Andrew Jackson and The Subjugation of the American Indian.* New York: Knopf, 1975.

Roubideaux, Ramon. "Essay." In *To Be An Indian: An Oral History,* edited by Joseph H. Cash and Herbert T. Hoover, 124–25. St. Paul: Minnesota Historical Society Press, 1995.

Roosevelt, Theodore. *An Autobiography.* New York: Macmillan, 1893.

———. "A Proclamation: June 23, 1902." In *Indian Affairs: Laws and Treaties,* vol. 1, edited by Charles J. Kappler. 1016–18. Washington, DC: Government Printing Office, 1904.

Rosebud Sioux. "Copy of Petition, January 15, 1897." Senate Committee on Indian Affairs File, RG233, HR54A-H13.1, box 193, Library of Congress.

Ross, John. "Annual Message, October 14, 1829." In *The Papers of Chief John Ross*, vol. 1, edited by Gary Moulton, 169. Norman: University of Oklahoma Press, 1985.

———. "Annual Message, November 11, 1831." In *The Papers of Chief John Ross*, vol. 1, edited by Gary Moulton, 169. Norman: University of Oklahoma Press, 1985.

———. "Letter to Andrew Jackson, March 12, 1834." In *The Papers of Chief John Ross*, vol. 1, edited by Gary Moulton, 279. Norman: University of Oklahoma Press, 1985.

———. "Letter to Lewis Cass, March 9, 1835." In *The Papers of Chief John Ross*, vol. 1, edited by Gary Moulton, 332–33. Norman: University of Oklahoma Press, 1985.

———. "Letter to Lewis Cass, February 29, 1836." In *The Papers of Chief John Ross*, vol. 1, edited by Gary Moulton, 388. Norman: University of Oklahoma Press, 1985.

Ross, John, and William Hicks. "The Cherokees." *Cherokee Phoenix*, vol. 1: 44 (January 14, 1829): 1, col. 4b–5a.

Rusling, James. "Interview with President William McKinley." *The Christian Advocate* 22 (January 1903): 17.

Sa, Zitkala. "Impressions of an Indian Childhood." *Atlantic Monthly* 85 (1900), 37–47.

Said, Edward. *Orientalism*. New York: Random House, 1978.

———. *Culture and Imperialism*. New York: Knopf, 1993.

Salisbury, Neal. "Native People and European Settlers in Eastern North America, 1600–1783." In *The Cambridge History of the Native Peoples in the Americas*, vol. 1, part 1, edited by Bruce Trigger and Wilcomb E. Washburn, 1–17. London: Cambridge University Press, 1996.

Satank. "Teach Us the Road to Travel." *New York Daily Tribune* (November 30, 1871), n.p.

Satz, Ronald. *American Indian Policy in the Jacksonian Era*. Lincoln: University of Nebraska Press, 1975.

Saunders, Alvin. "U.S. Congress, Senate, Debate on Bill to provide Lands in Severalty, January 20, 1881 from Congressional Record, 46th Congress, 3d session." In *The American Indian and the United States: A Documentary History*, vol. 4, edited by Wilcomb E. Washburn, 1700–1704. New York: Random House, 1973.

Schlesinger, Arthur M. *The Age of Jackson*. New York: Book Find Club, 1945.

Schudson, Michael. *The Good Citizen: A History of American Civic Life*. New York: The Free Press, 1998.

Schurz, Carl. "Annual Report of the Secretary of the Interior, December 7, 1879." *House Executive Document* no. 1, part 5, 46th Congress, 2d session, serial 1910, 5–6.

———. "Annual Report of the Secretary of the Interior, November 1, 1880." *House Executive Document* no. 1, 46th Congress, 3d session, serial 1959, 3–4; 11–13.

———. "Present Aspects of the Indian Problem," *North American Review* 133 (July 1881): 6.

Scrivner, Fulsom Charles. *Early Chickasaws: Profile in Courage*. New York: Vantage Press, 2006.

Sells, Cato. "The 'First Americans' as Loyal Citizens." *American Review of Reviews* 57 (May 1918): 523.

———. "Speech to the Indian Rights Association, October 2, 1920." In *The Great Father: The United States Government and the American Indians*, unabridged, Francis Paul Prucha, 801. Lincoln: University of Nebraska Press, 1984.

Seminole Nation. "Memorial of the Seminole, February 6, 1897." Senate Committee on Indian Affairs File, RG233, HR54A-13.1, box 193, Library of Congress.

Senier, Siobhan. "Allotment Protest and Tribal Discourse: Reading *Wynema's* Successes and Shortcomings." *American Indian Quarterly* 24, no. 3 (2000): 420–40.

———. *Voices of American Indian Assimilation and Resistance: Helen Hunt Jackson, Sarah Winnemucca, and Victoria Howard*. Norman: University of Oklahoma Press, 2001.

Shalhope, Robert E. *The Roots of Democracy: American Thought and Culture, 1760–1800*. Boston: Twayne, 1990.

Sherman, William T. "End of the Indian Problem." In *House Executive Document* no. 1, 48th Congress, 1st session, serial 2182, 45–46.

Shome, Raka. "Postcolonial Interventions in the Rhetorical Canon: An 'Other' View." *Communication Theory* 6 (1996): 40–59.

Shome, Raka, and Radha S. Hegde. "Postcolonial Approaches to Communication: Charting the Terrain, Engaging the Intersections." *Communication Theory* 12 (2002): 249–70.

Shanley, Kathryn. "Writing Indian." In *Studying Native America: Problems and Prospects*, edited by Russell Thornton, 130–51. Madison: University of Wisconsin Press, 1998.

Shullushoma. "It's Been a Great Many Years." In U.S. Congress, 23d, 1st session, *Senate Document* 512, vol.1, 240.

Silbey, Susan. "'Let Them Eat Cake': Globalization, Postmodern Colonialism, and the Possibilities of Justice." *Law and Society Review* 31 (1997): 207–235.

Sioux Man. "The Dead Did Not Return, 1891." In *Speaking of Indians*, Ella Deloria, 63. New York: Friendship Press, 1944.

Skinner, Thomas. "Debate on Bill to Provide Lands in Severalty," December 15–16 and January 18, 25, 1887, in *The American Indian and the United States: A Documentary History*, vol. 4, edited by Wilcomb E. Washburn, 1849. New York: Random House, 1973.

Sloan, Thomas L. "The Reservation System, Report to the Interior Department." In *Proceedings of the First Annual Conference of the Society of the American Indians* Washington, DC: Smithsonian, 1912. 112.

Smith, John Q. "Annual Report of the Commissioner of Indian Affairs, October 30, 1876." *House Executive Document* no. 1, 44th Congress, 2d session, serial 1749, vii–xi.

Smith, Linda Tuhiwai. *Decolonizing Methodologies: Research and Indigenous Peoples*. London: Zed Books, 2007.

Smith, Paul Chaat, and Robert Allen Warrior. *Like a Hurricane: The Indian Movement from Alcatraz to Wounded Knee*. New York: New Press, 1996.

Smith, Rogers. *Civic Ideals: Conflicting Visions of Citizenship in U.S. History*. New Haven, CT: Yale University Press, 1997.

Snyder, Homer. In *A Final Promise: The Campaign to Assimilate the Indians, 1880–1920*, Frederick Hoxie, 182. Lincoln: University of Nebraska Press, 1984.

Spivak, Gayatri. *In Other Worlds*. New York: Routledge, 1988.

———. "Can the Subaltern Speak?" In *Marxism and the Interpretation of Culture*, edited by Lawrence Grossberg and Cary Nelson, 271–313. Urbana: University of Illinois Press, 1988.

———. "Interview." In *The Postcolonial Critic: Interviews, Strategies, Dialogues*, edited by Sarah Harasym, 51. New York: Routledge, 1990.

Sprague, Peleg. "Remarks, April 17, 1830." *Gales & Seaton's Register of Debates in Congress*, Senate (April 17, 1830), 356.

Springer, William. "Debate on Bill to Provide Lands in Severalty," December 15–16 and January 18, 25, 1887. In *The American Indian and the United States: A Documentary History*, vol. 4, edited by Wilcomb E. Washburn, 1863. New York: Random House, 1973.

Starita, Joe. *Dull Knifes of Pine Ridge: A Lakota Odyssey*. New York: Putnam's Sons, 1995.

Story, William. "Indian Destiny." *Cherokee Phoenix* 1, no. 45 (21 January 1829), 1–2.

Storr, William. "Remarks, May 15, 1830." *Gales & Seaton's Register of Debates in Congress*, House (May 15, 1830), 998.

Stremlau, Rose. "'To Domesticate and Civilize Wild Indians': Allotment and the Campaign to Reform Indian Families, 1875-1887." *Journal of Family History* 30 (2005): 265–286.

Strickland, William. "The Rhetoric of Removal and the Trail of Tears: Cherokee Speaking Against Jackson's Indian Removal Policy, 1828–1832." *Southern Speech Communication Journal* 47 (1982): 292-309.

Stuckey, Mary E. *Defining Americans: The Presidency and National Identity*. Lawrence: University of Kansas Press, 2004.

Stuckey, Mary E. "'The Domain of Public Conscience': Woodrow Wilson and the Establishment of a Transcendent Political Order." *Rhetoric and Public Affairs* 6, no. 1 (2003): 1–23.

Takaki, Ronald. *Iron Cages: Race and Culture in 19th Century America*. New York: Oxford University Press, 1990.

Tecumseh. "Sleep No Longer." In *Indian Oratory: Famous Speeches by Great Chieftains*, edited by W.C. Vanderwerth, 54. Norman: University of Oklahoma Press, 1979.

Teller, Henry. "U.S. Congress, Senate, Debate on Bill to provide Lands in Severalty," January 20, 1881. From Congressional Record, 46th Congress, 3d session. In *The American Indian and the United States: A Documentary History*, vol. 4, edited by Wilcomb E. Washburn, 1700–1704. New York: Random House, 1973.

Thornton, Russell. *Studying Native America: Problems and Prospects*. Madison: University of Wisconsin Press, 1998.

Tisho Mingo, William M'Gilvery, and Stimoluet. "Indian Emigration." *Cherokee Phoenix* 1, no. 16 (June 11, 1828): 2, col. 1–2.

Trade and Intercourse Act, March 30, 1802, *U.S. Statutes at Large*, 2: 139–46.

"Transfer of Indian Affairs to the Department of the Interior" (March 3, 1849), *U.S. Statutes at Large*, 9, no. 395.

Treaty of Dancing Rabbit Creek, 1830. In *The American Indian and the United States: A Documentary History*, vol. 4, edited by Wilcomb E. Washburn, 2423–36. New York: Random House, 1973.

Treaty of Doak's Stand, 1828. In *The American Indian and the United States: A Documentary History*, vol. 4, edited by Wilcomb E. Washburn, 2377. New York: Random House, 1973.

Treaty of Fort Gibson, March 28, 1833. In *The American Indian and the United States: A Documentary History*, vol. 4, edited by Wilcomb E. Washburn, 2446. New York: Random House, 1973.

Treaty of Hopewell. In *The American Indian and the United States: A Documentary History*, vol. 4, edited by Wilcomb E. Washburn, 2275. New York: Random House, 1973.

Treaty of McIntosh. In *The American Indian and the United States: A Documentary History*, vol. 4, edited by Wilcomb E. Washburn, 2269. New York: Random House, 1973.

Treaty of Payne's Landing, May 9, 1832. In *The American Indian and the United States: A Documentary History*, vol. 4, edited by Wilcomb E. Washburn, 2443. New York: Random House, 1973.

Turner, Frederick Jackson. "The Significance of the Frontier in American History." In *Annual Report of the American Historical Association for the Year 1893*, edited by S. P. Langley.Washington, DC: Smithsonian, 1894.

Tuske-Ne-Hau (Creek), Hopithle-Ho-Lo (Creek), et al "To the Citizens of Alabama and Georgia." *Cherokee Phoenix* 2, no. 22 (September 2, 1829): 2, col. 1b.

Unnamed Mohawk Chief. In *The Iroquois and the New Deal*, edited by Laurence Hauptman, 6. Syracuse, NY: Syracuse University Press, 1981.

Unnamed Oneida and Seneca. In *To Be An Indian: An Oral History*, edited by Joseph H. Cash and Herbert T. Hoover, 124–25. St. Paul: Minnesota Historical Society Press, 1995.

Unrau, William. *The Kaw People*. Phoenix: Indian Tribal Series, 1975.

U.S. Congress, 23d, 1st session, *Senate Document* 512, vol. 1, 240.

Utley, Robert M. *The Indian Frontier of the American West, 1846–1890*. Albuquerque: University of New Mexico Press, 1984.

Vanderwerth, W. C. *Indian Oratory: Famous Speeches by Noted Indian Chieftains*. Norman: University of Oklahoma Press, 1989.

Vest, George. "U.S. Congress, Senate, Debate on Bill to provide Lands in Severalty, January 20, 1881, from Congressional Record, 46th Congress, 3d session." In *The American Indian and the*

United States: A Documentary History, vol. 4, edited by Wilcomb E. Washburn, 1700–1704. New York: Random House, 1973.

Wahunsonacock. "1622 Speech to John Smith." In *Travels and Works of Captain John Smith,* edited by Edward Arber, 137. Edinburgh: Edinburgh Press, 1910.

Wald, Priscilla. *Constituting Americans: Cultural Anxiety and Narrative Form.* Durham: Duke University Press, 1995.

———. "Terms of Assimilation: Legislating Subjectivity in the Emerging Nation." In *Cultures of United States Imperialism,* edited by Amy Kaplan and Donald Pease, 59–84. Durham: Duke University Press, 2000.

Walker, Cheryl. *Indian Nation: Native American Literature and Nineteenth-Century Nationalisms.* Durham, NC: Duke University Press, 1997.

Wallace, Anthony F. C. *The Long, Bitter Trail: Andrew Jackson and the Indians.* New York: Hill and Wang, 1993.

Wander, Philip. "The Third Persona: An Ideological Turn in Rhetorical Theory." *Central States Speech Journal* 35 (1984): 210–11.

Warren, Louis S. *Buffalo Bill's America: William Cody and the Wild West Show.* New York: Knopf, 2005.

Washington, George. "Third Annual Message to Congress, October 25, 1791." In *A Compilation of the Messages and Papers of the Presidents,* vol. 1, compiled by James D. Richardson, 96–97. New York: Bureau of National Literature, 1897.

———. "Fifth Message to Congress, October 25, 1793." In *A Compilation of the Messages and Papers of the Presidents,* vol. 1, compiled by James D. Richardson, 133. New York: Bureau of National Literature, 1897.

Weinberg, Albert K. *Manifest Destiny: A Study of Nationalistic Expansionism in American History.* Baltimore: Johns Hopkins University Press, 1935.

Wilkins, David. *American Indian Sovereignty and the U.S. Supreme Court: The Masking of Justice.* Austin: University of Texas Press, 1999.

Ward, John William. *Andrew Jackson: Symbol for an Age.* London: Oxford University Press, 1955.

Waselkov, Gregory A. *A Conquering Spirit: Fort Mims and the Redstick War of 1813–1814.* Tuscaloosa: University of Alabama Press, 2006.

Wickman, Patricia Riles. *Osceola's Legacy.* Tuscaloosa: University of Alabama Press, 2006.

Washakie. "Protest to Governor John W. Hoyt." In *Washakie,* edited by Grace Raymond Hebard, 212. Cleveland, OH: Arthur Clark, 1930.

Washburn, Wilcomb E., ed. *The American Indian and the United States: A Documentary History,* vol. 4. New York: Random House, 1973.

———. *The Assault on Indian Tribalism: The General Allotment Law (Dawes Act) of 1887.* Philadelphia: J. P. Lippincott, 1975.

Weiss, Richard. "Ethnicity and Reform: Minorities and the Ambience of the Depression Years." *Journal of American History* 66 (1979): 566–85.

Winnebago Indians. *To the Senate and House of Representatives in Congress Assembled—A Petition of the Winnebago Indians of Wisconsin.* Stevens Point, WI: Gazette Book and Job Office, 1889.

Winnemucca, Sarah. *Life Among the Piutes: Their Wrongs and Claims.* Reno: University of Nevada Press, 1994.

Wood Pecker, Roman Nose, Locust, Timson, Samuel Ward, Situagee and Ball Town George, "To Aquohee District." *Cherokee Phoenix* 1, no. 30 (September 24, 1838): 2, col. 4a.

Woodward, Grace Steele. *The Cherokees.* Norman: University of Oklahoma Press, 1963.

Wovoka. "Promise of the Ghost Dance." In *The Ghost Dance Religion and the Sioux Outbreak of 1891,* edited by James Mooney. Washington DC: Bureau of Ethnology, 1896.

Wright, J. Leitch. *Creeks and Seminoles: The Destruction and Regeneration of the Muscogugle People.* Lincoln: University of Nebraska Press, 1986.

Yagelski, Robert. "A Rhetoric of Contact: Tecumseh and the Native American Confederacy." *Rhetoric Review* 14 (1995): 64–77.

Yava, Albert. "We Want to Tell You Something." In *Native American Testimony: A Chronicle of Indian-White Relations From Prophecy to the Present, 1492–2000*, edited by Peter Nabokov, 246–50. New York: Penguin Books, 1999.

Yenne, Bill. *Indian Wars: The Campaign for the American West.* Yardley, PA: Westholme, 2005.

Yoholo, Tuckaubatchie Hajo, Tustenuggee, Smut Eye, et. al. "Memorial of the Creek Nation of Indians." *Cherokee Phoenix* 2, no. 48 (March 17, 1830): 4, col. 1a–4b.

Young, Donald. *American Minority Peoples: A Study in Racial and Cultural Conflicts in the United States.* New York: Harper & Brothers, 1932.

Young Joseph. "An Indian's Views of Indian Affairs," *North American Review* 128 (April 1879), 412; 433.

Zaeske, Susan. *Signatures of Citizenship: Petitioning, Antislavery and Women's Political Identity.* Chapel Hill: University of North Carolina Press, 2003.

Zagarri, Rosemarie. "Morals, Manners, and the Republican Mother." *American Quarterly* 44, no. 2 (1992): 192–215.

Zelizer, Barbie. "Reading the Past Against the Grain: The Shape of Memory Studies." *Critical Studies in Mass Communication* 12 (1995): 204–239.

Zinn, Howard. *A People's History of the United States: 1492–Present.* New York: HarperCollins, 2005.

Index

CPSIA information can be obtained
at www.ICGtesting.com
Printed in the USA
FSOW02n0408141016
25982FS

9 781496 809735